What is Money? And How to Make it Work Better for Everyone

What is Money? And How to Make it Work Better for Everyone

By

Ray Galvin

Cambridge Scholars
Publishing

What is Money? And How to Make it Work Better for Everyone

By Ray Galvin

This book first published 2026

Cambridge Scholars Publishing

Lady Stephenson Library, Newcastle upon Tyne, NE6 2PA, UK

British Library Cataloguing in Publication Data
A catalogue record for this book is available from the British Library

ISBN: 978-1-0364-7686-1
ISBN (Ebook): 978-1-0364-7687-8

TABLE OF CONTENTS

ACKNOWLEDGEMENTS

I'm very grateful to Professor Jared Sonnicksen of the Political Systems Faculty at RWTH Aachen University, for his encouragement and practical suggestions for getting the work done to write this book. Thanks also to my colleague and frequent research collaborator at Cambridge University, Professor Minna Sunikka-Blank, for her encouragement and enthusiasm for the topic and style of writing. Thanks too to my colleagues at FCN in the School of Business and Economics, RWTH Aachen University, for stimulating and challenging discussions on economics and the nature of money, and to Prof Reinhard Madlener for practical office support. My wife Fabiola Blum deserves special thanks for her support throughout the project and her very precise proof-reading of the manuscript. Finally, many thanks to the wider group of friends and family who consistently affirmed the value of the book's topic and the need to write it in straightforward language that would reach as many people as possible.

INTRODUCTION

Money touches on almost every part of our lives. We need it to be able to eat, clothe ourselves, travel, keep warm, get well, read books, communicate, bring up children, get educated, buy or rent a house or apartment, be entertained, bury or cremate our loved-ones, pursue hobbies, ensure a comfortable future–and for the lucky few, play the finance markets by investing in shares, bonds, mutual funds, and other forms of what economists often call "near money".

It may be surprising, then, that it's difficult to understand what money actually is–and not just for ordinary people who have little or no time to think about a question like this. It also seems to be difficult for many columnists, politicians, and even a large number of economists and leading bankers.

So, if most of humanity isn't sure what money is but the world keeps functioning anyway and money keeps flowing to-and-fro and doing what it's supposed to do, why should we be concerned about it?

First, it's a fascinating topic, even mind-bending. I hope that'll start to become clear when you read Chapter 1. This dives straight into explaining what an increasing number of researchers are now agreeing that money is. The clue is in the chapter's title: "Let there be money!" It explains how dollars, yen, euros or pounds come into existence out of nothing and are later dissolved back into nothing after they've done a circuit of very effective work among people like you and me.

Then, in Chapter 2 you may find the topic goes even beyond fascinating and becomes almost magical, and at the same time tinged with mayhem and chaos. Chapter 2 is about central banks. But don't think for a moment that central banks are boring. Just the opposite. These grey-suited institutions are the focus of some of humanity's cleverest ever practices–and biggest headaches.

Chapter 3 should fill a gap in everyday knowledge because it's about money's role in capitalism. But the chapter isn't a moralistic tirade against capitalists. Instead it's a brief journey through the history of our capitalist money system, starting in medieval Venice, migrating to Shakespeare's England, then developing into a powerful but little known, tacit agreement between governments and banks, often called the "memorable alliance", which pretty much holds the world of money together today.

Other chapters should also fill gaps in popular knowledge and bring some surprises: such as how cryptocurrencies, like Bitcoin, work and could collapse overnight (Chapter 10), and what central banks are doing to head them off with their "central bank digital currencies" (Chapter 9).

I hope you'll also find Chapter 6 thought-provoking. It looks at taxation, and how strange today's tax systems would look to an observer from almost any other period of history. The ancient Romans would probably say, "Why aren't you taxing the wealth of the super-rich? Why all that emphasis on income tax? That seems to us a lop-sided, ineffective way to collect revenue".

I hope Chapter 8, on foreign exchange, also gets your attention, because it addresses an intriguing puzzle: how does money shuffle its way across the world, between countries that all have different currencies? 99% of British pounds never leave Britain, 99% of Canadian dollars never leave Canada, and it's the same for almost all countries. Each country's currency is a closed loop system. Its money just goes round and round within that country. And yet every day over 7 trillion US dollars' worth of money shifts between countries. How can this be? Chapter 8 explains how the big corporate foreign exchange firms use "near money" to make this happen–and who the winners and losers are. The chapter also reports some good news for immigrants around the world who regularly send money home to their friends and families–and the bad news that the US has just started taxing this.

Chapter 5 has a very different theme, but it should also give an engaging take on what money is. It looks at money's roots in the primitive human need and practice of making obligations, one person to another and between different groups of people. What does an everyday pre-colonisation Polynesian social practice have in common with modern central bank money creation? What do these have in common with a couple of strangers sharing chocolates and ice creams on a very hot day in a busy city centre? This chapter is my attempt to go as deeply as possible into the question "What is money?"

So, the first reason we should be concerned about the question "What is money?" is that it's a fascinating, engaging subject and full of surprises. Why ignore a topic that can enrich our understanding of the world? If you only read this book to enjoy learning some intriguing things about humans and the sometimes clever, sometimes weird things they do, especially in the realm of money, I don't think you'll be disappointed.

The second reason there needs to be a straightforward, clearly understandable book about money is a lot more serious. Many people don't understand what money is, therefore those who do understand it have a huge advantage. They can run the money system to get maximum leverage from it, while the general public are left to assume that's the way it has to be. An example is "austerity". For the past 15 years, governments in western Europe, Britain, north America, Australasia and many other regions have complained that "there isn't enough money". Therefore, they've said, they've had to reduce spending on infrastructure, young people's education, health services, social housing, childcare, the railways, and in some cases even their defence forces.

That's why the mood of the book changes in Chapter 4, which looks at how (not) to grow an economy. It explains how we could all become better-off if there was just the right amount of money to power all our country's economic capacity into action. By "capacity" I mean brain-power, natural resources (consistent with looking after the planet, of course), workers, technology, industry and infrastructure. I use the example of the UK Labour government's 2024 budget and argue that this seems to have missed the mark by a long shot. More austerity!

The result of budgets like this has been a swathe of run-down countries with creaky services, cash-strapped young people, fraught parents–and for western European countries, weak defence against possible military aggression. Powerful figures in and around these governments have insisted this is the way it has to be because, they say, government money is limited. They've said that if we want better health services and railways, we'll have to hand these over to the private sector–who will of course make all the profits.

I attempt to show in the book that this reasoning is flawed. *Not* that one political viewpoint is necessarily better than another (the book studiously avoids being a party-political tract), but that the *understanding of money* that lies behind the dominant view is wrong. The *facts* are wrong. Austerity isn't inevitable and never was in countries where there's easily enough material wealth for everyone to have their basic needs met. The trick is for the state to create as much money as it needs to, to enable this material wealth to meet the needs of its people, and to intervene where necessary to ensure this money goes to the right places to make this happen. And of course it has to be careful to keep inflation under control–which means matching the amount of money in circulation to the capacity of the economy.

When I wrote the second-to-last draft of Chapter 7, on the euro, I criticised the dominant "austerity" view on the basis that it represented a misunderstanding of what money is, how it's created, and who has the power to create it and dissolve it back into nothing. This dominant view has been like a religious doctrine, an article of faith that shouldn't be questioned. The same issue comes up in Chapter 4.

But in mid-March 2025, when US President Trump appeared almost to swap sides in the Russia-Ukraine conflict, suddenly the dominant view lost some of its hold in Europe. Within a few days this hard-and-fast austerity doctrine that had held Europe's money systems in its grip for well over a decade showed signs of weakening. Germany, the arch-austerity advocate, suddenly stopped saying "there's not enough money" and the government introduced a bill to open the money taps. Government spending would increase massively, not only to revitalise the military, but also to provide hundreds of billions for the country's neglected and run-down infrastructure and its aspirations for climate protection.

A few days later, the spending taps were opened for the entire Eurozone–the countries that use the euro. Out of the blue, they were given permission to spend an extra 650 billion euros, over and above the limits that had previously been set in stone.

What can we learn from this? Austerity was all along a big charade. *It wasn't scientifically grounded.* It was just a doctrine, based on a misunderstanding of what money is.

So that's just one example of my second reason for claiming it's important to understand what money is. It's not just an intriguing, fascinating, magical subject. If the general public (and the politicians, columnists, economists and bankers) understand it well, this could save us from making costly mistakes.

The book also puts the spotlight on other examples of misunderstandings that deprive most of us of the full benefits of this amazing thing called money. One of these has to do with the relationship between government deficits, debt and bonds, which I discuss briefly in Chapters 4 and 7, then in detail in Chapter 11. Chapter 11 makes the case for what's probably the most original suggestion in the book, namely that there's a way that governments can go less deeply into debt, namely by developing certain, specific areas of cooperation with their central banks.

Because I think money is a subject everybody should understand better, I've done my best to write the book in a style that's clear and easy to follow. There are now some very good books on money but they're tough going. They tend to use highly specialist language–words we never come across in everyday speech–without explaining or defining them. Their sentences are often tortuous and contorted, and I sometimes think that to follow their reasoning you'd already have to know what they're trying to say.

So I've attempted to introduce the subject step by step, using plain language, together with examples and case studies from real life. This includes some very brief stories from my own experiences with money, and plenty of examples from history, including western, Islamic and Chinese history. I've also tried to explain the logic of the inner workings of the money system as clearly as possible. A difficulty is that many different and divergent aspects of our modern money system are closely interrelated and interdependent, so when you explain one feature of money you feel tempted to bring in all the related aspects, to make sure you've done the job properly. A lot of economics textbooks tend to do this, but I think it confuses readers: too much information overload all at once.

Because of this, an expert economist reading my Chapter 1 might say, "Oh but he hasn't explained this or that feature of the topic." But that's OK with me. That feature will be explained in Chapter 2 or 3 or 7 or 11. So if you feel there are gaps in the explanations in the first few chapters, please keep them in mind and look forward to them being filled in later chapters.

Finally, I want to assure readers that I've taken great pains to ground this book on solid, factual, empirical evidence, along with transparent, logical thinking, so that it's scientifically credible. I work as a scientist at two universities: Aachen in Germany, and Cambridge in England. My work is mostly in the field of energy policy and economics. In Germany I've done research in an economics faculty for over a decade, and in Cambridge I tutor postgraduate students in the university's sustainability institute. I've published over 90 scientific papers in the past 12 years and I'm Senior Associate Editor of the journal *Energy Research and Social Science*. So I have a stake in using only evidence-based, rigorously checked data and transparent, logical thinking.

But that doesn't mean the book is fool-proof. I hope you'll read it critically. Don't take what I say as gospel, check it out. Check the references, read the people I disagree with as well as those whose work has inspired and informed the book. If you can, talk to an economist or a banker, or just toss the ideas around in your head or among your colleagues, friends and families, and check whether my evidence and arguments hold together and make sense. I'm making some novel claims in this book, saying some things that, in some circles, would raise eyebrows. If I'm mistaken, please help demolish my arguments–but please read carefully what I'm *actually* saying, not a roughed-up, half-baked version of it. If I'm wrong, please prove it rigorously, then we'll all benefit.

But if most of what I say is right, we'd better get the message out to everyone: the general public, politicians, schoolteachers, teenagers, young people, columnists, bloggers and, yes, economists and bankers, including central bankers.

1. LET THERE BE MONEY!

It's probably true to say that most of us have little understanding of what money actually is, or how it comes into being and goes out of existence. In 1972 when I was an undergraduate student at Auckland University, we had an open-air, lunchtime forum where any student could come to the microphone and speak about any issue on their mind. It was often high politics: the Vietnam War, South Africa's apartheid system or equal pay for equal work. One day a dishevelled, hungry looking student came to the microphone waving a five dollar note. He said, "I've been trying to work out what 'five dollars' is, what five dollars actually means." Then he read us the words on the note: "'The Reserve Bank of New Zealand promises to pay on demand to the bearer of this note the sum of five dollars.'" He then said, "So if I take this to the Reserve Bank and hand it in and ask for my five dollars, what will they give me? Nothing but another five-dollar note." He paused to let it sink in, then concluded, "Brothers and sisters, we've been conned. Five dollars isn't anything. It's just a promise to give you another five dollar note that promises to give you another five dollar note ad infinitum."

The puzzle begins: What is five dollars?

The student was speaking just a few months after US President Richard Nixon had taken the US dollar off the gold standard. Until 15 August 1971 the US dollar was tied to the price of gold. Before that date the US Treasury (the ministry of finance) would guarantee to exchange one ounce of gold for every $US 35 handed in. The values of the currencies of other high-income countries like Canada, Australia, Britain, New Zealand and Japan were tied to the value of the US dollar. So, prior to 15 August 1971 the student could have taken his five New Zealand dollar note to a bank in Auckland and exchanged it for the equivalent value of US dollars–about $US 4.25 at that time–then handed the money to the US Treasury and received about one-eighth of an ounce of gold in exchange for it.

At the time he spoke at the forum, however, all he would have got for his $US 4.25 was another $US 4.25. Or if he'd handed the New Zealand $5 note to the Reserve Bank of New Zealand, all he would have got was a $5 note in return. So what *is* money?

Later in the book I'll talk about the history of using gold as a backup for the value of a currency and the pros and cons of doing this. For now, however, and for most of this book, I'll focus on money as it actually is in the world today. For the past 53 years the value of money hasn't been backed by gold or any other precious metal or commodity. The currencies of most high-income countries aren't tied to the US dollar or any other currency but are free to float in value in relation to each other on the international currency market. The student's dilemma has characterised money for the past 53 years–but also, as I'll aim to show, for many other periods of history. On the face of it, it appears that a dollar is nothing but a dollar, which is nothing but a dollar, ad infinitum.

Dollars as tax tokens

What, then, is a dollar? I suggest a useful way to start is to think of money as *a set of tax tokens.* A government, in order to function, needs people to work for it: clerks, teachers, air traffic controllers, probation officers, soldiers, politicians, and many others. To get them to work for the government, it has to reward them. It rewards them by giving them tax tokens. Every dollar it pays to one of its clerks or teachers can be redeemed for a dollar worth of the tax they have to pay–what we call their tax liability. Since almost every adult has to pay tax to the government, and since even children pay sales tax when they spend their pocket money, there's automatically a demand for dollars. The money earned by clerks, soldiers and teachers employed by the government gets spent on food, clothing, housing, entertainment, etc., and in this way it gets passed on to bakers, farmers, musicians, builders and others, who thereby get the dollars to pay their own tax. In turn, they pay other people further down the line, who thereby get the dollars to pay their tax, and so on as the dollars cascade through the economy. As they do so, the number of dollars is steadily reducing, as more and more dollars are paid to the government as tax. Eventually, almost every dollar paid out by the government in, say, January of this year will return to the government as tax payments. But there's always new money coming into circulation because clerks, politicians and teachers get paid all year round, so the supply of tax tokens keeps getting replenished as it keeps diminishing.

We can add to this the money the government pays out to contractors for projects like road repairs, research, space exploration and building new schools and kindergartens. This also circulates, and almost all of it eventually finds its way back to the government via taxes, and therefore out of the economy.

To complete the picture, I should really say the money comes back to the government "via taxes, fees, fines, student loan repayments and other payment obligations". Governments compel everybody to pay taxes, and some have to pay fines, fees, etc. All these are ways of withdrawing money from the economy. But since taxes make up by far the greater portion of these, I'll mostly just refer to taxes throughout this book.

Many governments today often speak as if they believe they should never pay out more money than they'll get back in taxes (and fees and fines, etc.). In other words, they say they should have a "balanced" budget, somewhat like a well-managed household or business. President Obama, for example, proclaimed he couldn't increase welfare payments or invest in infrastructure because "there is no money"[1]. In July 2024 Britain's newly elected Labour government repeatedly complained they couldn't spend very much on fixing the National Health Service or repairing run-down infrastructure because there was no money left to pay for these things. They were treating the government's budget like a household budget. In Germany the word for the government's budget is "Haushalt", meaning household.

When governments talk like this, they're falsely likening their budget to that of a household or private business. They claim they're aiming to pay out no more tax tokens (= dollars, pounds, yen, euro, etc.) each year, or at least in the long run, than they expect to get back in tax payments. Along with a growing group of economists, I'll argue in this book that this is a misguided and misleading approach, for four main reasons. First, it's not what happens in practice. I know of no government that actually behaves like this. The governments of countries like the US, Britain, New Zealand, Denmark, Switzerland, Australia and Canada almost always pay out more money each year than they get back. They also have some clever tricks to sometimes hide the fact that they're doing this. More on this in Chapters 4 and 11.

Second, many rather smart households and businesses certainly don't aim for a balanced budget in every financial year or even over several years, but instead they run a deficit in order to invest in projects that make them richer in the long run.

Third, and very important, the only way the total amount of money in the economy can increase over time is if the government pays out more each

[1] Wray (2015), pages 193-220

year than it gets back. If the total amount of money in the economy isn't steadily increasing, the economy can't grow and inflation can't be catered for–a fascinating topic I discuss in detail in Chapters 4 and 7.

Fourth, and most important, a government that issues its own currency is very different from a household or business, in that *a government creates all the money it spends. It doesn't have to get money from somewhere outside itself* to be able to pay a teacher's wages or invest in a project like a new railway line or research facility. If a government wants to spend money it has to create it. It creates it by spending it into existence.

Note that I'm not saying that governments *should* create money out of nothing, as if this were a novel suggestion from a fringe group of activists. I'm simply describing what actually happens. Governments create money out of nothing by spending it into existence, and when it comes back to them via taxes, etc., it's effectively dissolved back into nothing. The economist Warren Mosler brought this to the world's attention in 1993 in his book *Soft Currency Economics*[2]. This led to soul-searching among a certain group of economists, and Mosler's insights were further developed by others, most notably economics professors Stephanie Kelton[3] and L. Randal Wray[4]. Since then, a large number of others have taken up this insight and applied it to many fields such as banking practices, the wider economy, and the history of money.

This set of insights is usually called "modern monetary theory" or sometimes "modern money theory", both abbreviated to MMT. I'll be drawing on MMT a lot in this book, but it'll become clear that I don't accept all it has to say, and in some respects I think it needs to go further. Its basic insight, though, that governments create money by spending it into existence and dissolve it back into nothing by collecting taxes, fees, fines, etc., is now widely accepted.

In Chapter 2 I'll explain that there are some additional tricks governments and their central banks also use to create and dissolve money. The main point I want to emphasise here is that a useful way to begin to answer the question "What is money?" is to say it's a tax token created by the government. The five dollars our dishevelled student was waving around at the lunchtime forum was a promise to write off five dollars' worth of his or someone else's taxes. And because a dollar is a tax token, there'll always be

---

[2] Mosler (1993)
[3] Kelton (2020)
[4] Wray (2015)

a demand for it. It will always trade at its face value and people will work and offer their goods and services to get it.

I also need to add that money creation works a little differently from this in the European countries that use the euro. Although each of these countries spends money into existence and dissolves it again when taxes are paid, they each have to keep to a deficit limit imposed by the European Parliament. More on that in Chapter 7.

A dollar as an IOU: the magic of money

Another useful way to think about money is that it's an IOU ("I owe you")[5]. The twenty-dollar note I have in my wallet is an IOU written by and issued by the government. It certifies that the government owes me twenty dollars' worth of tax credits. When I was 5 years old and just beginning to learn to read, my older brother and sister and I got weekly pocket money from our parents, but it was never enough. One day when we were all broke, my sister wrote "IOU sixpence" on a small piece of paper, signed it "Marge" and said she would pay me with it if I polished her shoes. (In those days in New Zealand we used the old pounds, shillings and pence currency. Sixpence was later replaced by five cents, and due to over 60 years of inflation its value today would be equivalent to just under a dollar.) I believed at the time that Marge was economically sound (inasmuch as a five-year old can think such things), so I said yes. I polished her shoes and pocketed the IOU. Later that day I offered the IOU to my brother Frank if he would help me read a story. He said yes. The next day he got Marge to do a job for him, and paid her with the same IOU.

So this little IOU, which was nothing but a piece of paper with a handwritten promise on it, acted precisely like money. No actual money changed hands, but three jobs were done, the quality of life improved for us all, and everybody got paid for their work.

There's something almost magical about this. Money was created out of nothing. It circulated through an economy causing useful work to be done. Finally, it got back to its creator and was torn up and thrown in the rubbish

---

[5] While writing this I was surprised to hear from my German wife and Italian friends that there's no everyday equivalent in their languages for "IOU". This made the concept difficult to grasp for them.

bin, effectively dissolved into nothing. Governments use much the same mechanism that Marge used, to create and dissolve money.

There is, of course, another important dimension to this story. Both Frank and I knew that Marge was a reliable, well-resourced, honest person, four years older than me, two years older than Frank. We believed unquestioningly that she would and could keep her promise. She was able to create money out of nothing because the people who used this money were sure she wouldn't default.

A government has the same advantage but on a much bigger scale. By "government" here I don't just mean the particular political party in power at the moment. I mean the "state", the entire sum-total of the governing apparatus: a parliament, a cabinet and prime minister, a civil service, a central bank, a tax collection department, enforcement bodies such as the police, security forces such as counter-espionage agencies and the military, a vast rulebook of laws and regulations, a judiciary, and a population that on balance overwhelmingly supports this apparatus. If a particular prime minister or other government minister makes a promise, we may be wise to question its reliability. But if the state makes a promise, such as "We will put you in jail if you murder someone" or "We will issue you a passport that our border guards will always honour", we can believe it with extremely high confidence. In the same way, the state's promise embedded in the twenty-dollar note in your purse or wallet is the most trustworthy promise anyone can ever make regarding money and what it's worth. There's never any doubt at all that it will erase twenty dollars' worth of your or someone else's tax liability.

Some other metaphors for money

Not all money is created by the state. There are many different kinds of money, but the money created by the state as a tax token is the most reliable kind of money in countries with advanced, well-functioning economies. The Cambridge sociologist and economist Geoffrey Ingham analysed key periods in the somewhat chaotic history of money over the past 4,000 years and came to an interesting conclusion about money in general: money is a *social obligation*[6]. If I create money–whether I'm a medieval banker issuing a promissory note, an ice cream booth owner issuing a scoop token, a mafia boss issuing an IOU, or a government issuing a five dollar note–I'm putting

---

[6] Ingham (2008)

myself under an obligation. I'm promising to pay, to the bearer of the note, goods and services to the value of that note.

At the same time, the bearer of the note has an *entitlement*. She or he is entitled to request, or in some cases demand, certain types of goods and services to the value shown on the note.

Ingham argues that money is therefore an obligation and an entitlement, depending on whether you issued it or possess it.

Another scholar, David Graeber, who also studied the history of money, came to the conclusion that money is, in essence, *debt*[7]. If I issue a document or note to the value of five dollars, I'm putting myself in debt to the recipient, to the value of five dollars. The recipient can use it to demand goods and services of that value, but in the end I'll have to clear that debt: I'll have to give five dollars, or that value of goods and services, to whoever comes back to me with the note I issued. Graeber's notion of a debt is effectively the same as Ingham's notion of an obligation.

These are useful insights that are fully compatible with the idea of money as an IOU, and which can help us understand how all kinds of money work or have worked in the past, no matter who creates them. What they all have in common is that the money they describe doesn't exist in some abstract realm detached from people. Money is not a fixed quantity of stuff "out there", existing of its own accord, that humans can only access by competing against others who want it. Every unit or item of money that exists has been brought into being by a human creator. It circulates in a community causing work to be done and things to be made, bought and sold, and is dissolved back into nothing when it's repaid to its creator. Money creation is a social activity that operates according to rules that are set, explicitly or implicitly, by its creators and users.

State-created money is a special case of this kind of money. It can best be thought of as a tax token, or a government IOU that you can give back to the government for writing off taxes, which carries with it a solid, virtually unbreakable power. The money issued by the state is not just *any* obligation (as in Ingham's insight) or *any* debt (as in Graeber's). It's the *government's* obligation to reduce your tax liability by the precise amount that the money has as its face value. Therefore it's limitlessly tradeable among all the people who have tax liability to that government–namely everybody in the

---

[7] Graeber (2011)

country that issued it–and if it's issued by a stable, well-functioning state, it's as reliable and trustworthy as any money can ever be.

"Let there be money!" And there was money.

The insights of Mosler, Kelton, Wray, Ingham and Graeber outlined above came to light relatively recently. But similar ideas had been mooted in earlier decades. John Maynard Keynes (1883-1946), who was possibly the most influential economist of the first half of the 20th century, used a similar idea to prompt the US government to create billions of extra dollars to finance its Second World War effort[8]. And Mosler's insight that money is a creation of the state drew on an earlier idea called "chartalism". This term was invented by the German economist Georg Friedrich Knapp (1842-1926) in his publication "The State Theory of Money" in 1905. The word chartalism is derived from the Latin word "charta", which means a token or ticket. Knapp argued that money is a token or ticket produced by a state. He contrasted this with the so-called "metalist" theory, that money is essentially a quantity of gold or other precious metal and that banknote money is merely a representation of this. I'll discuss this further in Chapters 3 and 5 on the history of money, but the important point for now is that Knapp's and Mosler's insights have proved *factually* correct in today's world. Ever since the US abandoned the gold standard in 1971, the money you use every day has been chartalist: nothing more than a token or ticket produced by the state, created out of nothing.

This brings us to another important term: money today is called "fiat money". Fiat is a Latin word meaning "Let there be". For those who love grammar, "fiat" is the third person singular passive subjunctive of the infinitive *fieri*, which means "to happen" or "to come into being". For those who read the Hebrew Scriptures (the Old Testament of the Bible), it's in the Latin version of the key word in the Creation story in Genesis, where God says[9] "Fiat lux!", meaning "Let there be light!".

Fiat money is money that comes into being simply because a person with the right to do so declares it to exist. For state money, this is usually the head of the country's central bank or one of her or his deputies. This person follows a prescribed set of procedures authorised by a government minister,

---

[8] Carter (2020) provides an excellent biography of Keynes and his impact.
[9] The original Hebrew is יְהִי אוֹר.

makes a few keystrokes on a computer, and immediately a billion dollars or so comes into existence. Out of nothing.

This isn't as weird as it might sound. The philosopher J. L. Austin wrote a very insightful book called *How to do things with words*[10]. He explained how some of the most important things in life are achieved simply by the correct person using the correct words in the correct setting. For example, in January 2004 the late Queen Elizabeth II travelled to Southampton to launch a ship. In accordance with the prescribed tradition, she smashed a bottle of champagne across its bow and said, "I name thee Queen Mary the Second." In that instant, the name of the ship became Queen Mary the Second. In a similar way, every day thousands of couples around the world become married, simply by saying a prescribed set of words in an agreed place before a state-appointed celebrant. They sign a marriage register afterwards, but this doesn't make them married. It simply records the fact that their marriage took place at the instant they said the prescribed words.

Creating money is as simple as that. It doesn't require gold to be mined or coins to be minted or bank notes to be printed. It's all done with words. Let there be money!

A hierarchy of money

Anyone can create money–including a nine-year-old writing an IOU. While my sister's IOU was circulating among her siblings, the New Zealand economy effectively had sixpence-worth more money in it than before and after. The IOU was doing just what money does: inducing people to utilise their skills and time to do useful work. But some monies are more universally accepted than others, and this depends on the reliability of the creator of the money. Economists and governments recognise a hierarchy of money. Stable, high-income countries are the most reliable money-creators because they always accept their money back from you as payment for taxes, and everyone has to pay taxes. The money they create is called "narrow money" in this book, though in some contexts I call it "high-powered" money.

I need to warn the reader here that there's no standardization of the labels for different kinds of money. The labels vary among economists and between countries. While some economists and governments call this "narrow money" or "high-powered" money, as I do, others call it "the

---

[10] Austin (1955)

monetary base", "base money", "outside money" (because it circulates outside the everyday economy), "M1" or "M0". I'm calling this "narrow money" and sometimes "high-powered" money, but if you're reading other texts on money it's important to check what terms are being used for what.

The money in your bank account is far less powerful than the "narrow money" created by the state. I call it "broad money" in this book, and sometimes "lower-powered money". Some governments and economists call it "inside money" (because it circulates inside the everyday economy) or "M2", or other "M" labels. It is, literally, money that *your bank* creates. Just as the state creates money out of nothing by spending it into existence, commercial banks create money out of nothing by crediting it to your bank account, and also by issuing loans, as I'll explain more fully in Chapter 2. A bank balance of $1,000,000 means nothing more than "IOU $1,000,000, signed, Your Bank". It's only as dependable as the bank itself. If the bank goes bust, your money disappears. Actually, there's a little consolation in that some countries provide a government guarantee for the first $50,000 or so if your bank collapses, but you still stand to lose the remaining $950,000, or thereabouts.

You might respond to this by saying, "But that's not fair! That million dollars was the government's payment to me for building a new school gym. Why isn't it high-powered money that's as dependable as the state itself?"

The reason lies in how the banking system works. When the government pays you a million dollars for your services, its central bank doesn't deposit this high-powered money into your own bank account. Instead, the central bank gives the money to your bank. It does this by electronically depositing the money directly into an account that your bank holds, in its own name, at the central bank. This high-powered, narrow money now belongs to your bank, not you. Your bank then creates a million dollars of new money, its own-created, lower-powered, broad money, by crediting your account with a million dollars. It effectively writes an IOU in its own name for a million dollars and gives it to you. Your bank now owns a million dollars of high-powered, narrow money, but you have a million dollars of lower-powered, broad money.

In Chapter 2 I'll explain more about the banking system and how your bank uses its newly acquired $1,000,000 of high-powered money as collateral (alongside its other assets) to issue loans to other customers totalling *several million* dollars, loans which are also nothing more than the bank's IOUs, thereby expanding the broad money supply by creating a lot more money out of nothing. This is often called the "money multiplier" effect, though this can be misleading, again for reasons I'll explain in Chapter 2.

The distinction in this book between narrow money and broad money is quite simple. Narrow money has a government-backed guarantee. If you own some narrow money it can never become worthless, as long as your country survives. If you have broad money, it's only as good as the bank that issued it.

Economists generally recognise yet another level of money, sometimes called "near-money", which includes IOUs, bonds, and a vast array of exotic-sounding investment schemes such as futures, mutual funds, credit default swaps and hedge funds. An accountant friend of mine calls these "funny money", and they tend to balloon upwards and collapse from time to time, as in the great global financial crash of 2008-2009. What these examples of near-money have in common is that they're not actually dollars and cents, or pounds and pence, or euros and eurocents, etc. They may be valued at a particular amount of dollars and cents at any particular moment, but this depends on the mood of the market. They are "near" money because they are not quite the same as the money we save in banks and spend every day, but would first have to be exchanged for this money, and at the rate the market offers.

Cryptocurrencies such as Bitcoin, Ethereum ETH and Solana are also a form of money created out of nothing, but in Chapter 10 I'll argue that cryptocurrencies are far less reliable than the currencies of stable high-income countries, for three main reasons. First, they're not backed up by a guarantee, such as tax credits. Second, there are unanswered questions as to what will happen to their value when their planned maximum size is reached–a complicated issue that could hit like a time bomb. Third, their value depends entirely on people believing that *other* people believe these currencies are reliable.

This touches on a very important issue in economics: what other people believe about a currency or some aspect of the economy can have a far more powerful effect on it than material factors. If the masses believe, for no good reason, that the values of the shares in your company are going to collapse tomorrow, this can become a self-fulfilling prophecy and they'll most likely fall in value. The great 20th century economist John Maynard Keynes showed how this dynamic makes our economies potentially unstable and can lead to disastrous booms and busts[11]. As you'll see, this insight of Keynes will come up repeatedly throughout this book.

Money dissolved into nothing

What happens to the money you give to the government when you pay your taxes, fees or fines? Recall that when my sister's IOU was paid back to her, she tore it up and threw it in the bin. She did this because its job had been done. She could have kept it in case she wanted to issue it again, but it would be just as easy to write a new IOU. It wouldn't make any difference, in terms of her net wealth, whether she destroyed the IOU or kept it for later use. If she kept it, it would simply be a declaration that she owed herself sixpence. My guess is that she thought it would be a bit stupid to keep a note that declared that she owed herself sixpence.

The state is in a similar position regarding the money you pay it for taxes, fees and fines. This money is only useful when it's in circulation, as it's a promise to write off these liabilities. Once it's been used to write them off, it's no more use. The government can easily create more electronic money if it wants to in the future, so there isn't much point in preserving it in some active form. So I would argue, along with economists like Kelton and Wray, that at the moment the government receives your money *it's dissolved back into nothing*.

We can see this clearly in the mechanics of how your taxes are paid. I work internationally and pay two tax bills per year to the UK government (not to mention taxes I pay in the US, Germany and New Zealand!). I pay my UK tax by instructing my bank to pay money from my bank account to an account held by His Majesty's Revenue and Customs (HMRC), which belongs to the government and is held at the UK's central bank, the Bank of England. My bank responds in two steps. First, it reduces its IOU to me (which is in the form of lower-powered, broad money) for that amount from my account. Then it pays the same amount, but in *high-powered, narrow money, from its own account* at the central bank, into the HMRC's account at the central bank. The money thereby disappears from circulation. It can no longer be used by my bank as collateral for issuing loans to other people. It's as good as dead.

And as noted above, this high-powered money is nothing more than the government's own IOU, its pledge to write off tax, fee and fine liabilities.

---

[11] Keynes (1930); Carter (2020)

Therefore its job is done and it's no longer useful. Since it exists only in the form of electronic bytes, and since the government can create more of the same by spending it into existence, there's no practical reason to keep it. Further, it's now removed from the country's economy and cannot be used as collateral for creating broad money as loans.

Of course, government accountants keep a record of the comings and goings of government money, and their book entries may make it look as though this money still exists somewhere in the ether. But you won't find it anywhere in any tangible form. It can't power the economy because it's not represented by narrow money credits in the reserve accounts of commercial banks.

There's one further set of money labels we need to get to grips with before moving on. Some governments and economists use "M1" as a label for all the cash (notes and coins) in the country plus all the money *in current accounts* in the wider economy. I'll use "M1" for this kind of money, especially in Chapter 11. This is the money that can be spent at any instant of time. The money in savings accounts can't be spent until it's transferred into current accounts, and some governments and economists call this money "M2". I'll also use "M2" for this.

The importance of this distinction will become clear in Chapter 11, when I discuss how central banks estimate how much money people are likely to be spending at any particular moment.

But please note that not all economists use the same labels. An old friend of mine, who served for over a decade as governor of his country's central bank, told me that he and his colleagues scrupulously avoided using "M" labels, because different countries and economies attached so many different meanings to them. So please keep in mind that different people use different labels.

Deficit, credit and debt

The main effect of the government's bookkeeping is to map whether the government is in "deficit" or "credit" in any particular year. If the government creates more money than it receives back, in any particular year, it's said to be in deficit, and if it receives back more than it creates, it's said to be in credit. But this is not the same as a household. If my household budget is in deficit, I'll eventually have to fill the gap–not necessarily this year, but certainly in the long run. My money comes from *outside* my household, and I'll have to get money from outside, in order to be able to repay my creditors. But state money, namely narrow money (high-powered money), is created from *within* the government's own "household". The state does *not* have to get money from outside itself, in order to be able to spend money.

Further, there's an important difference between a government "deficit" and a government "debt"–a theme that's very important throughout this book. Government debt is the net amount of money a government owes to other people or institutions, and this money must eventually be paid back–more on this in Chapters 4, 7 and 11, where I talk about government and private sector bonds. But a government "deficit" is not a debt. It's simply the difference between what the government creates and what it dissolves, in any particular year (or other nominated period of time). If a government creates 20 trillion dollars over the course of a year and gets back only 19 trillion dollars in taxes, fees and fines in that year, it's run a deficit of 1 trillion dollars. But this is not a debt. It's simply the net increase in the narrow money supply over that year.

There's a very good reason why governments must *always* run up an annual deficit. As I argue in Chapters 4 and 7, this is the only way an economy can keep pace with GDP growth and inflation. A government deficit leaves more high-powered money, in total, in commercial banks' accounts at the central bank at the end of the year than at the beginning. Therefore, they have more collateral and can create more loans (as lower-powered money), so the economy can grow–but more of that later.

Why we shouldn't just print more money

As I write this, most governments of high-income countries are complaining they're short of money. In the UK this is seen in the running down of the National Health Service (NHS), overcrowded prisons, inadequate resources to process asylum claims, inadequate social welfare payments and a persistent increase in poverty. In Germany and France, governments' lack of resources for young people is in part contributing to the popularity of far right and neo-Nazi parties. But economists who advocate modern money theory argue that governments should stop saying they're broke when in fact they have the means to create as much money as the economy needs[12].

[12] Elliot (2024), and more generally Wray (2015)

In one sense this is true. As long ago as the 1930s, economist John Maynard Keynes provided the intellectual firepower for the US and other governments to make better use of their ability to "deficit" spend, to pull their economies out of recession, and later to finance their Second World War effort and post-war recoveries[13]. In these periods they put a lot more money into their economies than they were taking out. This built up the supply of narrow money from year to year and therefore enabled banks to build up the supply of broad money. The extraordinary growth in wealth and wellbeing in countries like the US, Australia, New Zealand, Canada and much of western Europe from 1945 to the late 1970s was in large part enabled by government deficit spending[14].

Deficit spending is a well-proven approach for stimulating economic growth among ordinary people, and it's severely under-used today (see Chapters 4 and 7). However, there are strict limits to how much money it's wise to create in any particular set of circumstances. The "new Keynesian" economist Thomas Palley points out a row of issues where caution is needed, and where a lot of careful, detailed information is needed on how different parts of the economy are functioning[15]. If a government creates more money than the economy needs, this will lead to inflation. The trick is to ensure that the supply of narrow money in the economy is at just the right level to stimulate commercial banks to create the right amount of broad money to ensure that no workers, production facilities or resources are sitting idle. Any more than this, and it feeds inflation. Any less, and we under-use the country's capacity and get austerity.

In Chapters 6 and 11 I'll argue that deficit spending needs to be used alongside major tax reform. I'll suggest we have a blinkered, 20th century view of what tax should be, centred almost entirely on *income* tax, which no longer suits the way modern economies work. We need to learn of other options from the long history of taxation and be more like the ancient Romans, who taxed *wealth* far more than income. More precisely, I'll explain some very encouraging moves by the G20 group of leading industrial nations to simultaneously adopt a carefully structured and costed billionaires' wealth tax. Currently this is being designed for the G20 by Gabriel Zucman, Emanuel Saez, Thomas Piketty and others from the Paris School of Economics[16].

---

[13] Carter (2020)
[14] Carter (2020)
[15] Palley (2020)
[16] G20 Brazil (2024). The rational for a wealth tax is explained in Zucman (2015)

In short, yes, the state can create as much money as it likes, and needs to make better use of this, but only in the right ways and alongside a profoundly reformed tax system.

Why all this is important

Why is it important to know what money is? Money is the substance that economies are built with. If we misunderstand what money is, we may misunderstand some of the biggest issues that affect the everyday life of billions of people around the world. One of the great puzzles in reading economics books and articles today is that so many economists, even some of great stature, either avoid the issue of what money is, or continue to convey the long-debunked idea that it's a kind of substance that exists of its own accord, which governments have to compete against the private sector for. In his critique of this approach, economist L. Randal Wray argues that this fuzziness benefits the super-rich. He points out that powerful, hugely wealthy corporations don't like governments to engage in economic activities, as this prevents markets from being completely free. In a completely free market there would be no welfare payments, no government-funded public services, and only minimal taxes, which would be mostly geared to support and enforce laws designed to keep markets free and protect people's wealth[17]. Economist Zachary Carter goes even further, tracking a history of wealthy funders of US universities successfully pushing to get John Maynard Keynes's writings expunged from economics courses through the 1950s-1980s[18]. Keynes's writings are fundamental to a factual understanding of what money actually is and how it works.

Once again, I'm not saying a government should feel free to create as much money as it likes, even though there are no physical restraints on doing this. I'm arguing that if we understand what money is and how it comes into and out of existence, we'll have a basic tool to begin to make it work better for everyone.

Summing up

Money is an IOU. It's continually being created out of nothing, then causing work to be done as it circulates in an economy, then being dissolved back into nothing when it's repaid to its (human) creator(s).

---

[17] Wray (2015), pages 193ff.
[18] Carter (2020), pages 370 ff.

Money creation is a widespread and common social activity. Anyone can create money by writing an IOU, which functions as an obligation or a debt. But whether or not people accept this money depends on how reliable they think its creator is.

The most reliable money is that which a stable, well-functioning state creates. It can be regarded as tax tokens, since the state will always accept it at its face value to write off tax liabilities (and fees, fines, etc.).

The money the state creates is called narrow money or high-powered money in this book. Different governments and economists often have different names for it.

Commercial banks create money regularly, by crediting your bank account and issuing loans. The money they create is called lower-powered or broad money in this book. When commercial banks issue loans they use their stock of state-created narrow, high-powered money as collateral for these, alongside other, "non-liquid" assets they own, such as government bonds– more on this in Chapter 2.

All other kinds of money are called "near money" in this book. These are usually the lowest-powered forms of money, and their value in terms of dollars and cents fluctuates continually. They can have enormously high values, but their values can crash to almost nothing.

Another important distinction is between money that can be spent right now, which I call M1 in this book, and money that has to be first transferred to a current account, to be spendable, which I call M2. But note that these "M" labels are often used differently by different writers.

Finally, some readers might misinterpret what I'm saying about money creation. I'm not saying that governments should create as much money as they like, the classic "printing money" scenario. I'm saying that money only exists because people create it out of nothing (thereby putting themselves under an obligation). This is simply a factual statement about how money comes into existence in today's world.

So far I've only told half the story of how high-powered money comes into being and gets dissolved out of existence. The other half has to do with central banks. Understanding central banks can be a rollercoaster ride because they can be weird, flabbergasting and magical all at the same time, and in doing so they hold the world's economic system together (more or less!). Please join me on this rollercoaster ride in Chapter 2.

2. THE MAGICAL, TUMULTUOUS LIFE OF CENTRAL BANKS

It would be wrong to think of "Central Banks" as a dull topic. In the 16th century, waves of Spanish soldiers, labourers and entrepreneurs looted hundreds of tonnes of gold and silver from the palaces and mines of South America, bringing disease, death and destruction in their wake. The Spanish king and his government were jubilant that their wealth was massively increasing, because to them, gold and silver were money. For a century Spain was the richest country in the world–until inflation and economic mismanagement made it one of the poorest in Europe[19].

Today, central banks create money on a scale that dwarfs Spain's 16th century gold and silver haul. They do it without ships, guns, canons, pickaxes, slave labour or direct foreign exploitation. They simply press keys on a computer in response to their own or their government's wishes. Compared to the effort and human cost of past centuries' goldrushes, this is pure magic.

In Chapter 1 I explained how governments create money, but that was only half the story. To recap from Chapter 1, when a government wants to pay a teacher's wages, let's say $5,000, it instructs its central bank to create $5,000. The teacher's commercial bank–let's say it's Wells Fargo Bank–has a special account at the central bank, and the central bank strikes computer keys to credit Wells Fargo's account with this $5,000. As I mentioned in Chapter 1, the commercial bank–in this case Wells Fargo–now owns $5,000 of high-powered money. Wells Fargo then credits the teacher's account with $5,000 of its own money, which is effectively Wells Fargo's low-powered IOU, which is also created out of nothing. The whole action takes place without any physical stuff like gold or silver changing hands or even being present in somebody's vault.

We also recall from Chapter 1 that when the teacher pays her taxes, the money she pays is dissolved back into nothing via the reverse route.

---

[19] Cartwright (2022), Charotti et al. (2022)

All this is somewhat magical, but very orderly and ultimately democratic. The central bank is acting according to legislation enacted by the elected government, which sets out clear rules and guidelines. Further, the annual total amounts of money it creates and destroys, as it provides this service, have been agreed in advance by the Parliament or Congress, whose members are elected by ordinary voters. Although the central bank has to create whatever amount of money the government tells it to, the government is not allowed to tell it to create more than Parliament or Congress has agreed. So, at least in theory, there's democratic control over this aspect of the central bank's money creation.

There's another side of central bank money creation which is also magical, but the rules are far more flexible and sometimes they could be said to border on mayhem. This has to do with a very broad mandate central banks are given by their governments, to keep the economy healthy. I'll outline this briefly in this chapter, then set it alongside a brief account of the tumultuous, often conflict-ridden history of central banking in Chapter 3.

Starting with the magic of interest rate control

Most governments give their central banks a mandate to keep inflation at around 2% per year. This is a rather crude way of controlling the amount of money circulating in the economy, as I'll explain in a moment, though some economists, such as Joseph Vogl, say it amounts to wishful thinking[20]. Here's how it's meant to work. If there's too much money in the economy compared to the amount of goods and services this money can buy, goods and services start to cost more. Economists often call this "too much money chasing too few goods and services". This is what happened in Spain in the 16th century, starting in the province of Andalucía where ships were arriving in great numbers, decade after decade, with cargos of gold and silver they'd extracted from the Americas[21]. Gold and silver were seen as equivalent to money, so the amount of money in the economy expanded enormously, but the "real" economy–the things people make and use and buy and sell–didn't. The number of olives, oranges, grapes, Spanish guitars[22] and matador capes in Andalucía didn't increase overnight but the amount of "money" on offer to buy them did, as each ship docked in port, so their price went up. Likewise, the number of carpenters, blacksmiths, clothmakers, matadors,

[20] Vogl (2017), pages 132-165

[21] Charotti et al. (2022). Leigh (2024)

[22] According to Johannes Tinctoris, who lived in the fifteenth century, the Spanish province of Catalonia was the birthplace of the guitar.

Spanish guitarists and orchard labourers stayed about the same but the money available to pay them shot up, so their wages increased. In other words, inflation took hold. The rule of thumb is: don't let the amount of money in the economy get too high for the value of all the goods, services, and workers on offer.

The opposite is also true. If the amount of money is too low, olives won't sell, the wages of orchard labourers will go down, labourers won't have enough money to buy grapes and attend concerts, therefore fewer grapes will be grown and harvested and the musicians will be out of work, so vintners and musicians won't be able to buy oranges, so the wages of orange grove workers will go down, and so on down the spiral. Less work will be done, fewer goods and services will be produced, and the material quality of life will go down. Economists call this deflation, and economic textbooks universally warn that deflation is to be avoided like the plague.

Even though today's money isn't gold or silver but tax tokens created out of nothing by computer keystrokes, the same balancing act applies. The amount of money in the economy has to match the potential production and consumption of goods and services in the real economy–plus a bit more to stimulate growth and a small, healthy dose of inflation.

Central banks aim to achieve this balance mostly by the rather mundane task of manipulating interest rates, but also by the more entrepreneurial task of buying and selling bonds. I'll explain what bonds are below. Let's begin with interest rates.

Central banks and interest rates

When the teacher, mentioned above, spends $1,000 of her salary on rent, she does so using her computer or mobile phone, by transferring this money from her Wells Fargo account to her landlord's bank account. Let's say the landlord banks with JPMorgan. Wells Fargo's online banking system immediately reduces the teacher's bank balance by $1,000 and informs JPMorgan of the transfer. JPMorgan's online system then increases the landlord's account by $1,000. Remember, this money is just bank-backed IOUs, which I call broad money, or lower-powered money in this book, not state-created high-powered money, which I also call narrow money. Wells Fargo's IOU to the teacher has reduced by $1,000 and JPMorgan's IOU to the landlord has increased by $1,000.

But because of this payment, Wells Fargo now owes JPMorgan $1,000 of *government-created, high-powered money*, and this has to be paid on the same day the transfer is made. Millions of transfers like this are being made every day, criss-crossing between thousands of banks. The US Federal Reserve Bank (the US's central bank, often called the "Fed") estimated that on 17 May 2024, 2,146 commercial banks in the US each had "domestic consolidated assets" of $300 million or more, a total of just over $22 trillion–much of which is deposited in the banks' special accounts at the central bank[23], usually called their "reserve accounts". The Fed estimated that about $4.5 trillion was transferred between banks that day[24]. Note that the monetary value of the total production of goods and services in the US in 2023–called the Gross Domestic Product (GDP)–was $27.36 trillion. So every day an amount of money equal to about one-sixth of a whole year's production criss-crosses between banks' reserve accounts. Far more money flies back and forth among banks accounts every year than is used to produce goods and services.

Getting back to our story, at the end of the day, due to all these transfers, most US commercial banks will owe most of the others a considerable sum of money, and even though many of these debts will cancel each other out, they won't all cancel out completely. Remember, too, as I explained in Chapter 1, that each bank is receiving new high-powered money from the central bank every day as teachers and other government workers get paid, and each bank is paying high-powered money to the central bank as its customers pay their taxes, fees and fines. This means that the commercial banks may also owe the central bank money at the end of the day, or the other way round. A crunch point comes at the end of the day, as banks are legally required to reconcile their reserve accounts with each other and with the central bank. After this super-reconciliation, all the banks have to owe each other nothing: $0.00 at midnight.

If a bank doesn't have enough money in its reserve account to make up its deficits to other banks or to the central bank on a particular day, it has to borrow the money overnight to clear its debts. It can borrow from other banks at an interest rate generally called the "overnight rate" (often called the "federal funds rate" in the US). Alternately it can borrow from the central bank, at a rate usually called the "discount rate", though it's called different things in different countries.

---

[23] Federal Reserve (2024)
[24] Fedwire (2024)

How central banks try to control inflation

This is where inflation management comes in. The central bank can simply set this interest rate that it charges banks for the money to reconcile their accounts with each other. Alternatively, it can influence the overnight interest rate through various investment techniques, called "open market operations" (which I'll explain more about in Chapters 4 and 7). If inflation is too high, it influences the overnight rate upwards and/or sets its own interest rate higher. This makes it more expensive for commercial banks to settle their debts to each other at the end of the day. The commercial banks pass this expense on to their customers by increasing the interest rates on the money they themselves create and lend, to people who ask for loans. As this interest rate goes up, fewer people apply for loans, and the loans people apply for are smaller. This reduces the amount of lower-powered money in the economy. There's therefore less money to spend on food, concerts, computers, new cars, travel and most other things people buy, and this puts downward pressure on inflation.

To summarize that rule: the central bank makes interest rates go higher, to make inflation go lower. On the other hand, if inflation is too low, the central bank drives interest rates downwards, so the entire mechanism works in reverse, and inflation trends higher.

You may have noticed that there's a clever trick in this. Why do banks have to reconcile their accounts *every day?* Why not do it on a weekly basis, with a busy exchange of money only on Friday nights? Wells Fargo might owe JPMorgan $5 billion at the end of Monday, but if they left it another day or two the credits and deficits between these two banks might balance out to near zero. In the late Middle Ages, when a crude form of this kind of banking system emerged in Italian cities such as Florence, Venice and Genoa, money lenders would often take months before reconciling their accounts with each other (more on this in Chapter 3). That saved them a lot of short-term interest payments, not to mention administration and travel. But the advantage of making commercial banks settle their accounts every day is that it gives central banks direct daily influence on interest rates. This gives them a reasonably useful tool to influence inflation.

So we can see that today's money system, where central banks actively influence the supply of broad money from day to day, by influencing interest rates on narrow money, is much more orderly and dependable than unpredictable cargos of gold and silver arriving at ports–or gold rushes happening at random as new deposits of the precious metal are found and mined.

When the method doesn't work: external shocks

Unfortunately, influencing interest rates is only a very blunt tool for controlling inflation, for two main reasons. First, inflation is also influenced by other factors besides interest rates. These are often called "external" factors, as they originate from outside the economy of the country they're affecting. A clear example is the price of energy. When Middle Eastern oil-producing countries suddenly hiked the price of oil in the 1970s, this sent waves of high inflation through the countries that depended on oil for transport, heating and industry. Inflation in the US had been hovering between 2% and 5% throughout the 1960s but rose to a peak of 11% in 1975, then dipped a little but rose to a new peak of 14% in 1981. In the UK it reached 24% in 1976[25]. When the banks tried to control inflation by putting up interest rates, this didn't work well because inflation wasn't being caused by an excess of money in the economy. It was being caused by a so-called "external shock", namely a sharp increase in the oil price. We suddenly found ourselves with both high interest rates *and* high inflation. In the UK, mortgage interest rates peaked at 17% in 1979. In New Zealand, where I lived and worked at the time, the mortgage interest rate on our house reached 21%.

A similar thing happened in the early 2020s when natural gas prices suddenly increased after Russia invaded Ukraine. Natural gas had been very cheap in Europe in the decade prior to that. For households in EU countries its price, not counting taxes, had hovered between 4 and 5 eurocents per kilowatt-hour from 2008 to mid-2021 and was at a low of 4 eurocents per kilowatt-hour in early 2021. It began to increase steeply in 2021, and in mid-2002 it peaked at just under 10 eurocents per kilowatt-hour[26]–a gas price inflation rate of about 150%–before starting to fall slightly. This had knock-on effects on the costs of virtually everything that runs on natural gas, leading to further knock-on effects on the things that depend on the things that run on natural gas–like food production, for example.

In Germany, by March 2023 the average price for all forms of energy was 50% higher than in January 2021, the price of food was 31% higher and the cost of goods and services overall was 20% higher. This put the overall

[25] World Bank (2025)
[26] Eurostat (2024)

annual inflation rate in the year ending March 2023 at 8.5% per year, more than four times as high as the European Central Bank's inflation target.

Note that the core of the problem was just one item, natural gas, but central banks had no means of focusing on just one key item in the economy. Their only tool was interest rate management, and interest rates affect many things in the economy that have nothing to do with the price of gas–such as mortgages, for example.

The European Central Bank used this blunt tool and increased interest rates progressively. At the start of 2021 the overnight lending rate was 0.25%. It reached a peak of 4.75% in September 2023 then reduced to 4.5% in June 2024[27]. By that date the inflation rate had reduced to 2.6% but was stubbornly refusing to fall to the coveted 2% target, so interest rates remained high.

This three-year-long hump in interest rates was disastrous for millions of homeowners. Many had mortgages at low interest rates that were due to be readjusted every few years. People who took out a mortgage in 2020 or earlier that was due for revision in the years since 2021 suddenly found themselves paying up to four times as much interest per month as they'd budgeted for. This happened in almost all high-income countries, because central banks in all these countries use the same very blunt instrument–interest rate management–to attempt to control inflation.

The situation could have been a lot worse, except that governments intervened directly by imposing high "windfall taxes" on energy companies. These corporations were making enormous profits simply because the commodity they were selling had become scarce. Governments used this tax to subsidize energy costs for households. This had a direct, well-focused impact on energy price inflation and therefore on inflation overall. But it wasn't enough to dampen inflation deeply, so the central banks were left to pick up the pieces–by continuing to use their very blunt tool of interest rate management.

[27] European Central Bank (2024)

The descent into mayhem

The second reason interest rate control is a blunt instrument for controlling inflation has to do with the nature of money. To explain this, we'll first take a step back.

Generally, if a government spends too much and taxes too little, this will lead to inflation. But if a government spends too little and taxes too much, this will lead to stagnation or even deflation. Governments have to spend just the right amount, and collect just the right amount of tax (and fees, fines, etc.), to ensure there's always just the right amount of money in the economy to match their country's capacity to use it, to produce goods and services–the balance has to be "just right", like Goldilocks' porridge. As we noted above, all the money governments create is narrow money, most of which never gets into the wider economy (which is why it's often called "outside money"). Instead, it sits in the reserve accounts of commercial banks at the central bank. The commercial banks use this narrow money as collateral to back up the much larger amounts of broad money they create by issuing loans.

All would be well if this was the end of the story. The government would spend and tax just enough to keep the supply of narrow money just high enough for commercial banks to create just enough broad money to match the capacity of the economy to produce goods and services. As long as there were no external shocks, the central bank would then use its interest rate management to smooth out any short-term fluctuations in inflation.

But there's another side to the story. I explained in Chapter 1 that money creation is a social activity, meaning that anyone can create money, and people have done so in many different ways throughout history. They create money by issuing what amounts to an IOU, and IOUs can take many different forms. People can denominate their IOU in any currency they like (or even in a non-currency, like cigarettes or jugs of beer), though they usually denominate it in the currency of the country they're in. So if a British finance company writes me a note saying, "We promise to pay on demand to the bearer of this note the sum of £200,000, plus 10% interest per year, redeemable on 04 July 2028, signed A. Smith, Director, 04 July 2024", they've effectively created £200,000 of new money. If A. Smith's finance company is known to be trustworthy and reliable, I can sell their note on to an investor, who can re-sell it, and so on. It can be sold and re-sold many times before it comes back to the finance company, when it pays out £200,000 of traditional, bank-created money, plus any interest still owing, to whoever owns it at that point. This is a description of a very simple and common form of IOU called a "bond". While the bond is in circulation, being sold and re-sold, it's acting somewhat like money, but not exactly like money. It can't be divided up into small amounts, like your wages can. And while it's circulating it can be sold for whatever price the buyer and seller negotiate–which can be higher or lower than its face value of £200,000.

Today there's a class of IOUs worth trillions of dollars, often called "near money"[28] or "shadow money", that make up what's often called the "financialisaton" of the economy. Many of these are much more complex and unstable than bonds–though bonds are also a form of near money. They have a huge impact on prices and wealth distribution, and *central banks are almost powerless to dampen their impact.* They have macabre-sounding names such as "mutual funds", "credit default swaps", "hedge funds", "futures", "forwards", "options" and, more generally, "exotic financial instruments".

The classic example of how these tend to confound central banks occurred in the early 2000s, when many commercial banks were offering so-called "sub-prime" mortgages to house buyers. These mortgages had very low interest rates for their first one or two years, which enabled millions of low-income people to buy homes. But the interest rates were due to increase after this initial period, to one, two or three percent above the rate that central banks charge commercial banks when they reconcile their accounts, as described above. This could drive the interest rate on these mortgages to 7% or higher.

The commercial banks knew they were taking big risks by offering these mortgages to low-income households, but they had a plan to reduce their risk. This involved various bank-like financial firms and institutions, including so-called "investment banks" and other more esoteric financial institutions. The commercial banks sold these mortgages to these financial institutions, which "chopped each of them up" into small slices and combined some of these slices together with slices of low-risk investments, to make very heterogeneous bundles of allegedly not-very-risky investments. These investments were called "derivatives", and they were offered for sale on the financial markets. This was effectively a form of downstream money creation, as each derivative represented a complex set of IOUs. These instruments became very popular among investors, and trillions of dollars'

[28] Ingham (2020), pages 121 ff.

worth were sold and re-sold among hundreds of thousands of investors looking for an easy windfall.

As we all know, in 2007-2008 these homeowners' mortgage interest rates sharply increased as their initial low-interest periods came to an end. Thousands of these homeowners began to default on their mortgages. As a result, investors suddenly realised that a significant proportion of their derivatives were plummeting in value. Investors also assumed that thousands of other investors would realise this, so there was a stampede to sell their derivatives before everybody else sold theirs, and the price fell through the floor. John Maynard Keynes's observation, mentioned in Chapter 1, that markets tend to do what people think other people think they're about to do, came true in a big disastrous crash.

In an insightful analysis of these events, economist Joseph Vogl points out how powerless central banks were against the ebbs and flows of these trillions of dollars of "shadow money" during this entire period[29]. During the early phase, when banks were offering mortgages at near-zero interest and the derivatives were burgeoning, this effectively expanded the money in the wider economy far beyond the bounds of regular broad money. Central banks couldn't increase interest rates to dampen this bulge in the economy, as it wasn't being caused by too much narrow money in commercial banks' reserve accounts leading to too much broad money creation. It was being caused by huge fluctuations in the supply of shadow money.

Besides, increasing interest rates further would have pushed homeowners' mortgage interest rates even higher when these rates came up for review.

Vogl also suggests that most central banks couldn't even see the problem. He suggests they were fixated on everyday inflation and didn't regard the expanding bubble of derivatives and other exotic financial instruments as a genuine form of money. Vogl, Ingham[30] and others point out that all forms of money should be of interest to central banks because they all affect the economy. We could add that central banks failed to recognise that money creation is a social activity which anyone can engage in. Every time someone issues an IOU of any kind, this acts as a form of money. Money-creation is therefore not just an activity of governments, central banks and commercial banks, but of many different kinds of actors.

---

[29] Vogl (2017)

[30] Ingham (2020), Chapter 7, pages 117ff.

A note about money creation

An interesting side-issue arose out of this financial chaos. Some people began to argue that only the state should be allowed to create money: that all money should be high-powered money and banks should be forbidden from creating lower-powered money. After all, the collateral for the shadow money that was created during the boom was mostly lower powered, broad money created by commercial banks. British economist Anne Pettifor describes a recent movement among a group of economists along these lines[31]. She disagrees with their view and argues that commercial banks, at least, should continue to be allowed to create money because this is done in response to people's need for loans. She points out that this gives a form of democratic influence to money creation, namely the influence of ordinary people. I would take this further and point out, along with economic historians Geoffrey Ingham[32], David Graeber[33] and others, that governments couldn't stop people creating money even if they tried, since money creation is a basic social activity, like creating new words and phrases in your native language or creating a new kind of music. Referring back to Chapter 1, how would a government stop a nine-year old issuing her own IOU? Or a business making a deal with a financial backer that's measured in dollars but uses no government-created dollars directly?

This leads to an important discussion on how central banks came to be what they are today, within a history of many competing groups creating their own money. I follow this up in Chapter 3. For now, I briefly mention that there's always been competition between governments and private commerce for influence and control over money creation in the economy. Anyone can create money, and currently governments and central banks more or less have the upper hand, but in some respects it's the law of the jungle. We also see this with the rapid rise of cryptocurrencies, outlined in Chapter 10.

Quantitative easing

Perhaps the biggest surprise in the aftermath of the 2007-2008 crash was the advent of "quantitative easing", when suddenly, out of the blue, central banks began creating billions of dollars of new money every day, out of

---

[31] Pettifor (2018), pages 93-130
[32] Ingham (2008)
[33] Graeber (2011)

nothing, for a thousand days or more. Let me begin by outlining the leadup to this.

The 2007-2008 crash is usually now called the "global financial crisis" or "great financial crisis", both abbreviated to GFC, and its long, slow aftermath is often called the "Great Recession"[34]. The crisis began in 2007, when thousands of US homeowners began to default on their mortgage payments. Ironically, the first big financial institution to teeter on the edge of collapse was the British bank Northern Rock. In many ways Northern Rock was in good health, but large financial institutions stopped lending it money because they were afraid thousands of its customers would follow their US counterparts and default on their mortgage payments. When these institutions stopped lending money to Northern Rock, its normal cycle of borrowing-to-lend was therefore interrupted, its share price plummeted to one-third of its pre-crisis level, and it no longer had enough "liquidity" (money available to flow in and out) to match its customers' normal daily cash withdrawals.

There's a small personal story enmeshed in this. In September 2007 I arrived back in Cambridge, England, from a research project in Freiburg, Germany, and had been out of touch with British news. The Cambridge train station is on the opposite side of the city from our house, so I was enjoying a pleasant walk through the city when I was surprised by a long, snaking queue outside the local branch of Northern Rock. I asked passers-by what was happening. They told me these unfortunate people had deposit accounts with Northern Rock and were queuing up to get their money out before the bank collapsed. It was a weird feeling, as I'd neither seen nor heard of a bank-run queue since watching wild-west movies some decades ago. It had never occurred to me that these things could happen in today's world and that I'd actually see one unfolding in the street.

Of course, the bank-run made Northern Rock even weaker–another example of Keynes's insight about self-fulfilling prophecies in the finance world: that financial markets often go the way that the masses think they're destined to go.

The Northern Rock story has a more or less happy ending because the UK government–not the central bank but the Ministry of Finance (called the "Treasury" in the UK)–stepped in and lent billions of pounds to Northern

[34] For a brief, broad overview of the GFC and the Great Recession from the perspective of the US Federal Reserve, see their essay "The Great Recession and Its Aftermath" (Weinberg, 2013).

Rock. The government also gave a guarantee of payment for all customers who wished to withdraw their money. It later gave the same guarantee for other banks, and for a while the crisis in Britain was well-managed, more or less.

In the US, however, the big crunch came a year later, when the hyper-large investment bank Lehman Brothers stood on the brink of collapse. Lehman had invested heavily in derivatives, the complex financial instruments that contained slices of sub-prime mortgages, described above. The value of these fell precipitously and Lehman no longer had sufficient assets to cover its losses. Its share value plummeted and it could no longer raise extra money by issuing new shares. It filed for bankruptcy on 15 September 2008. The fact that this was a Monday made matters worse, as I explain below.

At that time Lehman owed around $600 billion that it couldn't pay. This was a fairly large chunk of the US economy, but even then it was just the tip of the iceberg, because if Lehman could fail, so could hundreds of other investment banks, exotic investment institutions, and even commercial banks. Unfortunately, a Monday is followed by four more working days, so there was plenty of time for private investors to join the stampede and withdraw their money from banks and financial institutions throughout the US before the weekend was due to arrive and freeze everything in place for a few days.

To cut a long story short, within days the US central bank, the Fed, stepped in and created billions of dollars of new money (out of nothing) to inject into the markets to keep the economy afloat. When irresponsible governments do this, it's popularly called "printing money", but the Fed gave it a new, respectable name, "quantitative easing", or "QE".

Before explaining how QE works, I want to point out why this name change was very, very important. The term "printing money" is associated with economic disasters, hyper-inflation and social chaos, such as in Germany in the 1920s or more recently Zimbabwe. If the Fed had allowed its intervention to be called "printing money", this could have had the psychological effect of reducing confidence in the financial markets even more deeply. But by giving it the technical-sounding name "quantitative easing", they gave it a respectability that was designed to inrease society's confidence in the robustness and durability of the money created.

The Chairman of the Fed at that time, Ben Bernanke, was later questioned by a Congressional committee on where all the money had come from that he'd used to buy up and rejuvenate hundreds of half-defunct financial institutions. The committee first asked him if the Fed had borrowed this money, and he said no. Then they asked if it came from taxes, and again he said no. Congressional Representative Sean Duffy then asked him, "Are you basically printing money to buy those assets?"

Bernanke replied, "We're not printing money. We're creating reserves in the banking system."[35]

That sounds both intellectual and respectable. What it literally means, of course, is "We're creating money and depositing it in the commercial banks' reserve accounts." The average investor or congressional representative probably wouldn't have a clue what "creating reserves in the banking system" means, but would probably feel it sounds safe. It later came to be called quantitative easing. Language is very important in the financial world because, to return again to Keynes's great insight, if people think, rightly or wrongly, that the financial system is about to crash, it most likely will.

What, then, is quantitative easing and how does it work? I'll sum it up in one sentence, which may sound confusing at first, but then I'll unpack it and explain it phrase by phrase: *The central bank creates money and uses it to buy government bonds on the secondary market, as well as a limited portfolio of commercial bonds where necessary, depositing this money in the reserve accounts of commercial banks.*

It "creates money": The central bank creates money using keystrokes on a computer. Each dollar it creates is a promise to write off a dollar worth of taxes, fees and fines. The money it creates is narrow money, high-powered money, as dependable as the country itself. In this case, it was as dependable as the United States of America was at the time.

It buys "bonds": A bond is an IOU for a nominated amount of money. Anyone can issue a bond. You issue a bond by signing a particular kind of IOU and then selling it. Whoever buys the IOU from you earns interest from you at an agreed rate for a given number of years. At the end of that time, called the "maturity date", the bond is handed back to the issuer, in return for the nominated amount of money, called the bond's "face value", plus any interest that's still owed. In the meantime the issuer must pay the interest each year to the owner of the bond. To buy a ten-year bond with a face value of, say, $10,000, you agree on an interest rate with the issuer and pay them the $10,000. The issuer then has $10,000 of regular money which

[35] CBS News (2009)

they're free to spend however they like. You can then sell the bond on to another buyer, for a price you both agree on, which may be higher or lower than $10,000, depending on whether the bond's interest rate is currently competitive or not. After ten years the bond's maturity date arrives, when the original issuer has to pay the face-value of the bond, $10,000, to whoever owns the bond at the time. In the meantime they have to pay interest to whoever owns the bond.

"Government bonds": Governments issue bonds regularly as a way of borrowing money. In the US most of these are called "treasuries". The government usually sells these at a special kind of auction, often called a Dutch auction. This is a contorted-sounding process but, put simply, whoever offers to accept the lowest interest rate for the bond wins the auction and gets to buy the bond[36]. As you can imagine, potential buyers of bonds issued by a weak, corrupt, irresponsible government will demand very high interest rates if they're to buy the bonds. On the other hand, the German government can often sell bonds at zero or even negative interest rates. Germany's 10-year bond was paying 2.43% on 3rd January 2025, but Hungary's was 6.67% and Russia's was 15.12%[37]. Governments are creating and selling these bonds continually, while also getting back and paying out on the bonds they issued earlier and that have now matured.

Fortunately for the US economy, prior to the financial crisis there were tens of thousands of US government bonds already in circulation, worth billions of dollars. Many of these bonds were owned by banks that were on the verge of going bust. If someone would swoop in and buy these bonds, this would save them.

"The secondary market": When the Fed does its QE, it doesn't buy government bonds directly from the US government. Its aim is to put money into the hands of wobbly, half-broke financial institutions, to stop them collapsing. These institutions already owned millions of dollars' worth of government bonds, but during the great financial crisis they couldn't sell their government bonds for a good price on the open market, because other financial institutions were withdrawing money from banks rather than investing. So the Fed bought government bonds from them–i.e., it bought them on the secondary market–and thereby boosted the banks' stocks of

---

[36] The "yield" of a bond is the interest rate adjusted according to the price you pay for the bond at the time. For example, if you by a $10,000 government bond with an interest rate of 4%, but you pay only $9,000 for it (for example because the seller needs cash urgently), the yield is 4.445%.

[37] Investing.com (2025)

high-powered money. As noted above, the money it paid for these bonds was new money that it was creating out of nothing.

"A limited supply of commercial bonds": In case a half-broke commercial bank doesn't own enough government bonds to sell, the Fed can buy bonds which that commercial bank itself issues. Or, if the bank owns bonds that were issued by other, financially sound firms, such as Microsoft or BP, the Fed can offer to buy these. That's another way of increasing these banks' supply of high-powered money.

"Depositing this money in the reserve accounts of commercial banks": The money created by the central bank to buy these bonds from commercial banks and other financial institutions is high-powered money, narrow money. It gets deposited directly into the reserve accounts of these banks and institutions. They can use it to pay narrow money debts directly, or to serve as collateral to create their own broad money to pay debts in the wider economy.

That's how QE works. In my own words: The central bank creates money out of thin air and uses it to buy bonds from half-broke banks and other financial institutions so that they'll have money to pay their debts. Because they're now more able to pay their debts, the institutions they owe money to are also less likely to go broke, and so on through the chain of debtors and creditors. This breaks the cycle of bad debts and economic collapse.

On 17 September 2008, a Wednesday, two days after Lehman filed for bankruptcy and just before QE began, the total assets of the Fed amounted to $910 billion–meaning it owned that much worth of bonds. Within days that had doubled, and by 7 December its assets had increased to $2,000 billion. They reached a peak of $4,510 billion on 24 December 2014. Most of this was bought with QE money. The Fed created $2,290 billion via QE between 2008 and 2014, an average of just over a billion dollars a day for 6 years[38].

Other countries' central banks soon followed the Fed's example, putting trillions of dollars' worth of newly created money into the hands of commercial banks and investment banks around the world. Almost all these central banks followed the Fed's lead in calling their money-creation "quantitative easing".

---

[38] Federal Reserve (2020); Statista (2024a)

One of the last to act was the European Central Bank, which had left the Eurozone economy to limp and totter for five unhappy years. The European Central Bank then created €2,535 billion between October 2014 and December 2018 (over and above its regular topping up of the money supply). This was an average of €1.633 billion per day of newly created money, for 1,552 days[39].

Note that the European Central Bank also carefully avoided using the term "printing money". Officially they called it their "Asset Purchase Programmes", but it took the same form as US quantitative easing and is popularly called "QE".

In one sense, QE was a remarkably successful financial rescue throughout the world, in that it avoided a far deeper and widespread economic collapse. But it came with huge social costs. People who'd taken out sub-prime mortgages in good faith lost their homes, while commercial banks that had drawn them into these deals were rescued with enormous injections of central bank money. Households who'd lost their homes were plunged into debt and ended up spending less on everyday goods and services, leading to local unemployment and business bankruptcies. In the US, 6% of the workforce lost their jobs in 2008-2009[40]. US households' net worth reduced by $13 trillion between 2007 and 2009, equivalent to about $35,000 per person or $70,000 per household.

In the UK the Gross Domestic Product (GDP) fell from a peak of £445 billion in March 2008 to a trough of £419 billion in April 2009. The unemployment rate increased from 5.2% in February 2008 to 8.4% in October 2011[41].

It's been argued that a more appropriate response from central banks would have been to inject money into the households that were defaulting, or about to default, on their mortgages, for example by creating money to buy a stake in each house, rather than rescue the banks directly. This could have saved both the households and the banks they were indebted to, as the households could have continued to pay their mortgages[42]. It would also have prevented households' spending from tanking, and would have therefore also avoided the knock-on effects on local businesses and jobs.

---

[39] European Central Bank (2020

[40] Federal Reserve (2024)

[41] Office of National Statistics (2024)

[42] Galvin (2020)

But whatever view we have of the ethics or effectiveness of the methods central banks chose for injecting new money into the economy, Joseph Vogl's insight stands out. The system of regular everyday central bank practice is not fully suitable for keeping the economy stable in a world where anyone can create financial instruments that behave like money. Money creation is a social phenomenon which is impossible to fully control. As Ingham notes, "… governments and central banks have far less control of the monetary system than they would like to have and, indeed, claim to have", and there is "… a constant struggle between monetary authorities and private financial enterprise money creation[43]."

In Chapter 3 we delve more deeply into the intriguing history of contestation for the control of money between governments and private concerns, a contestation that's still alive today and is likely to continue long into the future.

Concluding remarks

In Chapter 1 we saw that governments create high-powered, "narrow" money, which forms the basis on which the wider economy is built. Meanwhile commercial banks create lower-powered "broad" money by issuing loans and by marking up deposits in their customers' bank accounts. In this chapter we've extended this to see how governments' money creation is not only *channelled through* their central banks, but also *supplemented by* their central banks.

We saw that central banks have an important role in linking commercial banks together and keeping them under a form of control. The central bank provides a home for their stocks of narrow money, which serves as the high-powered collateral for the lower-powered loan monies they create. Central banks also discipline commercial banks, in a sense, to restrain their money creation within realistic limits. They do this mostly by influencing the interest rates these banks have to pay, for the extra money they need, to make up the shortfalls in their daily reconciling of accounts with each other at the central bank. The central bank's aim in this is to keep the economy stable and to ensure that the amount of money in circulation more-or-less matches the value of the goods and services on offer.

We also saw that this can go terribly wrong, the main reason being that money creation isn't limited to governments, their central banks, and

---

[43] Ingham (2020), page 106

commercial banks. Anyone can create money, and its form can vary widely. Exotic forms of so-called "near money" that ballooned in the mid-2000s created a potentially devastating economic crisis that almost collapsed global economies.

Finally, we saw that central banks came to the rescue–more or less–via the magic of quantitative easing. They created vast amounts of money out of thin air. They called this "quantitative easing" to cleverly avoid the stigma of the term "printing money". They used this to prop up the large financial institutions whose profligacy had caused the crisis. This re-stabilised the economy, but hard questions remain as to whether the right people got the newly created money.

In Chapter 10 we'll look at another great challenge to central banks' influence on economic stability, namely cryptocurrencies, and in Chapter 9 we'll see how central banks are responding by developing a new form of virtual cash, called a central bank digital currency (CBDC). But next up, we'll look at how the advent of capitalism led to the money and banking system described in this chapter.

3. SPANISH GOLD, ITALIAN IOUS, AND THE RISE OF CAPITALISM

I wonder what comes to mind when you hear the word "capitalism". Or whether you feel complimented, insulted or confused if someone calls you a "capitalist". The words "capitalism" and "capitalist" tend to evoke strong feelings, or they miss their mark because we don't quite know what the speaker's talking about. What is capitalism? What is a capitalist? How is it related to capital? Is capital just another word for money or wealth?

To begin with, let's clarify what capitalism is not. The ancient Romans had a very unequal society of enormously rich landowners, thousands of utterly poor labourers, most of whom were slaves, and a relatively small middle-class. They used money, they lent at interest, and they paid taxes. But this isn't what we call capitalism.

In the 16th century the conquistadores flooded the Spanish market with the gold and silver they were looting from the Americas. Spanish kings were able to finance huge armies that cowed the western world and colonised peoples as distant as the Pacific. Spain became enormously rich–until inflation and the end of the gold bonanza severely weakened the economy. But this wasn't capitalism either.

There was also a huge influx of gold and silver into the Muslim cities of Mecca and Medina in Arabia in the 7th century. Islam was extraordinarily popular in its first few centuries and spread rapidly across North Africa, the Middle East and as far as India in the southeast and the Iberian Peninsula in the northwest[44]. Its tax system was efficient and effective, bringing "unimaginable wealth" to Medina and Mecca and a huge building boom. But under Islamic law most of the wealth was shared with people of all religions throughout the entire Islamic empire, with the poor being prioritised. This certainly wasn't capitalism either.

To understand capitalism and how it got started we can look to a group of 15th and 16th century Italian merchants writing IOUs. We can also note how Venice's canals and ocean port helped get the system up and running. Then

---

[44] Alkhateeb (2017), page 46.

we can delve into the history of a long-running, fiercely competitive relationship between governments and commerce for the control of money.

15th Century Italian IOUs

Let's start with the Italian IOUs. In Shakespeare's play *The Merchant of Venice*, Shylock the banker lends Antonio 3,000 ducats of solid, coin-based money. A ducat was a coin containing about 3.5 grams of nearly pure gold, modelled on the Florentine florin. If Antonio fails to repay the money by the due date, he'll forfeit a pound of his own flesh. In 1596, when the play is believed to have been written, a ducat was worth about $US150 of today's money, so a pound of Antonio's flesh was valued at just under half a million modern US dollars. In fact, however, late 16th century Italian financiers didn't lend people such large amounts of real money, but Shakespeare might not have known this. The system that Venice and other Italian cities were using at the time was based almost entirely on IOUs and was just beginning to get established in England when Shakespeare was writing.

The finance and loan system in north Italian cities such as Venice, Genoa and Florence during that period has been carefully researched by economic historian Niall Kishtainy and other economics scholars such as Geoffrey Ingham and Andrew Leigh[45]. About 150 years before *The Merchant of Venice* was written, several families in Venice believed they were wealthy enough to guarantee they could honour quite large IOUs they wrote and issued. A wealthy family might have a chest of real ducats plus jewellery and gold and silver bars. The family could act as a financier by using this as collateral to make a loan in the form of an IOU, to a trader. Traders and their clients would trust that the IOU would be honoured because they knew about the wealthy family's treasure chest and other assets.

Trade had the potential to boom because Venice's port enabled cargo ships to dock, and its canals enabled goods to be delivered close to retailers' and wholesalers' doors, plus the reverse of this for exporting.

Often a trader would need to outlay money to import a shipment of goods from one of Venice's trading partners, such as Constantinople, in what was then the Byzantine Empire. Suppose the trader needed 100 ducats. He could get a promissory note for 100 ducats–a form of IOU–from one of Venice's wealthy financiers. The trader would then owe the financier 100 ducats of

---

[45] Kishtainy (2017), pages 17ff; Ingham (2011), pages 70ff; Leigh (2024), pages 27ff.

real, solid money and have to pay it within a specified time, plus interest. In the meantime he would use the IOU to pay for the goods he was importing. He could then sell the goods to local buyers for regular, coin-based money. He would easily get enough, from these sales, to pay the financier his 100 ducats plus interest, and make a tidy profit.

Meanwhile, whoever ended up with the IOU could at any time hand it back to the financier and get 100 ducats of solid money for it–and it would be no problem for the financier to pay it because he would have got, or expected soon to get, the 100 ducats from the trader, plus interest. The financier would profit from the interest he'd charged the trader, and the IOU for 100 ducats would then be effectively dissolved into nothing.

Everybody benefited. The exporter got 100 ducats for the goods he sold to the trader. The trader got more than 100 ducats from his customers, so he made a profit. The customers got some useful goods (clothes, furniture, spices, etc.) which they wouldn't otherwise have had. The financier got the interest on the loan he'd created, *and he did this without actually opening his treasure chest and giving out any real coins or gold bars.*

Money and anti-money

It's helpful to see this process as the instantaneous creation of both credit and debt. When the financier wrote the IOU–the promissory note–he created both a credit for himself, and a debt against himself, at the same instant of time. The *credit* was the IOU for 100 ducats that began circulating in the economy the moment the trader got it from the financier. This credit would eventually return to the financier in the form of 100 actual ducats. The *debt* was the 100 ducats which the financier now owed to whoever would end up giving the IOU back to him.

So, although a form of money had been created out of nothing, at the same time a kind of anti-money had been created. The *money* circulates in the economy (as an IOU) and induces people to do work, make things, trade goods, and improve the quality of life. Meanwhile the *anti-money* sits in the background, waiting to destroy the money (the IOU) when its job is done. Fortunately the anti-money doesn't unmake things or ruin the quality of life. It just sits there, like a black hole, ready to swallow up the money when its life has run its course.

To be completely accurate, we can give a more comprehensive, but rather complicated, description of the situation: there are actually *two* sets of money and anti-money. First, the trader has both a credit (money) and a debt (anti-money). He has a *credit* of 100 ducats as specified in the IOU, and at the same time he owes a *debt* to the financier of 100 ducats. Meanwhile the financier also has both a credit and a debt. He has a credit (money) in that he's owed 100 ducats by the trader, but simultaneously he has a debt (anti-money) in that he has to pay 100 ducats to whoever gives him back the IOU.

This is always how it is with money. Wherever there's money, there's also anti-money. Each unit of money is shadowed by an equally large, but negative, unit of anti-money, waiting in the wings to swallow it up. The Italian financiers developed so-called "double-entry bookkeeping" to keep track of this: money in the left-hand column (called "Assets"); anti-money in the right-hand column (called "Liabilities"). If you add up all the money in a loan-based economy such as this, the total always comes to zero[46].

Capitalism, in a sense, rests on this foundation. It's more dynamic and stable than a gold-based economy because you can create the right amount of money to match the capacity of the real economy–the labour, skills, raw materials and technology that's waiting in the wings to get active. You don't have to wait till a goldmine is discovered, to activate this real economy. Conversely, you won't swamp the economy with "too much money chasing too few goods and services", as you would when a massive haul of gold arrives on the scene.

How the IOU circulates

Back to our story of the (non-Shakespearian) merchant of Venice. The trader would use the IOU to pay the exporter for the shipment of goods he was importing. The exporter would gladly accept it because he knew the reputation of the financier who issued it, and he also knew of the financier's connections with similar financiers in Constantinople.

When the exporter returned to his home port of Constantinople, he could hand the note to one of these financiers, who would gladly give him 100 ducats for it, or the equivalent in the Byzantine currency, the solidus. The financier in Constantinople would know the reputation of the financier in Venice, so he would be happy to exchange the note for coins.

---

[46] For an interesting discussion on this in the modern economy, see the Fed's report by Lagos (2006).

Hundreds of transactions and payments like this were taking place throughout northern Italy and nearby countries at the time, with IOUs criss-crossing between financiers. Every few months the financiers would meet up, work out who owed who how much, and settle their debts. The IOUs were then destroyed or marked invalid. The loan money they had created was thereby dissolved back into nothing. The financiers were richer due to the interest they had charged the original recipients of their IOUs. The interest was, of course, solid money. The traders would almost certainly be able to provide this because they got it from the sales of their goods. Life was better for Venetians because they could enjoy the goods that the importer brought them. Life was better for people in Constantinople because they got paid for making the goods that were exported, and they could spend the money on other goods from other places (like Venice!). Life was better for the trader and the exporter because they'd both made a profit. Life was better for the financier because he'd earned interest on the IOU.

The IOU no longer existed. The money that did all this wonderful work had been swallowed up by being reunited with its equivalent anti-money.

You'll notice that this is similar to what happens in the banking system today, as described in Chapter 2. Commercial banks create money by making loans to businesses and other customers. Like Venetian financiers, their loans are effectively IOUs (except that they're "fungible", meaning they can be divided up into smaller units–e.g., a bank loan of $100,000 can be used for four separate payments of $25,000). Meanwhile these commercial banks' "real" money sits in their reserve accounts at the central bank, just as the Venetian financiers' real money was safely locked away in their treasure chests. Also, like Venetian financiers, modern commercial banks regularly reconcile their accounts with each other, except that they do it at the end of every working day, not just once every few months. Their daily reconciliation of accounts at the central bank is a frantic, mostly electronic version of the more relaxed, sociable, occasional meetings of 15th-16th century financiers.

The money and anti-money in modern bank loans is the same, logically and in its effects, as in the Venetian system. Today's commercial banks get richer because of the interest they charge on the loan moneys they create, and this interest is "real" money (narrow, high-powered money) and increases the balance in their reserve account at the central bank. If the loans go to businesses that provide goods and services that humanity needs, everybody benefits from the system.

The beginning of capitalism?

As the northern Italian system developed and grew, it gave a huge boost to commerce. Financiers could issue IOUs totalling several times the value of the solid money in their coffers. The amount of IOU-money in the economy could expand to match the capacities of local traders to import, foreign traders to export, home industries to manufacture, and distant farmers to grow and harvest crops. Initially it was limited, of course, to major players, because the IOUs were usually for large amounts and weren't fungible like regular money: they couldn't be divided up into tenths and hundreds of their face value. But the system gave commerce a big boost and contributed to making northern Italy rich in goods and services.

This didn't necessarily increase the amount of solid metal money in circulation–the ducats, solidi or gold bars. Instead, it created a huge layer of what we might call broad money or near money, or what the ancient Chinese called "money on the fly"[47].

This is often seen as the beginning of capitalism[48]. Private financiers were creating money specifically to enable trade and commerce to flourish. The amount of money in circulation was no longer restricted by the number and face value of coins minted by governments or by the total weight of precious metals. Non-government entrepreneurs had found a way to make as much "money-on-the-fly" as traders and businesses wanted. The amount of money-on-the-fly expanded and contracted in response to the needs and demands of business, rather than the whims of the monarch or the successes and failures of gold and silver mining.

The Italian system soon spread to Holland, then to England. More on that below.

The reign in Spain

Meanwhile, in Spain, a very different story was playing out, as I mentioned in Chapter 2. The amount of solid money in the economy was rapidly expanding, as tonnes of gold and silver landed in Spanish ports after the ships and crews carrying it had survived storms, scurvy, plagues and pirates of the Caribbean (including a royally sanctioned English pirate named Sir

---

[47] Yulu (2014), pages 16ff.
[48] See especially Ingham (2008) and Ingham (2020) pages 61-85.

Francis Drake[49]). Not to mention the genocide of southern and central America's indigenous peoples through violence and European diseases, along with the deaths of thousands of Spaniards through violence and American diseases. This was much more dramatic and costly than writing IOUs.

The effect on the Spanish economy was tumultuous but short-lived. Gold and silver began arriving late in the 15th century. By the mid-16th century Spain was the richest country in the world. Traders in Europe equated gold with money, so the Spanish could import almost whatever they wanted. Spanish kings–who got 20% of all the new gold and silver–equipped a large army to conquer and exploit lands abroad.

But inflation quickly set in, because the thousands of new Spanish doubloons and escudos that were constantly being minted from newly arriving gold and silver flooded the market. This made local labour and goods more expensive, without significantly increasing the amount of work done or goods made. As the supply of new gold and silver began to run out early in the 17th century, Spain's economy stagnated. Spain became the sick man of Europe. The economic historian Carlos J. Charotti and his colleagues have estimated that by the end of the 16th century Spain's economy was 40% larger than it would have been without the influx of gold and silver, but 150 years later it had shrunk to 40% smaller than it would have been if Spain had not been the first to exploit America's precious metals[50].

It's worth noting that the Muslim world also had at least one hyper-inflation episode due to a sudden excess of gold. In the 14th century the West African Muslim kingdom of Mali, capital city Timbuktu, had huge deposits of gold in its legendary mines. In 1324 King Mansa Musa decided to make a pilgrimage to Mecca and Medina. He was accompanied by an entourage of 60,000 people, among whom 20,000 carried two kilograms of gold each (which would be worth around 3.4 trillion US dollars by today's gold price). Along the way, via North Africa, they gave small amounts of gold to the poor, but when they got to Egypt they became excessively generous. The Islamic scholar Firas Alkhateeb comments:

> In Egypt, Musa is said to have given out so much gold to the cities' locals, that unintended inflation wrecked the economy, and when the famous North

---

[49] Drake was an English world explorer and adventurer who supported the English monarchy and harassed Spanish shipping in the 16th century so successfully that he earned the nickname "El Draque" – meaning "The Dragon" in old Spanish.
[50] Charotti et al. (2022)

African traveller Ibn Battuta visited Egypt ten years later, he noticed that the local economy had still not recovered from the giant influx of the valuable metal.[51]

Why did all that gold lead to financial doldrums in Egypt and later in Spain? It was because the supply of money was out of step with the willingness or capacity of entrepreneurs, workers and consumers to produce and consume useful goods and services. By contrast, in the Venetian system the creation of money was closely attuned to the creation of specific commercial projects which were geared to improve the quality of people's lives and therefore be profitable. There's no shortage of popular criticism of capitalism, but this is perhaps its greatest strength.

Why Northern Italy's IOUs are capitalism

As the economist and sociologist Geoffrey Ingham points out, Northern Italy's system was one of the key events in the development of capitalism, because it enabled money to be created out of nothing to finance commercial ventures, then dissolved back into nothing when it had been round in a full circle. Ingham argues there are three essential elements to capitalism[52].

A. A monetary system for producing bank-credit money
B. Market exchange
C. Private enterprise production of commodities

We've looked at point A above. However, there's a big step from the somewhat informal IOU system of 16th century Italian city-states to the highly regulated, centralised system used today. I'll say more about this below. First, a few remarks about point B, market exchange.

Market exchange

The civilised world has always had markets. The ancient Greek philosopher Socrates once said, "I enjoy going to the market, because I love to go and see all the things I am happy without"[53]. He was probably thinking of small material goods like grapes, sandals and lyres, all brought together in a city

---

[51] Althateeb (2017), pages 171-172.
[52] Ingham (2008), page 52
[53] For a discussion of whether these were genuinely Socrates' words see https://www.reddit.com/r/Stoicism/comments/dwedws/i_love_to_go_and_see_all_the_things_i_am_happy/?rdt=48238

square for selling and haggling over prices. But markets can be scattered and dispersed over wide areas, such as the cotton market in the 18th and 19th centuries or the electricity market today.

What all these have in common is negotiation: sellers' attempts to raise their prices and buyers' attempts to lower them. Today we don't often hear this out loud as haggling, because most markets are not held in city squares but exist over wide expanses, even globally, and some exist only virtually, via computers and mobile phones. But the haggling can still be there in the background, as sellers attempt to make their goods cheaper than their competitors'–but not too cheap–and buyers attempt to outbid each other–but not by too much. Haggling tends to make prices converge to their most efficient levels, provided there's genuine competition between sellers and between buyers. The 18th century pioneering economist Adam Smith brought this clearly into focus. He argued that markets should be as free as possible so that the "invisible hand of the market" can make prices converge to their most efficient levels.

Smith's views are controversial, and the Oxford economic historian Linda Yueh gives a clear, readable outline of this controversy[54]. An obvious problem with Smith's view is that in his day, most markets were in-person, social events where people could genuinely bargain against each other for the goods laid out before them. Carolyn Steel describes these bustling, crowded markets, in particular food markets, in her book *Hungry City*[55]. We can see from her meticulous research how the meaning of the word "market" has shifted since the 18th century.

But Smith's views are still very influential. Capitalism requires relatively free "markets" if it's to be effective in making goods and services as realistically priced as possible. Unfortunately, this tends to benefit the better-off sections of society much more than the poor, as the poor can't compete against wealthier buyers in today's so-called marketplace, and often the wealthy, powerful players set the rules for their own benefit.

The main point here is that there have always been markets, and some markets are more "free" than others. It's also important to note that *Capitalism is not unique in utilizing free markets*–even the ancient Greeks had them. But the concept of free markets is an essential element of capitalism, alongside money creation via IOUs.

---

[54] Yueh (2018), pages 11-31.
[55] Steel (2013), pages 53-152.

The third feature of capitalism is the production of goods and services by private enterprise. I won't go into this in detail, except to say that creating new money by way of IOUs opens up huge possibilities for entrepreneurs to build factories and other enterprises, though it also provides a slew of options for exploitation. For readers who'd like a balanced, carefully reasoned analysis of this feature of capitalism, including both its nastiness and social successes, I highly recommend Ingham's book *Capitalism*[56] and Robert Reich's book *Saving Capitalism*[57]. Here, however, I want to continue to focus on the first of the three features of capitalism, namely money creation. I'll now explain how governments, banks and other private investors have battled for control of this since the dawn of capitalism in the late Middle Ages.

The battle for control of money creation

We've seen how private capital came to be created by wealthy financiers via their IOUs, and how these were backed up by the collateral of regular, state-created money in their coffers. The past 500 years have seen a battle for control of these two forms of money between the state and the private sector. This battle has been deeply affected by a long-standing and prevalent misunderstanding of what money is and how it functions. Today this battle has settled on a compromise, often called the "memorable alliance". But the structure of this compromise is weakened by the persistence of a deeply rooted misunderstanding as to what money is.

I'll begin by outlining the misunderstanding, as this will help readers see why the "memorable alliance" turned out the way it is. The misunderstanding is *the assumption that money always comes from somewhere else, somewhere apart from the person or institution that wants to spend it.* A longstanding form of this view is people's preoccupation with gold and silver: that you can get money by mining or looting gold and silver, and that this automatically increases the supply of money. But this view doesn't add up. When there's not enough gold, kings and rulers cheat by reducing the amount of precious metal in their coins. Alternatively, countries have issued paper money and tied its value to the price of gold, but the need for more money has often raced ahead of the amount of gold in their vaults, so they've eventually given up and let their currencies float in value. The last great abandonment of the gold standard was US President Nixon's, in 1971.

---

[56] Ingham (2008)
[57] Reich (2016)

A more recent form of this misconception is the belief that governments have to tax the private sector or borrow money from the private sector in order to have money to spend: that they have to get money from sources *outside* themselves, namely from the private sector.

This view would be fine if the total amount of money always stays the same. But it doesn't. There's far more money in the British economy today than there was in 1946, when the Bank of England was nationalised, and far more money in virtually every country than there was in 1971, when the US went off the gold standard. In New Zealand, for example, a typical modern economy, the amount of money in the economy increased about four-fold between 1988 and 2019. This mirrored population growth, inflation and a steady increase in gross domestic product (GDP) per capita. Where did all this new money come from, if money always has to be pulled in from somewhere else? The French economist Gabriel Zucman jokes, in a different context, that there must be money hidden away on another planet[58].

As I've argued in Chapters 1 and 2 and will go into in much greater depth in Chapters 5 and 11, money does *not* come from somewhere else. Most of it is created by the state, which spends it into existence, and by commercial banks, which lend it into existence. And note that the amount commercial banks can create, by issuing loans, depends crucially on the amount of state-created money or other real wealth they own. This phenomenon is the bedrock of capitalism, but it's often poorly understood. As we'll see below, this misunderstanding puts the state in a much weaker position in relation to private capital than it needs to be. It tips the balance of the "memorable alliance" in favour of private capital and enables billionaires to have much more influence on economic policy than they otherwise would.

A brief history of capitalist money-creation

Let's look again at the Merchant of Venice–the real Venetian financier, not Shakespeare's Shylock. I mentioned that the financier gave the trader an IOU, and the trader used it to pay the exporter who exchanged it with a financier in Constantinople, for Byzantine money, and the Byzantine financier eventually exchanged it for solid coin money with the Venetian financier. The City of Venice quickly realised they could make easy money by shortening this loop. They founded a bank which accepted reputable financiers' IOUs and exchanged them for solid coin money–at a profit, of

---

[58] Zucman (2015)

course. They then got their money back by reverse trading them with the original financiers who had issued them.

This system quickly spread across a swathe of Europe which happened to be enjoying a rare period of peace at the time[59], from northern Italy to Holland, then to England during the reign of Queen Elizabeth I (when Shakespeare was writing). In Holland the Bank of Amsterdam was established by the City Council in 1609, somewhat like the City of Venice's bank but on a much wider basis. Its name in Dutch was the "Wisselbank", meaning the "Bank of exchange". It accepted financiers' promissory notes, as well as coins, from many countries in Europe and exchanged them, at stable exchange rates, for its own precious-metal coins that were not debased, but of course at a tidy profit. This contributed to Holland's growing economic power, as it attracted commerce from throughout Europe during the period of expanding trade and colonial conquest.

In England the beginnings of the Venetian-style IOU system gave a huge boost to commerce, so much so that the commercial sector was becoming wealthy enough to make its own demands on the sovereign queen or king. It also represented a challenge to the sovereign's own exclusive right to issue money. It was especially a problem when the queen or king wanted to borrow money. Unlike in 15th century Spain, the English sovereigns never had enough gold or silver to finance their foreign wars, while the commerce sector was awash with money due to the growth of the IOU system. But it wouldn't do for a king or queen to have to go cap in hand to private financiers to get their enormous loans.

In passing, note the shifting assumptions behind this. On the one hand, money is believed to be essentially precious metal, a quantity of valuable material, and the sovereign doesn't have enough of it. On the other hand, the sovereign sees that IOU money works well in the commercial sector, and would like to make use of it even if she or he has to pay interest on it.

This led to a struggle in England between the commerce sector, the sovereign, and parliament. A compromise was reached in 1694 during the reign of William III (called William of Orange, due to his Dutch roots). A quasi "government bank" was established, styled somewhat on the Amsterdam model. It was called the Bank of England.

Today the Bank of England is owned by the state. It's subject to the government's wishes, which are subject to the dictates of parliament (at

---

[59] For a more detailed overview see Ingham (2020), pages 61-85.

least in theory), and it regularly makes money out of nothing. It does this through quantitative easing, as we saw in Chapter 2. It also does a very low-level version of quantitative easing on a daily basis, called "open market operations", which we'll look at in detail in Chapter 11. And of course, it regularly creates the money the government wants to spend.

But the original Bank of England was very different. It was owned by the private commercial sector. It was somewhat like a commercial bank but with just one customer, the British government. It financed the government by getting loans from the private sector. The more the sovereign borrowed, the higher the government's debt became. Effectively the Bank of England was issuing bonds, and when these became due, the Bank of England would simply issue more bonds to get the money to pay these back, plus more to finance the government's ongoing wars. The government also collected taxes, which were deposited in its account at the Bank of England, but taxes were unpopular and never enough to cover the government's outgoings.

To summarize thus far, city banks such as those in Venice and Amsterdam were established initially to act as clearing houses for the thousands of IOUs that were issued by financiers and that were criss-crossing between different firms and enterprises. The Bank of England added the additional role of being the government's bank. However, unlike financiers and commercial banks, the Bank of England was not, at that time, a bank that could create new money. Instead it acted as a straightforward deposit account for banking the government's tax takings, paying the government's bills, and borrowing to finance the government's excess expenditure.

The next phase in the evolution of capitalism was a gradual shift in central bank ownership. This was a slow, stop-start process, but fast-forward to 1946, when the newly elected UK Labour government nationalised the Bank of England. The Bank of England then came to be owned by the government rather than private shareholders, and its governors were then appointed by the government. Other countries followed suit, though the history of the US's central bank, the Federal Reserve, is more stop-start and complex[60].

A further development was that central banks became the channels through which governments minted new money–originally just coins, then paper money, and more recently electronic money, which is by far the largest proportion of money today. *The logic of government spending thereby*

[60] See Ingham (2020), pages 69ff.

reversed. Governments created new money by spending it into existence, then taxed it back, thereby avoiding flooding the economy with ever increasing amounts of money.

Yet another development was to give central banks a form of independence to influence the economy toward stability, which of course included an acceptable amount of inflation and growth. Central banks use a range of methods to do this. The main two are influencing interest rates and feeding extra money into and out of the economy via "open market operations". New Zealand was the first country to opt for this degree of central bank independence, in 1989, and others followed.

Success and ongoing problems

On the surface it might seem, then, that governments eventually got the upper hand in the "memorable alliance" between the state and the commercial sector. The government owns its own bank. Moreover, it has successfully split the money supply into two main portions, both of which are neither gold-backed nor predominantly coinage and notes: high-powered, narrow money and lower-powered, broad money. Narrow money consists of physical cash (which is relatively small) plus all the electronic money that sits in commercial banks' reserve accounts which are held at the central bank–effectively in the form of bookkeeping assets–as explained in Chapters 1 and 2. This makes up a large portion of the collateral, often called "reserves", on which commercial bank loans are based. Broad money, in contrast, sits in your and my accounts at our commercial banks, and its creation is influenced, at least indirectly, by the amount of narrow money in these commercial banks' accounts at the central bank.

A weakness of the "memorable alliance", however, was touched on in Chapter 2. Anyone can create money, as long as people accept it as money. There's not just narrow money created by the government and broad money created by commercial banks. There's a huge swathe of "near-money"–mutual funds, credit default swaps, bonds, futures and other exotic financial instruments–circulating in an enormous bubble of financial transactions that have little or nothing to do with material goods and services. Apart from government-issued bonds, which are usually stable in value (but not always), these are often high-risk investments and tend to get larger and riskier as time goes on, until they tend to collapse. As I mentioned in Chapter 2, central banks don't have the means to control these tidal waves of near-money and can find themselves having to bail out big financiers whose collapse would ricochet through the economy. This is a consequence of capitalism. The ascendancy of IOUs has made life better for millions of people but always leaves this bogey lurking in the background.

A further weakness in the system will be covered in detail in Chapter 11. It seems to be rooted in a misunderstanding of how modern money works and what its potential is. On the one hand, the state has to continually increase the money supply to cater for an acceptable level of inflation and a realistic level of GDP growth. This implies that governments should spend just a little bit more each year than they get back in taxes. But many governments appear to make two great mistakes. First, they borrow this excess from the private sector, by issuing bonds, to get the money for the extra that needs to be spent to facilitate inflation and GDP growth. This is self-defeating because, by borrowing, they're taking money out of the same pool they're trying to enlarge. The central bank then has to step in and inject new money into the economy via its open market operations. It does this by creating new money and using it to buy government bonds–with the result that a large portion of government debt is owned by its own central bank. This debt is routinely included in financial statements and news of the amount of government debt, which makes some governments look hopelessly deep in debt. But it's really just a kind of charade: "My right hand owes my left hand X-billion dollars".

The second mistake many governments make is to over-spend and under-tax, and borrow even more to cover this. Because of this they really do get heavily into debt, and their central banks are often left to manage the negative effects on the economy. I'll cover this very interesting issue in much more detail in Chapter 11.

Some takeaways

I'll finish this chapter by mentioning some of its key points. First, capitalism is not, essentially, the super-rich having all the economic power and the vast majority of the population living in poverty. This is, sadly, the way most of the world has been for millennia, long before capitalism arrived on the scene. I'll talk about at least one way to begin to reverse this, in Chapter 6.

Second, capitalism got started when moderately wealthy financiers learned how to create loan money in the form of IOUs. This had the advantage that the supply of money could quickly grow to match a country's or region's capacity to make useful goods and services. People didn't have to wait for the arrival of a shipment of gold to get their business and commerce up and running. And they didn't have to close their workshops when the gold stopped coming. There was always as much money available as they believed they could profitably make use of.

Third, the disadvantage of this system was that governments' control of money creation (through minting coins) was severely weakened. Entrepreneurs got the upper hand. The wealthy were able to use and abuse capitalism, often even more effectively than they'd used and abused other systems in the past.

Fourth, governments fought back, and this led to the "memorable alliance". One of governments' main achievements was to get their own bank, the central bank, under their control. Another was to make all private money creation dependent on collateral produced by the government itself: government-created money (high-powered, narrow money) serves as collateral for privately created money (lower-powered, broad money).

But there are still weaknesses here, as we saw in Chapter 2 and will look at in more detail in Chapters 4, 7 and 11.

4. How (not) to fix and grow an economy

When Britain's new Labour government was elected in July 2024, the Prime Minister and Minister of Finance (called the "Chancellor of the Exchequer", or "Chancellor" in Britain) immediately announced there was a "black hole" in the budget which would be difficult and painful to fill. The amount varied from announcement to announcement, but mostly there was talk of the government being £22 billion short in the current financial year. This means the amount it expected to receive in taxes, fees, fines, etc. was £22 billion less than the amount it would have to spend in order to keep public services at their current level.

By 15 October the Chancellor was announcing that this black hole would amount to £100 billion over the next 5 years[61].

In these announcements, "black hole" was slang for the technical term "deficit". The government deficit is generally defined as the government's excess of expenditure over income, in any particular year or other defined period. It's important to keep that word "deficit" in mind, and the definition politicians use for it, as you read on through this chapter, and in fact for the rest of this book. The "deficit" the government speaks of is the *shortfall* of income compared to expenditure, as measured over a defined period of *time*, usually a year.

Meanwhile the Office for National Statistics had announced on 20 September 2024 that government *debt* (note the word "debt", not "deficit") was now as large as Britain's gross national product (GDP)[62]. GDP was £2,720 billion in 2023, and by the end of 2024 the government's debt amounted to £2,822 billion. This represented money owed to enterprises, banks and individuals who'd bought and own government bonds. Remember that in Chapter 2 I explained that governments borrow money by issuing and selling bonds, and that a bond is a form of IOU.

Note the difference between government *debt* and the government's *deficit*. To repeat: the *debt* is the amount the government owes to its creditors. The *deficit* is the difference between what the government earns (through taxes,

---

[61] Guardian (2024)

[62] Bruce (2024)

etc.) and what it spends, in any particular year or defined period of time. You can have a debt without a deficit and a deficit without a debt.

Many reporters, commentators, bloggers, MPs and even some economists confuse these two, at least in their speeches and writings, if not in their thinking. They speak of "debt" when what they're really talking about is a deficit, and vice versa. Or they use them both in the same sentence as if they mean the same thing. In Germany, for example, until April 2025 there was a so-called "*debt*-brake" (*Schuldenbremse*) embedded in the constitution, which says the *deficit* may not exceed 0.35% of GDP[63]. The constitution limited how high the *deficit* in any year can be, but it's erroneously called the *debt-* brake.

Even when commentators don't confuse debt and deficit, they often mistakenly think an ideal world is where the deficit and the debt are reduced to zero, or at least where the deficit is minimal and the debt is falling. This is not just a harmless error of arithmetic. It's one of the main reasons Britain's economy has been languishing in the doldrums for the past decade. In Chapter 7 we'll see it's also one of the reasons Germany's economy and the economies of other countries that use the euro (the "Eurozone" countries) have been severely underperforming. More on the dynamics of this below.

There's also a third measure of state spending and income we need to think about, which politicians or economists don't speak of directly, though they almost always do so indirectly. It's always there in the background and it's very important for understanding the health of the economy. Note that we're talking about the *state* now, not just the *government*. The state includes the government together with its central bank. It'll become clear below why the central bank is a crucial actor in relation to government deficits and debt.

I call this third measure the state's "deficit-in-space", to distinguish it from the classic government deficit as measured over time, which I'll call the government's "deficit-in-time". The state's deficit-in-space is the same measure as the amount of narrow money currently in existence. The narrow money in existence at any given time is the money the state has spent into existence but has not yet got back in taxes, fees, fines, borrowings, student debt repayments, government debt purchases, etc.

---

[63] For more information about Germany's mis-named "debt-brake" see Kinkartz (2024).

The deficit-in-space exists because there's an important lag between the state's expenditure and the state's income. If this lag wasn't there–if the state's income was exactly timed to coincide with the state's expenditure–there would never be a bubble of narrow money in the reserve accounts of commercial banks at the central bank. Commercial banks wouldn't have stocks of narrow money, so they wouldn't have a pool of high-powered money to call on to reconcile their accounts with each other at the end of each working day. They'd also have less collateral as a basis to create their own broad money by making loans.

So the state needs to continually run a spatial deficit, for there to be any economy at all. The state needs to have paid out narrow money in advance, and while it's waiting for that money to be paid back (in the form of taxes, etc.), that money does the essential job of underpinning and powering the broader economy.

Further, this stock of narrow money has to build up over time, so that the total amount of money in the economy can grow, to match the increase in GDP and the effects of inflation. Fortunately, over the past decades the state has more-or-less continually spent more than it's earned (it's almost always run a deficit-in-time), and the result is an increasing deficit-in-space, the ever-expanding bubble of narrow money that underpins the economy as the economy grows. Generally, the more narrow, high-powered money there is in the reserve accounts of commercial banks at the central bank, the more broad, lower-powered money commercial banks can create by issuing loans, and therefore the more the economy can grow–except of course that when there's too much broad money this usually leads to high inflation.

There are several other factors at play in this, as I'll explain in more detail in Chapter 11, but generally speaking, the deficit-in-space needs to keep growing if the economy is going to grow.

We therefore have three different d-words to keep in mind as we think about how to make an economy grow: debt, deficit in time, and deficit in space. To recap:

Debt: the amount the *government* owes its creditors.

Deficit-in-time: the difference between what the *government* spends and earns over a given period of time, usually a year.

Deficit-in-space: the permanent bubble of narrow money that results from the lag between *state* spending and state earning. The "state" here includes both the government and the central bank.

It's useful to keep these three notions in mind and to avoid confusing them with each other, when we consider how an economy can be stimulated to reach its full potential.

Before explaining this, I need to mention that the economists L. Randal Wray, Stephanie Kelton, Eric Tymoigne, Andrew Berkely and others who advocate "modern monetary theory" offer one of the clearest understandings of the significance of government debt and deficit in a modern money system in a reasonably well-functioning "high-income" country[64]. The Cambridge sociologist-cum-economist Geoffrey Ingham also highlights the importance of these modern monetary theorists' insights on this topic[65]. The main point they make is that in a modern, sovereign country which controls its own currency, the state doesn't have to get money from *somewhere outside itself* to be able to spend, since all the narrow money that exists in such a country is created by the state. The state simply spends this money into existence. Therefore, they argue, there's no financial constraint on how large the deficit (in time) can be for a government. They agree there's certainly the *practical* constraint that if a state creates more money than the capacity of workers, businesses and consumers to put it to good use, this is likely to lead to inflation. But there's no *financial* constraint because all narrow money is created by the state.

However, there's a piece of the puzzle that's often missing in these economists' descriptions of money creation, or it's mentioned only obliquely in passing. This has to do with the role of central banks in continually stepping in to boost the narrow money supply when governments fail to do so because they feel morally obliged to cover their deficits by increasing their debt. I'll explain this step by step below. But first let's think for a moment about ordinary household debts and deficits.

Household debts and deficits

Josephine (a real person whose name I've changed for this story) had *debts* of about £50,000 at the start of 2022, due to her student loan, and by the end

---

[64] E.g., Wray (2015); Kelton (2020); Tcherneva and Tygmoigne (2024); Berkely et al. (2022)

[65] Ingham (2020), pages 33 ff.

of 2022 she had reduced these to about £45,000. Her annual take-home pay was £40,000, and she was saving £10,000 of this each year after paying her ordinary living costs, plus her student loan repayments, plus her rent in the shared house she lived in.

She had no *deficit* in that year, because she spent less than she earned, and her savings account increased from about £90,000 to £100,000.

This all changed in 2023 when she bought her own flat. It cost £235,000 including legal fees and government stamp duty. She paid all this with a bank loan of £135,000 plus the £100,000 she'd saved.

Therefore, her *deficit* in the year 2023 was close to £235,000: she spent about £235,000 more than she earned. And her total *debt* at the end of the year was £160,000, including the bank loan and what remained of her student loan debt.

Should Josephine be worried that her debt increased to £160,000 and that she suffered a deficit in the year 2023 of £235,000? Of course not. She now has an investment which is highly likely to increase in value each year, and even if it doesn't, her mortgage interest payments are only a little bit higher than the rent she was previously paying.

I admit this example has its limitations: buying an existing property isn't as productive as starting a business. Other people have invested similar amounts in starting businesses of various kinds. In addition to their investment advantages, these businesses can have positive knock-on effects on the wider economy, when they provide employment and produce goods or services that other people need, thereby increasing the wealth and wellbeing of society.

The moral of the story, however, is that *deficits can be a very good thing.* In fact, *we usually need to run a deficit to get a business or other profitable enterprise or investment up and running.* A second moral of the story is: *debts can be quite acceptable when they arise from wise investments.*

Are governments like households?

What about government debts and deficits? Are they like household debts and deficits? Broadly speaking, there are three main schools of thought on this among economists: Keynesianism; neoliberalism (which is often called economic orthodoxy); and modern monetary theory, which builds on Keynesianism but goes a step further.

Economists in the Keynesian tradition generally say that the story about the household also applies to governments. If governments want their countries' economies to grow, they should invest money in infrastructure, education, health, research, business and enterprise, especially in areas the private sector usually doesn't want to invest in. This, say Keynesians, will often involve going into debt and running deficits. The debts will incur interest, but government income will grow as the economy grows, so the debts will be easier to pay off.

Neoliberal economists have a different view. They say governments should have only a very small role in the economy. They should get out of the way and leave it to private enterprise to make the economy grow. They say government investments will "crowd out" private enterprise, meaning that if governments pay to start essential businesses or services like health and education, there'll be fewer profitable deals left for private enterprise to invest in. Neoliberal economists say governments should balance their budgets (i.e., avoid deficits-in-time) and avoid borrowing too much (avoid debt), so as not to saddle future generations with big interest bills[66].

In other words, both these views see governments as beholden to the same budget rules as households, but Keynesians say governments should act like entrepreneurial households, while neoliberals say they should act like extremely financially conservative households and leave the entrepreneurial investment to private enterprise.

Both these views omit two vitally important parts of the story. The first is covered, at least in part, by modern monetary theory. Modern monetary theorists emphasize that governments are *not* like households, and in a very basic way. *Households get their money from sources outside themselves, but governments create money out of nothing.*

This makes a huge difference. Wray, Kelton and others argue that the government of a state that issues its own sovereign currency doesn't need to worry about how big its budget deficit is. They argue that such a government should borrow all it needs to, to cover this deficit, and can always pay back this debt in the future because it can create more money to do so[67].

---

[66] For a detailed account of the contestation between Keynesian and neoliberal economics, and the power-plays this has led to in governments' economic policymaking, see Carter (2020).

[67] Kelton (2020), pages 75-126; Wray (2015), pages 103-124.

I agree that this fits with the idea of sovereign states being able to create as much money as they need to, to meet the real needs of the economy. However, it seems a bit topsy-turvy. If the state can create as much new money as it likes, why go into debt at all? Why would you need to go into debt to finance your deficit, if you can finance it up front by creating new money now rather than in future years? I'll say more about this below, and in greater detail in Chapter 11.

Another point where I disagree with modern monetary theorists is their claim that it doesn't matter how large a government's debt becomes, because it can always create more money to pay it back. In the first half of 2025 economists and investors throughout the world became increasingly alarmed at the size of the US government deficit. A recurring theme was, yes, the US government can create more money to pay its debt as it becomes due, but the amount it would have to create would massively increase the money supply. This would lead to unacceptably high inflation, which would reduce the value of the US dollar in relation to other currencies and, perhaps more worryingly, it would increase the interest rate the government would have to pay on any subsequent debt it issued.

Central banks to the rescue

The second part of the story that's often missing from popular deficit-debt discussion is the role of central banks. When a government funds its deficit by going deeper into debt, central banks get very active in the background and run what are called "open market operations" to help limit the damage.

There's a simple reason that central banks have to do this, as I've begun to explain in previous chapters. As an economy grows from year to year and decade to decade, the amount of narrow money has to grow in step with this. Your country cannot have the same amount of narrow money in 2024 as it had in 1954. The population has increased, GDP per capita has increased, and inflation has eroded the real value of each dollar, pound, yen, euro or renminbi. Broad money has had to increase to keep pace with this, and broad money can only increase substantially if narrow money also increases substantially.

We could illustrate this with any modern economy. In Chapter 3 I briefly mentioned the example of New Zealand. Now in more detail: Between 1988 and 2019 New Zealand's population increased by 43.5%, its GDP per capita increased by 56.5% and inflation led to a 98.1% increase in prices. To cover this composite set of increases, the amount of broad money in the economy in 2019 needed to be just under 4.5 times as large in 2019 as it had been in 1988[68]. This was made possible by an increase in narrow money, from $NZ 87.8 billion in 1988 to almost 3 times that much in 2019, namely $NZ 258.3 billion. This represents an average government deficit of $NZ 5.33 billion per year: the government spent $NZ 5.33 billion more each year, on average, than it got back in taxes, fees, fines, etc. Since the government was then spending an average of about $NZ 150 billion per year[69], the average annual deficit amounted to around 3.6% of government spending. This level of deficit was needed, on average, every year for 32 years, just to keep the economy steady and growing.

But, like most governments, the New Zealand government slavishly went deeper into debt, year after year, to fund its budget deficits. It did this by issuing bonds. In doing so, it pulled back money from the very economy it was attempting to grow. Each dollar it borrowed was ultimately narrow money. For example, imagine if government bonds were bought with money from your personal account at Kiwibank (yes there is such a bank!). Your account at Kiwibank is broad money, but when you buy government bonds, Kiwibank has to pay the required amount in narrow money from its reserve account at the central bank, to the government's account at the central bank. The commercial banking system therefore ends up with that much less narrow money to use as collateral to issue broad money loans in the wider economy.

So then, how does the narrow money supply keep on increasing? The answer is simple but somewhat contorted. Central banks come to the rescue with their "open market operations". They create new narrow money (out of nothing) and use it to buy back their government's bonds on the open market. They don't usually buy government bonds directly from the government (except in Canada), but from banks and other enterprises and individuals who already own government bonds. This injects narrow money directly into the accounts of commercial banks at the central bank. Effectively, then the state (in the form of the central bank) has bought back bonds that were issued by the state (in the form of the government), by creating new money out of nothing.

Because this is newly created money, it gives the economy the boost it needs, to compensate for inflation and to enable growth in GDP. It also provides additional liquidity in commercial banks' accounts at the central

---

[68] This is because 1.435 x 1.565 x 1.981 = 4.449

[69] He Tai Ōhanga, The Treasury (2024)

bank, enabling them to more easily reconcile their accounts with each other at the end of each working day. Central banks to the rescue!

Unfortunately, there are two downsides to this. One is that the money the central banks create to buy back government bonds isn't targeted to the sectors of the economy that the elected government believes need to be stimulated. I'll say more about this below, and more about open market operations in general in Chapter 11. The other downside is that central bankers have to make their own decisions about how much the economy should grow, contract or stagnate. In a state that can control its own money creation, it might be better if the elected government had more say in this. Again, we'll look at this issue in greater detail in Chapter 11.

Options for a cash-strapped government

In the light of this discussion, let's look at a case study of the options the new British Labour government had for its budget of 30 October 2024. Although this case study is centred on Britain, its lessons apply to any government in the modern world in a stable country that controls its own currency and is reasonably well endowed with resources, skills and infrastructure but is fearful of government debts and deficits. It's a little different in the European countries that share their currency, the euro, and we'll look at that in detail in Chapter 7.

The newly elected British government said it wanted to increase the quality of public services such as hospitals, schools, asylum seeker procedures, research, roads, welfare, the courts, the police and the military. It also said it wanted to stimulate businesses to produce more and better and more affordable goods and services. But it was deeply in debt and heading for a large budget deficit. Here are the 4 options it said it had, plus various combinations of these, plus the one option it never publicly considered or discussed.

1. Borrow money: finance the deficit by going deeper into debt. The main problem with this approach, as discussed above, is that it can't grow the economy overall. It takes money away from the very economy the government wants to grow. It robs Peter to pay Paul. This leaves the economy dependent on the central bank to increase the amount of money in the economy via its open market operations. The central bank can choose which enterprises it buys government bonds from, but this doesn't target the newly created money to the sectors of the economy that actually need it.

There's one mitigating factor in this. If a commercial bank buys government bonds, it can use them as collateral, alongside its cash reserves, for issuing loans. So *some* of the government's borrowing doesn't rob Peter to pay Paul. A downside of this, however, is that bonds aren't "liquid". You can't divide a bond up into separate dollars and cents to pay different creditors. For this reason, commercial banks can't use them to reconcile their accounts with each other at the end of each working day.

Another targeting problem is that the government doesn't know in advance what the current uses are, of the money that will be withdrawn from the economy when enterprises and individuals lend it to the government to buy its bonds. Governments usually know the proportions of their debt that are owned by various sectors of the economy, as they keep good records of this, but they can't know in advance which businesses or enterprises will win the bidding for which tranches of new bonds[70]. A government could be inadvertently taking money away from investment in new production of goods and services, and this could have knock-on effects that weaken the economy overall.

There are, however, some very positive uses for government borrowing which have nothing to do with deficit reduction, and I'll say more about these in Chapter 11.

2. Increase taxes. Another option the UK government considered was to increase certain types of taxes. In October 2024 a group of wealthy investors known as the IPPR thinktank urged the British government to increase capital gains tax[71]. Capital gains are increases in the value of certain types of investment, such as shares, or profits from the sale of a rental property. The IPPR estimated this would bring in an extra £14 billion per year if the tax rates for these capital gains were increased to the same level as income tax.

Other tax increase options that were discussed included increasing the top income tax rate (which the Chancellor said was a no-no), taxing the wealth

of the richest billionaires (to which the Chancellor said an even bigger no-no), and increasing employers' share of social security tax, called "National Insurance Contributions" in the UK.

---

[70] The UK's Office of National Statistics gives an overview from time to time. Its most recent update was in December 2023. See Office of National Statistics (2023).
[71] IPPR (2024)

For a government, increasing the tax take has a big advantage over borrowing: it avoids the government having to run a large deficit. It also gives the government more leeway to direct money specifically towards its social and infrastructural aims. However, it suffers the same disadvantage as borrowing, in that, overall, it also robs Peter to pay Paul. It doesn't increase the amount of economic firepower in the economy, and no-one knows what useful goods and services will be lost due to businesses having to cancel investments in new products and services as they pay higher taxes.

3. Austerity. Another option is simply to reduce government expenditure on services, welfare, infrastructure, research, education, healthcare, etc. This had been the overriding policy of Britain's Conservative government from 2010 to 2024, as well as most of the governments of the Eurozone countries. It has two advantages, but only in terms of bookkeeping: it avoids increasing government debt, and it reduces, eliminates or even reverses the government deficit-in-time. Its disadvantages, however, are obvious. It robs both Peter and Paul. It makes poor people poorer and therefore sicker and less able to work, and it fails to stimulate the kinds of enterprise that could produce more and better goods and services that make society better off[72]. It also runs down public services. For example, in Britain, hospital waiting lists almost tripled between 2010 and 2024, the cost of a university education increased more than 3-fold, and many young people couldn't afford the education they needed, which society needed them to have, to make for a prosperous future for everybody.

The other big disadvantage is that austerity doesn't bring stimulus for private enterprises that could develop and produce new goods and services, in fact it reduces this, so the wider economy tends to stagnate. We rob Paul directly, and we deny Peter the money he needs to make us all better off.

4. Reshuffling the economic pack. Another option was to increase expenditure on some public services by reducing expenditure on others. Again, the advantages are that debt and deficit don't increase. But in this case we rob Pauline to pay Paul–we take money from one government department and give it to another. And as for Peter, again we deny him the money he needs to increase the supply and quality of goods and services.

5. Create money. The fifth option is for the government to create the money it needs–rather than leaving it to the central bank to create it via buying back government bonds. Once again let's walk through the logic of this option.

---

[72] Krugman (2024)

To begin with, as I've explained at length in this book, the government doesn't need to get money from some outside source, to be able to spend it. All narrow money is created by the state. The government simply spends money into existence. It does so by instructing its central bank to mark it up in the reserve account of the recipient's commercial bank, whereupon that bank credits the same amount to the recipient's account, but as a commercial bank-created IOU. The narrow money in the commercial bank's account at the central bank is thereby shadowed, in effect, by the same amount of broad money in the recipient's bank account.

More broad money in the economy is created by commercial banks when they issue loans, but these banks must have narrow money in their reserve accounts to reconcile their debts with each other at the end of each working day. The narrow money in their reserve accounts therefore also serves as collateral, along with their other assets, for the broad money loans they issue.

In short, the entire edifice of money in the economy originates with governments creating money. Governments spend money into existence to achieve their goals for society and to ensure there's just the right amount of narrow money in existence

Governments therefore do *not* have to tax people (or collect fees, fines, student loan repayments, etc., or borrow) to *get* money. They collect taxes (etc.) to reduce the amount of money in the economy–or more precisely, to prevent the deficit-in-space (see above) from increasing ad infinitum.

This gives a government enormous power to spend as much as it needs to, to achieve its goals. It only needs to beware of two dangerous pitfalls.

The pitfalls of over-enthusiastic money creation

First, *the amount the government spends into existence must not race ahead of society's ability to make good use of it.* The money a government spends must match the potential productive ability of society. For example, following Keynes's ground-breaking *Treatise on Money*[73] in the 1930s, if there are unemployed bakers and carpenters but insufficient bread is being baked or not enough houses are being repaired, some extra investment money can get this production up to speed. The bakers and carpenters will now have more money to spend locally, and the locals will have easier

---

[73] Keynes (1930)

access to bread and house repairs. As long as the extra money more-or-less matches people's needs and their capacity to fulfil these needs, this is unlikely to lead to inflation. The government must be careful that its extra spending increases the production and consumption of goods and services, and doesn't merely result in more money chasing the same amount of goods and services.

The opposite is also true. If the government spends too little, or takes too much away from the economy, this will reduce the amount of goods and services, and make everybody poorer–a classic case of austerity leading to economic stagnation. Spending too little is one of the main reasons the economies of most Eurozone countries have stagnated over the past decade.

A further warning is: *be careful not to spook the financial markets.* On Friday 23 September 2022 the short-serving British Prime Minister Liz Truss and her Chancellor Kwasi Kwarteng seriously spooked the financial markets[74], though with a very different tax and spend policy from the Labour government's budget. They announced £45 billion worth of income tax reductions for high-income earners, in a surprise effort to stimulate the economy. But, far from being pleased, financiers assumed this would lead to massive government borrowing to cover the resulting deficit. This expectation led to a sudden jump in interest rates for government bonds, from just under 3.8% on the morning of Friday 23 September to just over 4.2% by Monday morning 26 September. Interest rates had already risen from just over 3.5% when trading opened on the morning of 23 September, due to action by Britain's central bank, the Bank of England, on the day the budget was delivered. By October the cost of government borrowing had increased to over 5%, which at the time was higher than that of Italy, the US, Canada and France.

Higher interest rates for bonds make their tradeable value go down. Large investment firms such as pension funds, which hold much of their assets as government bonds, therefore suddenly found their assets' value had fallen precipitously.

Another effect was that the British pound began to plummet in value. This led investors to sell their pounds for euros and US dollars, which put more downward pressure on the pound. This made pension funds even weaker, as they're largely made up of British government bonds, which are denominated in pounds.

---

[74] BBC (2022)

It was only because the Bank of England intervened with a large dose of quantitative easing (see Chapter 2 for an explanation of QE), that the pound stabilised and pension funds began to recover their value.

Why were the markets spooked? There are two main reasons. First, investors rightly saw the dangers in what the government had announced. Suddenly depriving itself of £45 billion would lead to a massive increase in government borrowing and thereby reduce the value of the government bonds that were already in existence. Ironically, the government wouldn't have needed to borrow this money to keep the deficit low (at least according to modern monetary theorists), but the assumption of all the players (government, press, financiers and others) was that governments always borrow to reduce their deficits.

The second reason is that financiers knew that other financiers would be spooked, so they acted to divest themselves of government bonds before other investors divested themselves, which of course led to the value of their investments falling even lower. Once again John Maynard Keynes' observation proved true: if investors think the markets will crash, this will steeply increase the likelihood of them crashing.

What kind of budget did it turn out to be?

The budget announced by the Labour government's Chancellor on 30 October 2024 was a mixture of options 1 and 2 above. She increased government spending on services such as health, education, the military and housing by £70 billion, and got back more than that amount by increasing specific taxes by £40 billion and increasing borrowing by £32 billion[75].

The first thing to note is that this reduced the net flow of narrow money into the accounts of commercial banks at the central bank, by £2 billion.

If these banks follow the international guidelines of the Bank for International Settlements[76] (a Swiss-based, international service organisation for central banks) and create around 12.5 times as much in broad money loans as they have in their reserve accounts, this will reduce the broad money supply by about £25 billion. This means about £25 billion less will be available for business growth, home loans, private research and other ventures.

---

[75] For a succinct summary see Elliot (2024a).
[76] Bank for International Settlements (2024).

The second thing to note is that the budget aimed a direct hit at businesses. By far the greatest share of the tax increase, £25.7 billion out of a total of £40 billion, came in the form of an increase in National Insurance contributions from employers. The rate they pay increased from 13.8% of their workers' wages to 15%. This equates to an 8.7% increase in the amount of National Insurance they have to pay. The UK's Office for Budget Responsibility (OBR) is tasked with estimating economic impacts of government spending, taxes, borrowing and other financial operations. It estimated this would increase employer's payroll costs by about 2%[77].

To get a rough idea of what this means, a business employing 100 workers would suddenly find it could only afford to employ 98–unless it could cut back in other areas, but this can be very difficult. It can also be counter-productive, for example if it leads to a delay in the installation of more efficient manufacturing technology or causes a firm's research money to be cut. The OBR predicted this would lead to a fall in economic output.

The Bank of England reacted immediately after the announcement of this particular tax increase. It said the tax increase would allow interest rates to fall, because the tax increase would put downward pressure on inflation, *since it would lead to reduced employment and lower wages*. Reduced employment and lower wages lead to less local spending, which leads to harder times for local businesses, which leads to further reductions in employment, and so on down the spiral. Sadly, at the time of writing these predictions have come true.

A further issue concerns the government's increase in borrowing. No-one really knows what kinds of useful (or useless or speculative) investment the £32 billion was previously servicing, which was lent to the government over the course of the year to cover its increased borrowing. It's obviously a good thing if the money the government borrows goes to public health or education, via government spending, rather than speculation on the financial markets. But the enterprises that lend it could be directing it away from societally useful ventures such as wind farms, privately run homes for the aged, or medical research. There's no control on this.

More generally, however, the government didn't need to borrow more or tax more, to get the money it needed for improving public services–since the state creates money out of nothing. This assumes, of course, that these were entrepreneurial investments which would pay back in subsequent

[77] Office for Budget Responsibility (2024), pages 20-21.

years by their positive effect on the economy. By borrowing–going deeper into debt to finance its deficit–the government most likely shrunk the wider economy by about £25 billion. And by increasing National Insurance contributions it made it much harder for businesses to employ workers and to keep production at current levels.

I suggest it's useful to think of three very positive types of government spending and one very questionable or even toxic type. The positive types are: (1) Normal financing of regular state services such as schools, police, hospitals, welfare, etc. This could generally be about the same level as the tax take, so it wouldn't normally require deficit budgeting. (2) A small amount of deficit budgeting to ensure the narrow money supply grows sufficiently to cater for an acceptable level of inflation and a realistic amount of GDP growth. This has to be funded by new money creation. (3) A further small deficit to cover entrepreneurial spending, such as establishing a research centre for the use of artificial intelligence in medical science, or building a new rail link, both of which can bring extra economic growth in the longer term. These could be funded by borrowing.

The questionable, toxic type of government spending is running a deficit just to keep the normal financing of regular state services going. If extra money is needed for these services, the emphasis should be on raising taxes. I'll say more on tax in Chapters 6 and 11.

What would happen if the debt-deficit link were broken?

What would happen if a government decided not to increase its debt to finance the portion of its deficit that's necessary to cover an acceptable level of inflation and a realistic amount of GDP growth, or that can provide a genuinely entrepreneurial investment in the economy? Economist Stephanie Kelton has served on US congressional budget committees, and reports that she's often made the suggestion that the government can create as much money as it needs to, to meet the real needs of the economy. But whenever the subject of money creation comes up for discussion, Kelton says there's a howl of fearful derision from various members of Congress: "How dare you print money! The US will end up like Zimbabwe or 1920s Germany!"[78]

This fear and derision are in part based on the common misunderstanding that governments have to get money from somewhere outside themselves, to be able to spend money. This myth is even perpetuated in economics

---

[78] Kelton (2020), pages 75-100

textbooks. The Bank of England itself complains about this myth. In the words of the Bank of England's Monetary Analysis Directorate, "The reality of how money is created today differs from the description found in some economics textbooks"[79]. As long as this myth persists, many investors and elected representatives will get nervous if they see their government spending money without borrowing to make up for the deficit–even where the spending is on genuinely sound investments that can give a long-term boost to the economy, or where the spending simply has to occur so that inflation and GDP growth are catered for.

But of course, a reason for legitimate fear of large government deficits is that government over-spending can lead to high inflation. Again we need to remember that the aim should be to ensure there's just enough money in the economy to match the potential production, including education and welfare which can pay off in the long run, and that this money is well aimed to stimulate this productive potential.

Another point is that it's logically absurd to have no deficit at all, because as discussed above, if the state never increases the money supply but just keeps recycling the existing supply at the same level, there'll be no more money in the economy today than there was in 1950, or even 1900. A further absurdity is that the state, via its central bank, *does* increase the money supply over time, as I explained above, but governments wash their hands of this forbidden money creation and leave it to the central bank to implement. The result is that this newly created money isn't targeted to the areas the elected government sees as the neediest or most societally entrepreneurial.

I suggest two strategies to overcome this problem. The first is education. We need to make special efforts to explain the profound differences between government spending and ordinary household or business spending. The Bank of England is already attempting to do this, inch by inch, in some of its quarterly bulletins[80]. Hopefully this book will make a further contribution in this direction. In the long run we need to build up a strong narrative in society that challenges the deficit-debt prejudice and replaces it with a more factual account of how the state actually creates money, spends it into existence, and taxes it back out of existence.

---

[79] McLeay et al. (2014)

[80] At the time of writing, the latest tranche of BoE quarterly bulletins can be found at https://www.bankofengland.co.uk/quarterly-bulletin/2024/2024

Second, governments need to be cleverer with words. The US central bank was very smart with words when it invented the term "quantitative easing", as we noted in Chapter 2. QE is really just the same as the much-feared "printing money" (though both of these are now done electronically, rather than on paper notes), but US central bank director Ben Bernanke resisted Congress's attempts to call it that. Instead, he and his team invented this wonderful, magical, technical-sounding term "quantitative easing".

What clever term can we use for a government's action of spending extra money into existence to rescue public services and stimulate useful production? I suggest something like "quantitative stimulus". By re-using the word "quantitative", this gives it an air of safety and respectability, as it reminds us of the success and respectability of quantitative easing. Meanwhile the word "stimulus" is a standard, Keynesian word for spending government money sensibly to help the economy grow.

In short, governments should avoid being cowered by outmoded, unfounded fears of crashing the economy if they act precisely in accordance with the actual, factual nature of the money they spend. They should educate themselves and the public, use words that give people confidence, and get busy with quantitative stimulus–but just the right amount to match the real needs and capacity of the economy: no more, and no less. That's an essential element in growing an economy.

5. THE POWER AND OOMPH OF MONEY: MONEY AS A QUANTITY OF SOCIAL STUFF

In this chapter I'll attempt to break new ground in explaining what money is and why it works. I'll also try to make aspects of it clearer than in the books and papers currently available on the subject. Some readers might find this chapter a bit abstract and distant from the practical issue of how to make money work better for all of us. That's fine, skip it for now if you want to. It's aimed more at the concerns of money theorists and social scientists than the cut and thrust of our everyday dealings with money.

There are three main theories as to what money essentially is: a measurement scale; a quantity of stuff; and an IOU. Regarding the first of these three, some economics textbooks talk of money as a kind of background measurement scale, like the centimetre markers on a ruler or the kilogram markers on bathroom scales. They call it a "neutral medium", that sits in the background as a scale for measuring and comparing the various values of our goods and services.

Another view is that money is a quantity of something valuable, like gold or silver. In this view, money is what I would call "stuff", something that exists in the real world, that already existed before human beings started using money, and that we co-opted to use as money.

Many economics textbooks combine these two views, or flick between them, depending on what issues they're discussing at the time.

A third view is that money is an IOU. This is the view I've argued for throughout this book so far. It's advocated by an increasing number of economists today, including leading lights such as the British scholars Geoffrey Ingham and the late David Graeber, US "modern money theorists" such as L. Randal Wray and Stephanie Kelton, more mainstream US economists such as Thomas Paley, the Chinese economist and central banker Chen Yulu, and the Bank of England staff who write the Bank's monthly bulletins and occasional books. This view of money fits nicely with the way money works in today's world. However, in this chapter I'm going to expand on it and attempt to show that it might be incomplete without some input from the other two views.

This is likely to be the most controversial chapter in this book, because here I'm attempting to push the discussion of money into territory that's not usually explored in writings on money.

Money as a quantity of stuff

The "quantity" theory says that money is material stuff, usually gold or silver but sometimes other precious metals or valuable goods like cocoa beans or shellfish. The Spanish conquistadores believed they were acquiring money when they looted hundreds of tonnes of gold and silver from the palaces and mines of the Americas. The 18th century economist Adam Smith needed the quantity theory of money to make his theory of free-market economics work, so he modelled money as iron nails, which in those days were scarce and precious[81]. The quantity theory states that money is a physical, material substance that has value in its own right. So when we save it, we're building up a stock of valuable goods. When we spend it, we're simply exchanging one valuable quantity of goods for another.

On the other hand, as I noted above, the writers I tend more to agree with– Ingham, Graeber, Wray, Yulu, the Bank of England essayists and others– regard money as an IOU, a formal, signed debt issued by a merchant or bank, or in fact by anyone who believes they can back up their IOU with something of real value, something people want for its own sake, like food or shelter or a shortened prison sentence or a tax writeoff.

I agree with these writers that the quantity theory of money fails to explain how money has evolved over the past few thousand years. For example, in England in 1351 the Pound Sterling was a coin containing 258.9 grams of silver and 23.21 grams of gold, plus other, non-precious metals (it never had a pound of sterling silver in it). The gold and silver content gradually diminished, and by the year 1771 a newly minted pound coin contained only 111.5 grams of silver and 7.32 grams of gold[82]. But people still accepted it as legal currency for one pound Sterling (£1), so there was something else about it that gave them that confidence and made it worth one whole pound.

A similar story is seen with ancient Roman currency. In 211 BCE the Romans introduced a new coin, the silver denarius, which became the principal coin of the Roman Republic and later the Roman Empire until the 3rd century CE. During this 400-year period the amount of silver in newly

---

[81] Yueh (2018) pages 11-31.
[82] Shaw (1896)

minted denarii gradually reduced to almost zero. Again, however, people trusted it and treated it as if it was worth a whole denarius. What was it that gave it this dependable value when most of it was cheap, common metal?

Presumably it was that people knew it was minted and stamped with their government's royal seal. It wouldn't take much depth of intellect to conclude that it therefore represented a promise by the government to always honour it at its face value. If the emperor's stamp says it's worth one denarius, then it's at least as reliable as the empire.

The history of money in ancient China takes this a little further. A fascinating account of the trials and tribulations of ancient Chinese coinage is given by Chen Yulu, an economist who was governor of China's central bank, the People's Bank of China, from 2015 to 2022 and later President of Nankai University[83]. The Chinese seem to have been more reluctant than the Europeans to reduce the amount of precious metal in their coins. This led to a succession of currency crises. During the Tang Dynasty in 600-900 CE there were periods when food production and other forms of real wealth increased far beyond the supply of silver and other precious metals for coinage. There wasn't enough money to oil the wheels of the growing real economy. This led to what Yulu calls "money-on-the-fly": coinless forms of money similar to what we would call IOUs and letters of credit. The idea of coinless money became firmly established, and a few centuries later, during the Song Dynasty in the 10th–13th centuries, China became the first country in the world to issue paper money. This was called "jiaozi", meaning "a voucher for exchange".

So, whatever we think about the quantity theory of money, it's clear that it's never been successful for long, even on its own terms, at least with regard to the material quantity of valuable stuff in it. It suffers the practical problem that the supply of precious metals seldom matches the power of the economy. Usually there's too little precious metal to cover the needs of the economy. In some cases, such as Spain in the 16th century, there's far too much, leading to runaway inflation, as I mentioned in Chapters 2 and 4.

The interesting point in all three of these situations, Ancient Rome, Medieval England and Old-World China, is that people generally trusted the currency despite knowing that the quantity of precious metal in it was either diminishing or had reached zero.

---

[83] Yulu (2014), see especially pages 1-24.

Introducing power and oomph

If you look closely at the above paragraphs, you'll see that I've used the word "power" in quite a different way from how physicists use it. I've talked about "spending power" and "the power of the economy." We use the word "power" in all sorts of ways in English, quite apart from how physicists use it to mean "energy expended per unit (of) time". We say, "Mao came to power in 1948"; "Wow, that herb has a powerful taste"; "I'd love to get you out of prison but I'm powerless to help you."; "Jennifer Rush sang her song, 'The power of love' at the concert last night." My German friends talk about a successful businesswoman as a "Power-Frau".

I'm now going to use the word "power" in this broad, general sense. I'm on good grounds here because one of the greatest philosophers of the 20th century, Ludwig Wittgenstein, famously wrote: "The meaning of a word is its use in the language[84]". A word means what people use it to mean.

But just to be extra clear that I mean power in this general sense rather than in the sense that physicists use it, I'll expand the word to "power and oomph."

The central point I want to make is that the history of money shows that when money has worked properly (whether it's coins or shellfish or paper notes or IOUs), it's because it has a particular kind of power and oomph. I'll now explain this in more detail.

Money in closer detail

When we say, "I have twenty dollars", we're actually saying four things simultaneously.

1. I own some stuff that has a specific type of *power and oomph.*
2. This type of power and oomph can best be described as *credit*.
3. Its power and oomph has a specific *magnitude* (i.e. size, strength, impact).
4. In this country the *measuring scale* we use for this magnitude of that type of power and oomph puts it at twenty dollars.

This has the same logical structure as other types of power and oomph that we talk about every day. Examples are speed, distance and volume. For

[84] Wittgenstein (1953), p. 43.

example, when we say, "I'm riding my bicycle at 25 kilometres per hour", we're saying four things simultaneously.

1. I 'm doing something that has a specific type of *power and oomph.*
2. This type of power and oomph can best be described as *speed.*
3. Its power and oomph has a specific *magnitude.*
4. In this country the *measuring scale* we use for the magnitude of this type of power and oomph puts it at 25 kilometres per hour.

It's very important to notice that the number on the measuring scale differs from country to country, even if the magnitude of the power and oomph is the same. When I ride my bicycle in Britain, in exactly the same way as I ride it in Germany, I'm riding it at a speed of 15.53 miles per hour, but it's exactly the same speed as 25 kilometres per hour in Germany. If I ride it near the CERN laboratory in Switzerland I'm riding it at a speed which the CERN workers would call "2.319×10^{-8} *c*", where *c* is the speed of light. But it's still the same speed.

It's the same with money. A particular amount of credit has the same amount of power and oomph whether we measure it in euros, US dollars, Japanese yen, British pounds or Chinese renminbi.

I'll illustrate this with an example from my own freelance work. From time to time I evaluate book proposals for an international publisher based in Switzerland. Each evaluation takes about one-and-a-half hours. After I've done and submitted my evaluation, the publishers are in debt to me for the value of my work; they have an obligation to me of that value. Expressed around the other way, I'm in *credit* to the publishers for the value of my work. I own some stuff which has a particular type of power and oomph, which we call credit. This credit has a particular *magnitude.* In Switzerland the *measuring scale* the publishers use for the magnitude of that amount of credit puts it at 100 Swiss Francs.

This gets more interesting because the publishers know I don't have a Swiss bank account. So they always say, "We can pay you 100 Swiss Francs or 90 British pounds or 106 euros." (though the amounts of pounds and euros differ from month to month depending on the exchange rate). Each of these represents the same amount of debt or obligation (from their point of view), and credit (from my point of view)–the same amount of power and oomph. The debt/credit itself is the thing that has power and oomph, not the number associated with it. The francs, pounds and euros are just different countries' measuring scales for the magnitude of this type of power and oomph.

A critic, reading this, might say I'm getting a bit too close to the "quantity" theory of money–the idea that money is a quantity of stuff, such as a specific amount of gold or silver, that we hoard and then exchange for goods and services like shirts or plumbing repairs (or evaluations of book proposals). And actually, *I am indeed saying that money is a quantity*. But it's not a quantity of *material* stuff like gold or silver. It's a quantity of *social* stuff. This particular social stuff is *credit* (if you own it) or *debt* (if you owe it). Money is solid, very solid indeed, and it's a quantity, but in the *social* sense, not the material sense. Money is a social form of power and oomph.

As a child I had the privilege of being brought up and educated alongside indigenous Māori people in New Zealand, in a district called Māngere (which, incidentally, means "lazy" in the Māori language). This resulted in a lifelong interest in Māori culture, language and politics, not to mention rewarding friendships. Before the Europeans arrived, Māori people had a counting system very much like Europeans, and they used numbers to count things like trees and sweet potatoes, but they had no numerical units for measuring things like speed, distance, weight or debt/credit. They would *not* say "Rangi can run at a top speed of 30 kilometres per hour", or "We harvested 20 kilogram of root vegetables today", or "Kura is 1.754 metres tall", or "Kiri sings at 50 decibels", or "Waka owes Aroha 150 dollars". But they certainly *would* say "Rangi can run incredibly fast" [85]; "What a big harvest of root vegetables we had today"[86]; "Kura is the tallest woman in the community"[87]; "Kiri sings very, very loudly"[88]: and "Waka owes a very big debt (obligation) to Aroha"[89]. They were fully aware of the differing magnitudes of speed, distance, weight, volume and, importantly, debt (i.e., obligation) and credit, but unlike us, they didn't use numbers to measure these.

Generally they used the word "utu" where a debt had to be paid back or a wrong or offence had to be righted and there was a sense of reciprocity: the payback had to fully cover the debt or hurt. They used the word "koha" where there was a sense of gratitude, such as when a visitor would bring a gift to their host. In both these situations there was the idea that "mana" (prestige) had to be restored.

---

[85] Ka taea e Rangi te oma tere.

[86] He aha te nui o te hauhake o nga huawhenua pakiaka i a tatou i tenei ra.

[87] Ko Kura te wahine teitei o te hapori.

[88] Ka waiata a Kiri, tino kaha.

[89] He nui rawa te mana a Waka ki a Aroha.

Although their concepts of debt were different from the idea of a specific magnitude of debt that can be measured in dollars or euros, the notion of debt and reciprocity was deeply ingrained. Debt was real, as real as speed, loudness, distance and weight. It had its own kind of power and oomph.

There are plenty of modern, European examples of the same kind of debt, as power and oomph, that don't use a number to measure its magnitude. My wife and I were recently visiting Oxford. It was a hot day and I stepped into a supermarket to buy a topsy–a chocolate ice cream on a stick. But the supermarket only sold them in packs of three, and my wife didn't want one. They were very cheap, so I bought a pack, and as we were walking down the high street, me eating the topsy and wondering what to do with the other two, we passed by two men sitting on a bench, busily engaged in conversation but looking rather hot. I stopped and explained about our unwanted ice creams and asked if they would help us out by eating them. They accepted our offer graciously, with plenty of laughter and thanks. Then one of them immediately opened his bag, pulled out a handful of individually wrapped chocolates, and offered them to us. "Please, you must take these", he said. So we graciously accepted them, also with plenty of laughter and thanks.

This seemed to me to be an example of a basic, fundamental social phenomenon of the power and oomph of debt and reciprocity. The men felt indebted, obligated. There was no formal obligation to repay the debt, but it seemed to them socially right to do so, and it seemed to us socially right to accept their gesture.

I give these examples, not to claim that feelings of debt and reciprocity always work like this, nor to suggest that Māori culture is a template for all indigenous or pre-measurement cultures. Rather, I simply want to point out that debt/credit is a *real entity* with power and oomph, just as speed, distance, weight and loudness are. The difference is only that speed, distance, weight, and loudness are *material* forms of power and oomph, whereas debt/credit is a *social* form of power and oomph.

One of the remarkable things about human beings is that we've developed measuring scales for many different kinds of power and oomph. In relation to physics, we have scales to measure force, speed, density, acceleration, power (in the sense that physicists use that word), loudness, spatial volume, electrical charge, and many other forms of material power and oomph. But note carefully that these scales are all arbitrary, and many of them differ from country to country. There's nothing absolute about saying that Rachel is riding her bike at a speed of 25 kilometres per hour. She's also riding it at a speed of 2.319×10^{-8} *c*. We humans have invented scales for physical forms of power and oomph, and we've also invented scales for a social form of power and oomph. This scale represents the quantity of our money.

So money is, in fact, a quantity, but not a quantity of material stuff like gold or silver. It's a quantity of social stuff, namely credit (if you own it) and debit or obligation (if you owe it). Like any other quantity, it can be collected, hoarded, added up, and traded for different kinds of stuff.

Of course, the scale we use to measure the quantity of money–the quantity of debt/credit–differs, in an important way, from the scales used for these material quantities. It's almost always a continually shrinking scale. Because of inflation, the Swiss publisher's debt to me for jobs done next year will be measured by a larger number of Swiss Francs (I hope!), even though the amount of power and oomph in the debt remains the same.

This is also the case with state-created money. In Chapter 1 I argued that the money the government spends into existence can best be thought of as a tax token. Each 10 dollar note you have in your wallet or purse can be used to write off 10 dollars of your tax liability. It will always write off 10 dollars' worth, regardless of inflation or the relative value of goods and services. However, the number of dollars of your annual tax liability is highly likely to increase from year to year, as your income increases due to inflation. Therefore if you hoard your 10-dollar note it will write off a smaller proportion of your tax liability each year. The amount of power and oomph you've hoarded actually diminishes over time, due to inflation. Even though the quantity remains the same, the measuring scale keeps shifting as its value in relation to quantities of other kinds of stuff is slowly diminishing.

So our scaling of the power and oomph of debt/credit is less certain and stable than our scaling of material forms of power and oomph. The main point, though, is that money is *both* a social relationship *and* a quantity. I would argue that a comprehensive theory of money needs to acknowledge both these aspects of it. The mistake made by many commentators in times past was to see the quantity of money in terms of material stuff, like precious metal or cocoa beans. On the other hand, the mistake some recent economic theorists make is to focus so much on the abstract social side of money that they ignore the quantity aspect of this relationship, as measured by the quantity of power and oomph in the debit/credit relationship. Money is indeed a quantity of stuff, but social stuff, not material stuff.

Money as a neutral measuring device

The view of money I haven't yet said much about is the idea that it's a neutral measuring device: that it sits in the background and provides a scale against which we measure and compare the values of different goods and services. In one sense this is true, as long as we don't make the mistake of thinking this scale is just a neutral set of hypothetical numbers, like the numbers on a ruler. You can trade a bag of 10 kilograms of wheat, but you can't trade 10 kilograms in itself. That's just the scale that sits in the background. With money, the scale that sits in the background is a measurement of the amount of power and oomph in social obligations. If we say a lampshade is worth $40, we mean its value is equivalent to $40 worth of human obligation, one person to another. The scale only has meaning because it originates and arises out of real stuff: the social stuff of debt and obligation. I'll return to this point below.

Implications for the meaning and functions of money

The idea of money as a form of social power and oomph has major implications for the meaning and functions of money. First, the power and oomph of obligations between people exist whether or not they're translated into money. You can have obligations in societies where there's no such thing as money, but you can't have money without obligations.

Second, when a government creates money (by spending it into existence– see Chapter 1) it's thereby putting itself under an obligation. The money *represents* the obligation it has taken on by creating the money. If you have the money it created, you can use it to get something from the government, such as a reduction in your tax liability or a new passport. This is one of the reasons a government should be careful how much money it creates. The more money it creates, the higher its obligations. I've mentioned in previous chapters that creating too much money can lead to runaway inflation, or that creating too little can lead to deflation or stagnation. But another way of looking at this is to say that when a government creates money (by spending it into existence) it's increasing its obligations–such as the obligation to write-off a certain amount of tax liability.

Third, the money a government creates isn't just the government's means of exercising its power and stimulating the economy. An additional, basic function of money is to provide a *measuring scale* for the amount of power and oomph in the millions of obligations being formed in society from day to day. Without this measuring scale, a complex society simply cannot function.

Economists call this measuring scale the "money of account". Different countries have different measuring scales (US dollars, Australian dollars, Japanese yen, British pounds, Swedish krone, and many others). Having a specific money of account provides a clear, agreed measuring scale for our obligations and transactions.

The economist Daniela Prates, of the UN Conference on Trade and Development, makes this point in detail in her critique of modern monetary theory[90]. She stresses that people are compelled to use their country's currency not just because it's a tax token, but also because it's the only really convenient and robust way to settle their debts, i.e. to discharge their measurable obligations. The "money of account" is the measuring stick for the magnitude of our obligations, and also the medium we use to discharge them. Without it, we couldn't assess the magnitude of our obligations–what I call the power and oomph of these obligations, and we couldn't pay off these obligations at their precise level of magnitude. Therefore we couldn't do business in an orderly way in a large, complex society.

I find this is a profound insight, and it pushes our understanding of money further than the groundbreaking work of modern monetary theorists. However, Prates takes it even further. In her own words:

> Hence, the sine qua non condition for the existence of a monetary economy is private contracts for spot and deferred settlements denominated in the money of account defined by the state and discharged by the thing the state defines as the economy's money (state money and bank money), which differs from the obligation to pay taxes to the government, which are debt contracts between private agents and the state.

Prates is effectively saying that money exists and has been devised *primarily* to measure and discharge our obligations to people who provide us with goods and services, and that its use in paying taxes is only a kind of spinoff from this. This appears to be grounded on the assumption that our obligations to the tradespeople, sellers and businesses who enable our everyday life to run smoothly are somehow more fundamental than our obligations to our government (or, in some societies, our chiefs or clan leaders). I'm not sure I can go along with this. I know of no society that doesn't have political leaders of some sort (elected governments, tribal

---

[90] Prates (2020)

chiefs, etc.), and I wouldn't like to say whether my obligations to my tribal chief or to the woman who harvests my sweet potatoes are paramount. I certainly can say, however, that our chiefs or governments are likely to be far more effective than our tradespeople and vegetable growers in forcing us to fulfil our obligations to them.

This does, however, raise a further interesting question. Would societies invent a money system even if their government didn't issue a reliable currency? There's evidence that they do. In Chen Yulu's history of money in China, there were periods and regions where the state's currency was inadequate, and cities and regions simply invented their own currencies[91]. In Europe after the breakup of the Roman Empire there was currency chaos, and people tended to use whatever coins they could find, from any regime anywhere, for estimating the value of their business obligations and paying them off. In Argentina today, where the official currency, the peso, is weak and its future value unpredictable, the province of La Rioja has created its own currency, the chacho[92]. If you visit the Ashmolean Museum in Oxford, England, you'll see displays of coins issued by tradespeople in the year 1652, alongside those minted by the government of the day.

But a further point which I think Prates and many other economists miss is that money is not *just* a scale to measure the size of our obligations, it's also *the means of paying them off*. It's real stuff, solid stuff: power and oomph. It carries within it the obligation of the person or institution or government that issued it. If it's in your pocket, then from your point of view it's a credit, an entitlement, a unit of power and oomph. It seems to me (and to an increasing number of thinkers) that the source of this power and oomph lies in the authority which the state exercises over every one of its citizens. The state has the power (whether we approve of this or not) to oblige each of us to contribute to its goals. It exercises this power by demanding that we pay taxes: that we give it back these tokens it has issued in return for our work and services to it. These tokens not only measure our obligations to the state, but also encapsulate and discharge these obligations. Therefore they're made of real stuff, real power and oomph, that derives from the state's creation of them as it spends them into existence.

This leads me back to the conclusion that money is, essentially, a tax token created and issued by the state. But it's also a quantity: a quantity of human obligation.

---

[91] Yulu (2014), pages 1-18.
[92] Doll (2024)

Conclusions

I began this chapter by mentioning three common but different theories as to what money essentially is: a measurement scale for the values of goods and services (the "money of account"): a quantity of coveted material stuff that can be traded for goods and services; or an IOU that anyone can issue as a debt to be repaid.

The main point I've attempted to make in the chapter is that money is indeed a quantity of stuff, but social stuff, not material stuff. It's composed of people's social obligations to each other. These obligations arise because a person does a service for you or provides you with goods that you want. While all human societies have recognised that such obligations exist, a country with a money of account provides a measurement scale that can robustly and credibly enable numerical values to be put on these kinds of obligations, and the money can therefore be used as payment to discharge these obligations precisely.

I've also argued that money can only serve as both a measuring scale for our obligations (the "money of account") and a means to discharge them, because it's a quantity of stuff. But it's a quantity of social stuff, not of precious metals. And it's measurable, because the money created by the state is calibrated on a scale. It's also an IOU: a promise to pay. When the plumber receives her $200 from me, she's receiving a quantity of social stuff that can be used further down the line to fulfil her own social obligations. This is partly because society has agreed that money serves this function, but it's ultimately because money is the state's IOU. The owner of the $200 has in their hand the state's promise to reduce their tax obligations by $200, or to renew their passport, write of their speeding fines or give them a TV licence. In essence, then, there's a fine balance between these three definitions of money. But in the end, they only hang together because the state creates money as tokens for taxes, fees and fines.

6. TAXATION: ITS ROLLER-COASTER HISTORY AND FUTURE POSSIBILITIES

What would be a fair and sensible way to tax people in a modern, high-income, reasonably well-functioning country like Britain, the US, Australia, New Zealand, Japan, Canada or the countries of western Europe? This question should concern all of us, because we all have to pay tax. Even children pay tax when they spend their pocket money.

This is a burning question today because more and more observers are saying our current tax systems are unfair. The richest people pay some of the lowest tax rates and the poorest pay some of the highest, since everybody has to pay sales tax or value-added tax on the everyday essentials they buy. Juila Davis, a wealthy investor and founding member of the UK lobby group "Patriotic Millionaires", complains that the taxes on wealth are "minuscule", while everyday work is taxed very solidly[93].

At the same time, the gap between the richest and the rest of us is growing at a runaway pace. When French economist Thomas Piketty wrote his classic tome *Le capital au XXI siècle* in 2013[94] (English version *Capital in the 21st Century*) he pointed out that the richest 1% in the US owned 34% of the country's private wealth. In Britain this was 29% and in continental Europe 25%, though in Sweden it was lower, at 10%[95]. These shares have continued to increase since then. Oxfam estimated in September 2024 that the "World's top 1% own more wealth than 95% of humanity"[96].

There'd be a windfall for government tax departments if this increase in wealth was taxed. On the one hand, in the US in 2021 the highest 1% of earners paid an average *income* tax rate of 26% on their income (note the word "income", not "wealth"), compared to an average rate of 10% for the lowest-paid 50%[97]. But almost all the increase in *wealth* among the richest

---

93 Neate (2024)
94 English translation Piketty (2014)
95 Piketty (2014), pages 340-349
96 Oxfam (2024)
97 Federal Reserve (2024a)

1% comes from increases in the value of capital (real estate, exotic financial instruments, etc.), which is *hardly taxed at all*. The effective tax rate on the wealthiest is therefore around 1% of their actual income, if by "income" we include increase in wealth. Meanwhile the poorest 1% still have to pay sales tax of around 20% on the essentials they buy just to stay alive. And since they have to spend their entire income just to stay alive, they effectively pay a rate of at least 20% on their entire income.

There's now a coordinated movement among some economists, politicians, NGOs, citizens' organisations and a small but significant number of billionaires to change tax systems globally so that a higher portion of tax comes from the wealth of the super-rich. In fact, our current system of taxing income from work rather than wealth is a strange historical anomaly. So in this chapter I'll give an overview of how tax has changed and developed over the centuries. But before I embark on this journey, here's a very brief overview of what gets taxed, and how much, in most countries today.

What's taxed today

Broadly speaking there are six different kinds of tax in most countries: personal income tax; social security contributions; corporate income tax; property taxes; taxes on goods, services and trade; and "other". These categories are used by the Organization for Economic Cooperation and Development (OECD) in its detailed analysis of global tax regimes[98]. Some countries, such as Australia, New Zealand and Denmark, count social security tax as part of personal income tax, since both these taxes rise and fall with your income. In most OECD countries these two together make up more than 60% of the total tax take, reaching over 70% in the US and Iceland. This means that 60-70% of tax is, effectively, income tax. As I mentioned above, this represents a huge historical anomaly. Income tax is a very modern trend. Most people who lived before the 20th century never paid income tax at all.

The next largest share is tax on goods, services and trade, which is generally about 20% of the total tax take.

Next down the list is corporate income tax, a tax that corporations pay on their profits. This varies from 4% in Italy to around 22% in Norway and

[98] OECD (2023), and see summary on page 8.

Australia, with a global average of about 15%. Again, this is a historical anomaly, a new form of tax that only recently emerged.

Property taxes make up the smallest share of the tax take (apart from "other"), at around 10%. This, too, is a historical anomaly. As we'll see below, for all but the last 150 years of human history, property taxes were often the biggest source of income for emperors, monarchs, caliphs and most other forms of government.

But before we embark on this journey through history, a few more introductory points need to be mentioned.

Why tax?

In Chapter 4 we saw that governments treat taxation as a mechanism to boost their budgets. The popular belief is that if governments want to spend money, they have to get it from a source outside themselves. So they take it from you and me. Where you and I get it from is usually left to the imagination in these discussions.

So far in this book I've suggested this view is deeply flawed. It's factually incorrect, since the state itself is the ultimate source of the official, legitimate money that circulates in the economy (the so-called "money of account"). The state creates this money by spending it into existence, via its central bank, using computer keystrokes for most of it, and printing and minting a small portion of it to be used as cash. This is especially clear in a modern economy where there's no gold standard or other ultimate source of money outside the state's own governing apparatus. The popular view is also logically contradictory. If the state has to get its money from you and me, then you and I must have some magic source that *we* get it from, whereas in fact we get it from each other and, if we're civil servants, from the government.

I've argued in earlier chapters that the basic effect of taxation (along with government fees, fines, etc.) is that it creates demand for the currency the state issues its money in. People value their country's particular form of money because, in the end, the state will accept it as payment for their and everyone else's tax liabilities. They happily use it to buy, sell, lend, invest and pay off debts, because the state guarantees its value, via the tax system. The state absolutely guarantees to write off $20 of your hairdresser's tax liability for every $20 she gives the government, so she's highly motivated to demand that you pay for your haircuts in $s (or yen, renminbi, euros or whatever her country's currency is).

I also pointed out that there's a lag, in time and space, between the state's creation of money (as the state spends money into existence) and its withdrawing of money from the economy (via taxes, fees, fines, etc.). Because of this lag, a great pool of state-created money (narrow money) has accumulated. Most of it sits in the reserve accounts of commercial banks, which they hold at the central bank. I called this the government's deficit-in-space. Commercial banks use this narrow money as collateral for the broad money they create as loans, and this powers the wider economy. Tax is therefore an essential element in keeping the money-making machinery going.

This understanding of money and tax developed and crystalised throughout the 20th century and early 21st century via the cumulative insights of economists and social scientists such as George Friedrich Knapp, Joseph Schumpeter, Hyman Minsky, John Maynard Keynes, David Graeber, Geoffrey Ingham, L. Randal Wray, Stephanie Kelton and others. The Bank of England's regular publications also reflect this understanding, though they sometimes shy away from its implications[99].

In this chapter I won't argue this point further. Instead, I'll build on the point all economists agree on: that in almost every economy there need to be taxes. I say "almost" because there are some oil-rich countries that don't tax their citizens. Kuwait and Bahrain are examples. They withdraw money from the economy, not by collecting taxes, but by taking a large share of their countries' vast oil revenues.

Other purposes of taxation

Taxation has further uses besides creating demand for the money the state creates. It redistributes wealth. In most tax regimes throughout history, the rich have paid more tax than the poor, and often the poor have paid none at all. This has enabled governments to redirect money toward shared public services, as in ancient Greece (more on this below) or directly to the poor. Examples of taxes being used to alleviate poverty are seen in early Islamic

---

[99] Patel and Meaning (2022). In Chapter 10 they claim that government revenue has to match government expenditure in the long run, so that broad money doesn't increase. If this were so, the broad money supply could never grow to accommodate inflation and increases in population and GDP.

societies[100] and in England and Wales's so-called "poor laws", of the 16th and 17th centuries.

Taxation has also been used extensively in the 20th and 21st centuries in high-income countries to redistribute income from rich to poor. These countries generally use progressive income tax rates and social welfare programmes: "progressive" meaning that high-income earners are taxed at a higher percentage rate than lower-income earners. This could be vastly improved, as we'll see below. Thomas Piketty gives a thorough and detailed account of the rise and fall of progressivity in income tax rates over the past 100 years, in his groundbreaking books *Capital in the Twenty-First Century* and *Capital and Ideology*[101].

Another important use of taxation is to put downward pressure on inflation. Ideally a government should spend just enough money to stimulate the economy to work at its full capacity. If it spends less, there'll be people out of work, and unused tools and raw materials, when useful jobs could be done, and there'll be businesses operating below their capacity to produce useful goods and services. On the other hand, if the government spends too much, there'll be too much narrow money in the reserve accounts of commercial banks, leading to too much broad money being created by way of bank loans, and we'll get the classic inflationary situation: too much money chasing too few goods and services. The state can pull this excess money back by increasing taxes.

Unfortunately, this can be a bit hit-and-miss, because it can take a long time for tax increases to get approved by Parliament or Congress, and even longer for the new taxes to be paid[102]. So using taxation to dampen inflation is at best a long-term strategy.

For a short-term, immediate impact, a second mechanism is useful, namely government bonds. Governments borrow money from the private sector by issuing bonds. This can happen literally overnight. When the government borrows, money is paid to the government directly from the reserve accounts of the lenders' commercial banks at the central bank. This reduces the supply of narrow money immediately, putting downward pressure on inflation. Conversely, if the government wants to fend off a downward trend in the economy, it can reduce its regular bond-buying, so that more money is being paid back into the economy from old bonds that are maturing, than

---

[100] Alkhateeb (2017), pages 33ff.

[101] Piketty (2014); Piketty (2020)

[102] See the discussion on this in Palley (2020).

money that's being withdrawn due to new bonds being issued. The downside of this is that the government can't control precisely where in the economy the money comes from when it borrows, or where the money goes to when it pays back the bonds that mature. It might be inadvertently depriving an under-financed manufacturing sector of capital for necessary growth, or stoking inflation in a sensitive sector.

Yet another use of taxation is to attempt to change people's unhealthy or unsociable habits. This is seen in sugar, alcohol and tobacco taxes, taxes on CO2 emissions, and other so-called "sin taxes".

Without wanting to complicate matters too much at this point, I should also add that in almost every epoch in history, taxation has been used extensively to finance wars. This applies whether the state sees taxes as a way of getting money to finance its spending, or as a means of avoiding inflation by reducing the narrow money supply as it gets bloated by the big increase in military spending. Since the Napoleonic wars in the early 19th century, government borrowing has also been used extensively for this purpose. In earlier times governments tended to increase taxes while their wars were raging, then reduce taxes again afterwards.

With these thoughts as a background we'll now look at some of the ups and downs in the history of taxation. We'll do this with some major questions in mind: what would be a fair and sensible way to tax people today, and what can we learn from history? It's also useful to keep in mind the fact that today, income tax dominates the tax landscape. Work, as in employment and self-employment, contributes well over half of today's tax take–but is this normal in human history?

A brief history of taxation: beginning with ancient Egypt

The earliest written records of taxation that have survived come from ancient Egypt some 5,000 years ago, in the 31st century BCE. During the reign of Pharaoh Hor-Aha (c. 3100-3050 BCE), in what's now known as the First Dynasty, Hor-Aha appointed a vizier to assess people's real wealth each year: how many cattle they had, the amount of crops their fields produced, the amount of cooking oil in their stocks. Hor-Aha took prescribed portions of these for his own household and for his armies and public works.

These taxes were effectively wealth taxes. The vizier noted how much of each commodity you had at the end of each tax year and assessed you on that basis.

Over the next 3,000 years there were many variations on what various Pharaohs taxed and how. One important addition was a tax on cross-border trade, the ancient equivalent of import taxes. Another was a tax on labour. According to your ability, you had to give a certain number of days each year to help with ongoing public works such as dredging the Nile. Taxes were also imposed on women in proportion to their household food preparation. In fact, reading the history of taxation in ancient Egypt can be bewildering because of the many changes and variations that took place under different Pharaohs and dynasties. What seems to be consistent, though, is that a person's real wealth was quite a good predictor of how much tax they had to pay.

As far as we know, Egypt had no cash currency until the 30th dynasty, in the 4th century BCE, when Pharaoh Teos introduced the Gold Slater. Taxes had been collected in the form of produce and labour for some 3,000 years before cash money arrived on the scene.

Ancient Egypt also gives one of the earliest examples of tax exemptions. This comes, surprisingly, in the scripts on the Rosetta Stone, which dates from about 190 BCE. The Rosetta Stone is hugely important because it enabled modern linguists to begin to understand Egyptian hieroglyphics. It's written in ancient Egyptian alongside an ancient Greek translation, using three different scripts: hieroglyphics, the Greek alphabet, and a cursive form of Egyptian known as demotic script. Since ancient Greek had been well known and widely understood consistently for centuries, this gave 19th century linguists the keys that opened the door to our modern, comprehensive understanding of hieroglyphics.

The Rosetta stone is a declaration by a group of Egyptian priests that their temples are tax-exempt. The Macedonian conqueror Ptolemy governed Egypt at that time and had imposed heavy taxes, but to get the priest's cooperation he was persuaded to exempt their temples from tax. Tax evasion was heavily punishable, so the priests composed the text, translated it into Greek, the language of the conquerors, added the demotic version of Egyptian which was more accessible to many local people than hieroglyphics, and carved it into stone. Presumably they set up the stone in or near one of their temples, to remind Ptolemy's tax agents that they were tax exempt. The stone was later used as a building block in the construction of Fort Julien near the town of Rashid, also known as Rosetta, in the Nile Delta. One of Napoleon's officers, Pierre-François Bouchard, found it there in 1799, and when the British defeated Napoleon in 1801 they looted it and put it in the British Museum, where it's still on display today.

The Rosetta stone is an early example of tax exemption. Tax exemption is part of a wider phenomenon called "tax avoidance", which refers to all the possible legal ways of paying as little tax as possible, and this, too, is evident in different ways throughout history. It's different from "tax evasion", which refers to *illegal* ways of avoiding paying tax. Recently a group of economists, finance experts and historians headed by German historian Korinna Schönhärl published a detailed overview of the long history of tax avoidance, evasion and resistance[103]. It shows how "throughout history, wealthy and poor taxpayers have tried to avoid or reduce their tax burden by negotiating with tax authorities, through practices of legal tax avoidance or illegal tax evasion, by filing lawsuits, seeking armed resistance or by migration …" It seems there's almost always and everywhere been a cat-and-mouse game between states and the populace, where people find loopholes and escape routes from taxes, almost as fast as states find ways to close them off. This is also a major theme in recent research by French economists Thomas Piketty, Emmanuel Saez and Gabriel Zucman on how to design a modern wealth tax. They note that a challenge in instituting any new tax is to design it in such a way that wealthy, privileged people don't find ways to avoid it[104].

So, from ancient Egypt we see five features of taxation that have occurred and recurred in many societies over the past few thousand years: the dominance of wealth taxes; the advent of taxes as a fact of life even before cash money arose; taxes on goods that are bought, sold and traded; the preponderance of a large number of other sorts of taxes; and the phenomenon of tax avoidance.

We'll now take a brief look at tax regimes and types of taxes that stand out, in different places and times in history

Tax in ancient Greece and Rome

In ancient Greece around 500 BCE taxes were inconsistent compared to the orderly and predictable regimes we're used to today. There were sudden

103 Schönhärl et al. (2023)
104 Piketty et al. (2023)

bursts of heavy taxation to pay for wars–something that's been repeated in many countries throughout history. But in Greece an interesting variation was that the government would often pay any excess back to its taxpaying citizens after the war was over.

Another unusual practice was the way Greece funded its public works, such as concert arenas, sports stadiums, bridges and public buildings. The government simply ordered specific wealthy individuals to fund specific projects. The chosen funder would have to pay for the whole project but would have the honour of having it named after him or at least associated with his reputation. This is different from the modern phenomenon of a rich firm funding or part-funding a project and then profiting from it, as with the Emirates Football Stadium in London, for example[105]. In Greece the completed project belonged entirely to the state, not the funder. Interestingly, it seems the wealthy class not only approved of this system, but sometimes even competed with each other for the prestige of paying for a project and being known as the funder.

Ancient Rome was much more vigorous and systematic in its revenue collection. As we've seen in Chapter 5, in 211 BCE the Roman Republic introduced the denarius, a silver coin. They did this to make it easier for wealthy landowners to pay their wealth taxes. Like the Egyptians, the Romans also tended to link tax liability to wealth rather than income.

Rome also developed an extensive system of goods and trade taxes. It was relatively easy to tax seaborne trade because ships had to dock at ports. Caravan trade wasn't so easy to identify, but the Romans developed a comprehensive system to identify tax liabilities at all scales, from large ports to local markets. It's called "tax farming".

Tax farming was the collection of taxes by private citizens who got a commission from the government for the tax they raised. The government "farmed out" its tax collection, hence the tax collectors are often called tax farmers. The Roman government delegated tax collection to its provincial governors, who used the services of tax farmers to raise their quota of tax money to send to Rome.

In the early 1st century BCE a man in Judea named Matthew was a tax farmer, until he simply walked away from his desk and his piles of coins and lists of tax-liable Judeans, to join the growing group of disciples of an itinerant preacher named Jesus. If we treat the Gospels–the first four books

---

[105] Emirates invested some £100 million in the stadium in return for naming rights.

of the Christian New Testament–as typical ancient historical documents, we get an interesting insight into how a conquered, subjugated people viewed tax farmers.

In short, tax farmers were hated. This hatred was no doubt much stronger and probably far more justified than some modern taxpayers feel toward their own countries' tax bureaucrats. To begin with, tax farmers were working for a foreign power. Matthew was doing the work of Pontius Pilate, the Roman governor of Judea. A large portion of the money was therefore simply extracted from the local people and used by the conquerors for their own luxuries and distant wars. Second, tax farmers usually set their own commission rate and added it to people's tax liability. By setting a high rate they could get rather rich at other people's expense and enjoy the protection of the occupation troops if they came under threat.

Perhaps it's not surprising, then, that in writings attributed to the reformed Matthew, he quotes Jesus as lumping tax farmers together with prostitutes and other "sinners"[106]. His readers would no doubt have nodded approvingly. Tax farmers were not only hated, but seen as morally reprehensible–though it seems that all could be forgiven if they walked away from their profession and left their piles of money and lists of tax-liable citizens behind.

Another interesting insight along similar lines concerns a hugely successful Muslim reform movement in North Africa in the 15th century, known as the Murabitun. North African Islam at the time had been fractious and over-complex, and the Murabitun offered a much-simplified version based on what they saw as Mohammed's original insights. Their leader, Ibn Yasin, maintained there were just three basic demands in Islam: personal moral behaviour; social justice (especially looking after the poor); and taxation only in accordance with Islamic law, i.e., only taxation that most Muslims would agree was fair[107]. This simple, pared-down version of Islam united North African peoples, and their military support for the Muslim provinces in Spain delayed the Pope's armies' conquest of their territories by about a century. Fair taxation had a positive effect on national solidarity and military strength!

Another insight about people's craving for fairness in taxation concerns the American revolution. In the late 18th century the British government was deeply in debt, mostly due to financing its many wars. The British were

---

106 In the Christian New Testament an example is Matthew 21:31.

107 See the interesting discussion of the Murabitun movement in Alkhateeb (2021), pages 149ff.

already heavily taxed, so the government turned to its American colonies to increase its tax take. In 1764 it passed the Sugar Act, taxing the colonies for imports of molasses, sugar and wine. This was followed by the Stamp Act in 1765, taxing printed material such as newspapers and legal documents. Finally in 1767 the Townsend Act was passed, introducing or increasing taxes on 72 items, including tea. This was a step too far for the colonists. They staged a demonstration at the port of Boston, boarding ships and throwing tonnes of tea overboard–which became known as the Boston Tea Party. This helped trigger the revolution that led to independence from Britain in 1769. The taxes were seen as unfair, the government pushed them too far, and in the end it lost far more than it would have gained.

The general insight from these events, seen throughout history, is that people have repeatedly advocated and agitated for fairness in tax and its collection. A fair tax regime has often promoted patriotism and military solidarity, while an unjust tax regime has sometimes led to rebellion.

One final point about the Romans: they also collected money via tribute and booty. Tribute is a term for taxes imposed on a conquered territory. What Matthew was collecting was, technically speaking, tribute rather than what we today would call tax. A large portion of it went to finance Rome's enormous military legions, and this would also have contributed to people seeing it as unfair.

Booty was precious metal coinage and other valuables the Romans looted when they sacked a city or defeated a territory. Looting for booty was common practice. Genghis Kahn's armies did it to the Muslims in Persia; the Pope's Crusader armies did it to Eastern Orthodox Christian towns in the Turkish regions while on their way to do it wholescale to Muslim cities in Palestine; the Spanish did it to cities and mines in the Americas in the 16th century; and the Portuguese, Dutch, British and French did it to the lands they colonised. Armies tend not to do it today because their conquered territories use fiat money rather than gold coins, and the currency of a conquered state tends not to be worth much.

Income tax

Income tax is a relatively modern phenomenon, at least on the scale it happens today. Wealth tax, as we've seen, is at least as old as the ancient Egyptians. Roman Emperor Augustus introduced a form of income tax in the late 1st century BCE, but this seems to have had little impact and didn't last long.

In later centuries, attempts to introduce income tax were associated with governments' need to finance wars. In Britain one of the first serious attempts to tax income was made by Prime Minister William Pitt in 1799. Britain's war with France, beginning in 1793, was draining the government's coffers, so Pitt sought to widen the tax base. His Parliament imposed an income tax of 10% on annual incomes over £200, the equivalent of £29,000 today. The Parliament then set a graduated rate from 0% to 10% on incomes between £60 and £200 (today's equivalent of £9,000–£29,000), and 0% on incomes below £60. The tax rates were low compared to today's, which range from 20% on incomes over £12,500 to 45% on incomes over £150,000.

Today's UK Parliamentary papers comment on how people reacted to William Pitt's income tax:

> At first the tax was highly unpopular and was widely evaded, particularly among merchants and manufacturers. It was thought to be too intrusive into people's private financial circumstances. In time, though, the tax came to be accepted as a vital price for winning the war against Napoleon. Indeed, many regarded paying the tax as a patriotic duty.[108]

But the income tax didn't last long. It was abolished by Prime Minister Henry Addington in 1802 after the Peace of Amiens brought the war to a halt. Addington reformed the tax system and reintroduced income tax at a lower rate. Over the next 70 years a succession of governments tried to abolish it, but usually just reformed it and lowered the percentage tax rate. In the 1870s, under Prime Minister Benjamin Disraeli and his Chancelor Stafford Northcote, the rate fell to 1%, with most earners exempt.

It wasn't until the First World War of 1914-1918 that income tax in Britain began to resemble the form we have today. The top rate was increased to 17.5% in 1915 and 30% in 1918.

The US was even slower at getting income tax established. A bewildering range of different types of taxes had been tried and had often failed among the early American colonies and again after the American Revolution, but none of these included a stable, comprehensive income tax[109]. The first major attempt to tax income systematically was by Abraham Lincoln, who introduced an income tax as an emergency measure during the Civil War of

---

[108] UK Parliament (2024)

[109] For a detailed account of taxes in the American colonies see King and Case (2020).

1860-1864. His Revenue Act of 1861 imposed a 3% tax on income over $800 per year (today's equivalent of about $18,000). This was modified in a new Revenue Act in 1862, which introduced a progressive scale of tax rates–the higher your income, the higher the percentage tax rate. This was further modified in 1864 with more income tax brackets and higher tax rates.

The tax lapsed when the Civil War ended. Congress passed a bill for a new income tax in 1894, but the following year the Supreme Court struck it down as unconstitutional. It wasn't until 1913, when Congress got the support of 36 states to add the 16th amendment to the constitution, that income tax was finally reintroduced. The 16th amendment states:

> The Congress shall have power to lay and collect taxes on incomes, from whatever source derived, without apportionment among the several States, and without regard to any census or enumeration.

This was the beginning of today's major focus on income tax in the US.

Although income tax rates in both Britain and the US started at relatively low rates, they steadily increased in these and other countries during the 20th century. Piketty's *Capital in the 20th Century* gives graphs of the top tax rates for the US, Britain, Germany and France from 1900 to 2014[110]. The top rates steadily increased from the mid-1910s to the 1940s, reaching 90% and higher in Britain, the US and Germany and over 80% in France. They then slowly declined to a range between 35% and 45% by the 2010s, where most of them lie today. The Scandinavian countries retained higher top rates, with Denmark now leading the pack at 55.9%. The lowest in the EU are Hungary and the Czech Republic, each with 15%.

But these are just the top tax rates, which apply to the highest incomes. In most of these countries, lower income earners pay a lower percentage rate, but this is still substantial if their income isn't high. Britain is typical, where you pay 20% on all income between £12,500 and £50,00 per year, 40% on income between £50,000 and £150,000, and 45% on income above £150,000 (in Scotland the rates are slightly higher). When you add social security payments to this, the result, as I mentioned above, is that over 60% of government revenue in most high-income countries comes from income tax.

---

[110] Piketty (2014), page 499

So, what we have today is a reversal of what's happened throughout most of history. In the past, most of the tax take came from wealth taxes, with very little coming from income tax. Today it's the other way round.

In the 1950s-1970s this made good sense, especially in high-income countries such as the US, Canada, Australia, New Zealand, Britain, Ireland and the countries of western Europe. In that period a very large portion of the increase in private wealth came from people's income, and most of this income was earned by working, not by speculation. In these countries you could work at almost any kind of job and earn enough to save up the deposit for a house. Income from work was the main source of increase in wealth.

Back to wealth tax?

So it made sense in the 1950s-1980s to tax income. Income and wealth were closely related. If you taxed income, you were effectively taxing wealth.

Now this is no longer the case. Today most of the increase in wealth comes from capital gains and financial speculation. If you have money, you make money by investing, reinvesting and betting on the financial markets. We see this, for example, in what's often called the "financialization of housing". Economists Rodrigo Fernandez and Manuel Aalbers were among the first to seriously investigate this phenomenon in depth[111]. Wealthy individuals and finance cartels buy houses and apartments because real estate is almost guaranteed to increase in value, steadily and persistently. This creates an increased demand for residential property, which drives its value even higher. Investment firms buy up large portfolios of houses and apartments, and these portfolios are sometimes carved up into shares and sold on for even higher prices. Over time, fewer and fewer people can afford to buy a house or apartment to live in. Housing is "financialized", turned into a speculative money-making enterprise that makes rich people richer, without their having to do any productive work. For example in Auckland, New Zealand, in the 1960s through to the early 1980s the average price of a house was about three times the average annual wage. Now it's about 18 times the average wage. It's much the same in Britain, western Europe, the US, Canada and Australia. Instead of productive work leading to an increase in wealth, now wealth itself leads to an increase in wealth.

This type of cycle is repeated in hundreds of investment schemes and exotic financial instruments. Money begets money, which begets more money.

[111] Fernandes and Albers (2016)

According to the US's central bank, the Federal Reserve, in June 2024 the poorest 50% of Americans owned just 2.5% of the wealth, while the richest 1% owned 36.5%[112]. The wealth of the top 1% increased from $30 billion to $45 billion in the three years 2020-2024, an average increase of around 17% per year. This represents an average increase in wealth of over $3 billion per person per year among this privileged group. This didn't come from work, so income tax didn't touch it. It was tax-free. This situation is echoed in almost every country around the world today.

I mentioned above that French economists Emmanuel Saez, Gabriel Zucman and Thomas Piketty are designing a modern wealth tax[113]. Their scheme is being promoted by Brazilian President Lula and has won the support, at least in principle, of a number of prominent leaders, including the prime minister of Spain and the former Social Democrat prime minister of Germany. The details of how such a tax would work are beyond the scope of this book, but I would highly recommend that readers follow the publications of Saez, Zucman and Piketty closely over the next few years.

Things to think about regarding tax

I'll finish this chapter by briefly mentioning some key points to think about regarding taxation.

First, there's plenty of evidence from history that people expect tax to be fair, and are likely to rebel or plot against it if it's not. Governments need tax revenue (whether they see this as giving credence to the money they spend into existence, or getting money from outside themselves), and societies tend not to like taxes in general and to despise them when they're seen as unfair. Unfair taxes were the trigger that set the American Revolution in motion. A return to fair taxation was a key component in the simplified creed that united North African Muslims in the Middle Ages, enabling them to support their Iberian cousins against papal-led invasions for over a century. A huge and complex practice of tax avoidance has always existed alongside tax regimes–evidenced as far back as the Rosetta Stone– and tax avoidance is much more deeply ingrained and hard to combat when tax is seen as unjust. Tax has to be fair.

Second, there's a passive, complacent acceptance among most people today that *income* tax should continue to be the main source of government

---

112 Statistics given in Statista (2024b)

113 An outline of their reasoning is given in Saez and Zucman (2021).

revenue. I suspect this is largely because most people don't realise that income tax is a peculiarly modern phenomenon. Benjamin Franklin is reported to have said, "In this world nothing can be said to be certain, except death and taxes." But for many people the two great certainties are death and *income* taxes. For most of history this certainly wasn't the case. And it doesn't have to be the case in future. We need to be critical of our acceptance of today's tax structures as somehow inevitable. There are many more ways to design tax regimes than our current one.

Third, high rates of income tax were appropriate in the decades after the Second World War, when much of the increase in wealth was gained through regular productive work. Now, however, work makes very few people substantially richer. By far the greatest increases in wealth come from investing and reinvesting large fortunes. This makes an ideal situation for the introduction of a tax on wealth–coincidentally in line with most of history. It's now time to look seriously at reducing income tax to a minimum and getting a large chunk of government revenue from wealth taxes.

Finally, recall that taxation is a necessary component of modern money. State-created money gets its value and credibility from the fact that we all have to pay it back to the state in our taxes. Therefore, if the tax system is unfair or unjust, money itself is morally tainted, and the $20 note in your purse or wallet is an instrument of injustice or even exploitation. We can't afford to have an unfair tax system because it pollutes the very basis of the money we use every day.

7. WHY THE EURO IS A PROBLEM-CHILD AMONG MODERN CURRENCIES

In the summer of 1977, I toured eight European countries with two other UK students in our second-hand Sunbeam Rapier car. We slept in a very small tent or stayed over with European friends we'd met in Cambridge. There wasn't much mass tourism in those days, so we had easy access to museums, city squares, castles, Alpine lakes and sunny Italian beaches. Our main problem was how to pay for things. Eight countries, eight different currencies.

It was complicated. Before we left England we went to the bank and got small stocks of French Francs, Swiss Francs, Belgian Francs, Austrian Schillings, German Marks, Dutch Guilders and Italian Lire. That would cover the small change. We couldn't get Slovenian Tolars, so we decided we'd solve that problem when we got there. For larger amounts we got travellers cheques, denominated in US dollars. A travellers' cheque was an elaborately decorated stiff paper note that represented a bank's promise to pay the amount stated, in the currency stated, usually US dollars. We got them from our UK bank but had to pay about 5% more than their face value. Later we handed them to banks in the foreign countries and they gave us their own currencies in return, but only at about 95% of the value of the cheques, sometimes even less. In one Italian bank we had a long wait while the clerks put our travellers' cheques through an elaborate proofing process, to make sure they were genuine. And of course, we'd also suffered substantial losses on the foreign cash we'd bought.

Things actually turned out to be easier in Slovenia because our friends there were eager to get western money (Slovenia was part of Communist Yugoslavia at the time) and happily exchanged some of our leftover Lire, Marks, Schillings and Francs (especially the Swiss ones) for Tolars, at a rate we all thought was fair.

When we got back to Britain we had the remains of several currencies in our wallets and a jangling diversity of coins in our pockets, but the summer holidays were over and no-one seemed interested in buying them.

I vaguely remember our discussing the fact that thousands of other tourists must have been having similar experiences. All over western Europe, banks were making tidy profits exchanging travellers' cheques in pounds, dollars and yen for their local currencies. What a huge amount of clerical work was going into this purely bureaucratic process, and at what cost to travellers.

But you have to upscale the problem to see what it was like for businesses. The value of trade between European countries is typically more than one-and-a-half times as high as the total value of European trade with other countries. In 2023, for EU countries the ratio was 4.13 trillion euro to 2.56 trillion euro. In other words, over 60% of EU countries' trade flowed between EU countries. If the value of each shipment of today's imports had to be converted to the exporting country's currency there'd be a huge and expensive bureaucracy to make the currency conversions, plus of course the losses through commissions. An alternative would be to value all trade in US dollars, as happens between many other trading countries, but this would syphon off commission to US banks, while reinforcing the global power of the US dollar.

Early attempts to form a European currency

The desire for a common European currency goes back at least as far as 1865, when the so-called Latin Monetary Union, or LMU, was formed. Its four founding members, Belgium, France, Italy and Switzerland, produced a common coinage based on the French "Gold Franc". This included 13 denominations of metal coins, each containing a specified amount of gold, silver and/or brass, ranging from a gold coin worth 100 francs down to a brass coin worth 1 centime. Each member country could produce as many of these coins as it wished to, because their value was fixed by the amounts of precious metal in them.

Unlike the euro, these coins were used alongside the countries' own separate currencies, so goods and services could be bought and sold cross-border using the LMU coins, without having to continually exchange currencies, while ordinary commerce continued in each country with its own currency.

Greece joined the LMU in 1867, followed by Finland, Serbia and Bulgaria. The Papal states also joined, but they debased the currency by minting coins with a lower precious metal content and were expelled from the LMU in 1870, owing the equivalent of 20 million Italian lire.

Later, other member countries began to debase the coins as the costs of precious metals rose, and some member countries produced paper notes which promised to pay the metal coinage on demand, but these were not well accepted as there was uncertainty as to how this would be honoured. This reflects a more general problem of a joint currency: how to prevent cheating. As we'll see below, this is also a problem for the euro even though there's no precious metal involved.

Despite the suspicions of cheating, the LMU survived until the First World War of 1914-1918, and remnants of it lived on until its formal end in 1927. Two years later German Prime Minister Gustav Stresemann called for discussion of a new European currency. This was partly motivated by the increased number of small European countries that had formed after the First World War. Since each country had its own currency, the cumbersome and costly inefficiencies of cross-border trade and commerce had multiplied.

After the Second World War the countries of western Europe found a great deal in common due to their proximity to the Communist regimes to the east and the formation of NATO in 1949. In 1952 the Treaty of Paris established the European Coal and Steel Community, a free trade zone comprised of Italy, West Germany, Belgium, the Netherlands, France and Luxembourg. This was expanded and deepened in 1957 under the Treaty of Rome, to form the European Economic Community, also called the European Common Market, which over the following years came to include Britain, Ireland, Spain, Portugal and Denmark. In 1993 this was renamed the European Community and in 2009 it was modified to become the European Union, or EU, which continued to expand–except for Britain's formal departure in January 2020.

Serious discussion of a common European currency began in the 1950s, but the need for it became more pressing when exchange rates between different European currencies began wavering heavily, after President Nixon abolished the gold standard for the US dollar in 1971. In March 1979 the European Monetary System (EMS) was formed. This fixed the European countries' exchange rates onto the European Currency Unit (ECU), a kind of bookkeeping quasi-currency, to stabilise exchange rates and dampen inflation.

In 1988 the European Commission began to outline possible steps of cooperation toward a common currency centred on a European central bank, but Britain opposed this. There were then ad hoc discussions between EU countries, leading in 1989 to the Delores Report, which set out a 3-step programme for introducing a common currency. This was based on a new quasi-currency called the European Monetary Unit (EMU), which turned out to be the precursor of the euro.

In Step 1 of this programme, exchange controls between participating European countries were abolished on 1 July 1990, so their individual currencies could find their natural values in relation to each other; and the Maastricht Treaty was signed on 7 February 1992, agreeing to a future common currency but without Britain.

In Step 2, on 12 January 1994, the forerunner of the European Central Bank was established, and in December 1995 the term "euro" was agreed for the forthcoming currency while the date of 1 January 1999 was set for the currency's launch. It was also agreed that the values of each country's currency for conversion to euros would be based on the exchange rates of the day before the launch.

In Step 3 the euro was launched. It initially covered only electronic transactions, travellers' cheques and government bonds, without euro notes or coins. The individual countries' old notes and coins remained legal tender until January 2002, when the new euro notes and coins were introduced.

Although this may sound like a somewhat tedious list of dates and agreements, it's actually a remarkable story of cooperation and coordination between 11 diverse countries, each with good reasons to want to remain attached to their own currencies but even stronger reasons to share a common currency. Since then, the number of euro countries–the "Eurozone"–has steadily increased, with 19 now either members or candidates for membership.

How the euro works

In non-euro countries like the US, China, Australia, Japan and Britain the central bank is the government's own bank. It has two main functions. One of these is to handle the government's payments and receipts, which, as we saw in Chapter 2, are all made in narrow, high-powered money: money which the state creates out of nothing. The government spends it into existence, via its central bank, and effectively dissolves it back into nothing when it receives it back as payments for taxes, fees, fines, student loan repayments, etc.

Each of the euro countries also has its own central bank, which performs this same function. For example, when the German government pays a contractor 1 million euros for building a new motorway off-ramp, it orders its central bank, the Deutsche Bundesbank, to credit the contractor's bank's account at the central bank (again the Deutsche Bundesbank) with 1 million euros of narrow money, effectively creating this money out of nothing. When a German resident pays 1,000 euros of tax to the German government, their bank transfers 1,000 euros of narrow money from its account at the central bank to the German government's account at the Deutsche Bundesbank, effectively dissolving it into nothing. This is just the same as if we're talking about Britain, China, Japan, New Zealand, or most other non-euro countries.

The second function of non-euro countries' central banks is to continually attempt to stabilize the economy. Again as we saw in Chapter 2, they do this by setting overnight interest rates for lending narrow money to commercial banks for their daily reconciliation of accounts with each other. They also create and dissolve money by buying and selling bonds, to slow down or speed up the economy when they think this is necessary–their so-called "open market operations".

In the euro countries most of these functions are still carried out by the individual countries' central banks. However, the European Central Bank has three powerful, over-arching functions that govern how the individual countries' central banks have to operate.

First, the European Central Bank adjusts the interest rate of its so-called "marginal lending facility", often called the "overnight interest rate", through which commercial banks get overnight loans for reconciling their accounts with each other's after each day's commerce (on which see Chapter 2). For example, on 18th September 2024 the European Central Bank reduced this rate from 4.50% to 3.90%, then down to 3.65 % on 23rd October, and down further to 3.40 % on 18th December. The central banks in all Eurozone countries are required to keep their own overnight interest rates very close to these rates. This effectively means that all commercial banks in all Eurozone countries pay these rates for their overnight loans, or very close to them, regardless of the state of their economies.

It's important to note that the overnight rate directly influences the interest rate the commercial banks charge on loans to businesses and individuals. The higher the interest rate on these loans, the less demand there is for them, therefore the less broad money is spent in the economy, therefore the inflation rate begins to fall and unemployment tends to increase.

Second, the European Central Bank has a further set of tools to attempt to stabilize the economy, namely by buying and selling bonds (open market operations) and using quantitative easing–in other words, by creating and dissolving whatever small or large sums of money seem appropriate to prevent bubbles and crashes and to ensure the money supply keeps up with GDP growth and an agreed level of inflation, about 2% per year.

Third, the European Central Bank, together with committees of the European Parliament, sets limits on how much deficit and debt the member countries' governments are allowed to incur.

The Eurozone countries have thereby surrendered part of their sovereignty to the European Central Bank. An individual member country that's suffering from under-utilized capacity cannot stimulate its economy by reducing interest rates or by substantially increasing its budget deficit and borrowing heavily. Likewise, it cannot increase interest rates substantially to dampen inflation or reduce them to boost employment, because all Eurozone countries have to keep close to the rates set by the European Central Bank.

Fairness and the risk of stifling the economy

To understand why there are these restraints on member countries, it's helpful to look at the issue of fairness: the need for the euro to be fair to all member countries. Recall that each Eurozone government can spend euros into existence via its own central bank. Without a regulated restraint, this would enable a Eurozone country to get rich at the expense of the others simply by spending to excess. For example, Portugal could spend an extra trillion euros into existence by financing the construction of a new elite university, plus another few billion per year to run it, plus more on promotional activities to attract top professors from all over the world. Portugal would get the benefits, but the whole Eurozone would effectively pay for it, because of the way inflation is controlled. Portugal's huge tranche of spending would increase the average inflation rate across the Eurozone, and the European Central Bank would have to respond by increasing the base interest rate for the whole Eurozone. So, while Portugal's economy would boom due to all the new euros flowing into the elite university project and out from it into the wider Portuguese economy, the economies of other

Eurozone countries' economies would be slowed down due to overly high interest rates.

Economists and bureaucrats thought of this when they designed the euro. So the negotiating countries decided that to become a member of the Eurozone, a country would have to agree to two further restraints. These have to do with *deficit* and *debt*.

First, the deficit rule: a government's spending in any year was not allowed to exceed its income by more than 3% of its country's gross domestic product (GDP). In other words, it should never have a budget *deficit* higher than 3% of GDP.

Second, their level of government *debt* was never allowed to exceed 60% of their countries' GDP.

These restraints would obviously put the brakes on any project like the elite university outlined above, as spending that much excess would clearly break the deficit and debt rules. But these rules can also stifle economic growth in general. In particular, the deficit rule can make it very hard and costly for a country to shake free of poor economic performance, or to invest entrepreneurially in projects with large future returns for the economy.

Before we look into this in more detail, note that it has similarities and differences with the problem that dogged the LMU in the late 19th century: the problem of restraints and cheating. In those days the restraint was that the LMU was made up of coins, each with a precisely prescribed amount of precious metal in it. As long as a country could pay for the precious metal for its coins, it could mint as many as it liked. If it wanted to import bricks and mortar from the country next door to build an elite university, it would almost certainly have to sacrifice some other project to buy the precious metals for the coins it used as payment. It couldn't make the coins out of nothing. No cheating there.

The cheating started when precious metals became too expensive and countries started debasing the coins.

In the Eurozone the restraint is not the cost of precious metal, but those two very severe percentages. And as we'll see below, cheating has already started here, too. We'll also see that in March 2025 the restraints were suddenly relaxed. Meanwhile, let's look more closely at these restraints.

The deficit restraint

What does the deficit restraint mean? Up until March 2025 a Eurozone country's budget deficit was not allowed to ever be higher than 3% of its GDP. Take Spain as an example. In 2023 Spain's GDP was 1.462 trillion euros, and its budget deficit was 51.46 billion euros. This is 3.52% of its GDP. So Spain didn't come in under the 3% limit. It cheated, so to speak. But this was better than in 2022, when its deficit was 4.59% of GDP.

Compared to other Eurozone countries, Spain was about in the middle. 10 Eurozone countries had deficits higher than 3% of GDP. The highest was Italy, at 7.2%. All Eurozone countries reported a deficit, the lowest being Portugal's, at 1.2% of GDP.

But you'll recall from Chapter 3 that a budget deficit can actually be a good thing, because it increases the amount of narrow money in the economy. Narrow money is the basis on which broad money is built, and broad money powers everyday commerce, industry and household spending. So if we don't let the narrow money supply grow over the years and decades, the broad money supply is restrained and it's difficult for the economy to grow.

So then, what would be a healthy level of narrow money supply growth? To address this, it's helpful to look at the budget deficit *as a percentage of a country's budget,* i.e., of government expenditure, rather than as a percentage of its GDP. In 2023 Spain's budget was 678.8 billion euros and its deficit was 51.46 billion euros, so its deficit was 7.58% of its budget. It spent 7.58% more than it received back in taxes, fees, etc. If it had met the euro target of 3% of GDP, this figure would have been 6.46%.

Looking at it that way, it seems quite a generous allowance. If a government spends 6.46% more than it gets back in taxes, fees, fines, etc., its narrow money supply will grow. This will provide an increase in collateral for commercial banks to give loans that make the broad money supply grow. Therefore the economy will grow, and as long as the broad money makes its way to socially useful industries, this will increase the wellbeing of society.

But there's a catch, and this has to do with the *debt* restraint: the limit on government debt.

The debt restraint

If Eurozone governments have a budget deficit–if they spend more than they get back in taxes, fees, fines, etc. in any particular year–the Eurozone rules say they have to borrow money to cover the deficit. When they borrow money, they increase their level of debt. The restraint on this is that their total debt is never allowed to be more than 60% of their GDP.

Just to put this in perspective, US government debt reached 112% of its GDP in 2023[114] and 124% at the end of 2024. Japan's debt was a huge 205% of GDP in 2023, but if it weren't for the excessive government spending that's contributed to this level of debt, Japan's economy would almost certainly be even deeper in the doldrums than it's been in for the past two decades. The UK's debt in 2023 was 110% of its GDP, but it's probably fair to say that many UK economists would support the excess spending that led to this. Without it, the UK, like Japan, would be even deeper in the economic doldrums.

On the other hand, most high-income countries outside the Eurozone had debt levels under 60% in 2023: Australia's was just under 35%, New Zealand's 46%, Canada's 60% and Norway's 14%.

There are three issues with government debt in Eurozone countries that need to be considered: balanced economies, cheating, and borrowing. First, regarding balanced economies, I've argued in this book that governments need to be free to spend as much or as little as is needed to keep their economies running at full speed: to keep the economy finely balanced between recession and overheating. In the words of economist Stephanie Kelton, policymakers should "focus on delivering a balanced economy rather than a balanced budget. That might require persistent deficits, but it might also require a balanced budget or even budget surpluses."[115]

For example, Japan's government needs to spend to excess because its people are net savers: its aging population doesn't spend enough to power its economy at its full potential. Because there's no rule in Japan limiting the government's level of debt, Japan's government is free to spend the amount it needs to. And because Japan also has a rule that government

---

[114] See IMF (2024) for data on over 100 countries' debt levels in 2023. I'm rounding these percentages to their nearest whole number. For example, US debt was112.26% of its GDP, rounded to 112%.

[115] Kelton (2019), page 2

deficits must be covered by borrowing, Japan's debt has now reached 205% of its GDP.

Italy, Greece Portugal and Spain also have aging populations, but their debt is limited by Eurozone rules. They're only allowed a debt of 60% of their GDP. Clearly, they're finding it necessary to spend more than this, because in 2023 Italy's level of debt reached 140% of its GDP, Greece's reached 185%, Portugal's 105%, and Spain's 98%. These are way above the permitted levels, but their economies haven't imploded and the Eurozone is still intact. But doesn't this mean they've broken the rules? Isn't this a form of cheating?

Cheating and Eurozone rules

Since governments spend money by creating it out of nothing, the more a Eurozone government creates, the bigger the portion it's taking from the shared pool–or more accurately, the more it's adding to the shared pool but taking back all that extra share for itself.

The rationale behind the debt and deficit rules, therefore, is that in any particular year a Eurozone government should be permitted to create an amount of money *only in proportion to the size of its economy in that particular year*: no more than 3 % higher than that year's GDP. And a government's accumulated debt in any particular year is never allowed to be more than 60% of the country's GDP. This stops tiny Luxembourg from creating 10 trillion euros while Germany only creates 3 trillion, or Portugal, with a population of 10.53 million, creating more than France, which has a population of 68.17 million.

But there's no *physical* constraint on how much these governments can create, because money creation is just keystrokes on a computer. And when all the southern Eurozone states apart from Slovenia go way over their allowances, this becomes an existential problem for the Eurozone.

But it was solved–after a fashion–in the true spirit of European compromise. In April 2024 the EU approved a set of "New Fiscal Rules"[116] designed "to foster investment" and "strengthen the social dimension"[117] of the Eurozone. The compromise rule for government debt is:

---

[116] European Parliament (2024)
[117] European Parliament (2024a)

> Countries with excessive debt will be required to reduce it on average by 1% per year if their debt is above 90% of GDP, and by 0.5% per year on average if it is between 60% and 90%.[118]

So this means that Greece, for example, has over 120 years to get its level of debt down to 60% of its GDP, Italy has at least 70 years, and Portugal at least 45.

This clearly represents a stunning relaxation of the rules, but some would argue it's not enough. After all, it still requires Greece, Italy, Portugal and Spain to *reduce* their debt continually for the foreseeable future.

The French economist Thomas Piketty questions the very basis of the 60% debt and 3% deficit rules. He comments: "The precise economic logic behind these rules has never been completely explained." "It's difficult", he says, "to justify any particular level of public debt on rational grounds."[119] Like Stephanie Kelton and others, he argues that levels of government spending–and therefore government debt and deficit–need to be calibrated to serve the needs of the economy. If there's a slump, such as the 1930s Great Depression or the aftermath of the 2008 global economic crisis, the way to climb out of it is for the government to spend, so as to get the unused capacity in the economy fully utilized.

Nevertheless, Piketty is all too aware of the danger of cheating, where there's a shared currency, but he suggests a novel solution. The EU Parliament should be able to decide, on a case-by-case basis, what the limits of a Eurozone country's budget are allowed to be, especially in times of economic crisis. He points out that large economies such as the US, Britain and Japan "have never imposed these arbitrary rules on themselves". Since he wrote that, of course, Britain *has* imposed arbitrary budget debt and deficit rules on itself, and in Chapter 4 I argued that this is one of the reasons its economy is so sluggish.

Piketty's suggestion is worth considering because it might solve the problem of cheating, while leaving the door open for sensible deficit budgeting.

More recently, however, the tumultuous events of early 2025 presented an existential challenge to the dogmatism of the Eurozone's deficit rule. In mid-March US President Trump appeared to back Russia in the war in Ukraine and called into question US commitment to NATO. Eurozone

---

118 European Parliament (2024)
119 Piketty (2014), page 565

countries, along with the UK, were confronted with the reality of their substandard military forces and their 8-decades long reliance on the now vacillating US for national and regional defence.

Within days, the European Commission and the European Central Bank agreed to a major relaxation of the deficit rule. The Eurozone countries could increase their deficits by a further 650 billion euros. This represents about 4.2% of their GDP. The 3% constraint was suddenly increased to over 7%. Meanwhile Germany, which had an even tighter, self-imposed deficit limit embedded in its constitution, scrambled to repeal it so it could spend up to a trillion euros on defence plus half a trillion on fixing its crumbling infrastructure and meeting its climate protection goals.

Readers might like to ponder what this means for the scientific credibility of the Eurozone's original deficit rule. It wasn't based on science but on three very questionable pillars: first, the false belief that there's only so much money in the world and therefore there's not enough for the things we want and need to spend it on. The panic of mid-March 2025 showed this up as an unfounded belief, a complete misunderstanding of what money is. Suddenly the Europeans switched beliefs. They could spend an extra trillion euros or more, and there'd be plenty of money around to finance that.

Another questionable pillar is a kind of moral law that a government that spends more than it earns is profligate, wasteful, and immoral. Joesph Vogl traces this doctrine from its origin in Germany's post-war economics discourse, into the philosophy that was embedded in the founding of the euro[120]. Ironically, the incoming German government, led by the party and leader that had most vigorously supported this doctrine, is now leading the charge to relax the deficit rules and turn on the spending taps.

A third questionable pillar is the notion of 3% of GDP as the right level for government deficits. Prominent US billionaire hedge-fund managers, such as Ray Dalio and Scott Bessent, are often heard promoting this idea. Dalio proclaims the "3% solution" as the best level of government deficit, as it enables inflation and GDP growth to be catered for. Bessent proclaims the "3-3-3-plan": a government deficit of 3%, aiming for GDP growth of 3%, alongside an annual 3% increase in oil production.

But Dalio and Bessent suggest these merely as rules of thumb, not laws of economics. On *average* 3% might be reasonable, but different countries' economies are in different phases and require different rules. This is the

---

120 Vogl (2017)

value of Piketty's suggestion. The EU Parliament could form a subcommittee, enhanced with professionals from banking and commerce, to make recommendations as to what level of deficit is fair and appropriate for each country, given its economic capacity and its current economic performance.

Government debt and bonds: when are they necessary?

A further issue concerns government debt. Eurozone governments borrow and go deeper into debt by issuing bonds, to finance their budget deficits. Is this really necessary? And doesn't it stifle the very growth it's designed to stimulate?

Let's remind ourselves what happens when governments borrow by issuing bonds. To begin with, all the money that goes into or out of government coffers is high-powered, narrow money. A government will accept narrow money only, in payment for the bonds it issues. If I buy a government bond worth, say, 10,000 €, my bank first reduces my account by that amount. It thereby reduces its liability to me by 10,000 €. You'll recall from Chapter 2 that the money in my bank account is broad money–bank-created, lower-powered money. The next step is that my bank has to pay 10,000 € out of its own account at the central bank, to the government's account at the central bank. This is narrow money, high-powered money, since all the money in commercial bank's accounts at the central bank are government-created narrow money.

So, by borrowing 10,000 €, the government has reduced the amount of narrow money in a commercial bank account by 10,000 €. The commercial bank therefore has 10,000 € less collateral to back up the loans it issues. If the bank generally creates about 10 times as much in loans as it has on reserve in its account at the central bank, it can create about 100,000 € less than it could previously, and the economy is therefore smaller.

But let's also recall that the reason the government issued this bond of 10,000 € was to be able to spend 10,000 € more than it otherwise would have (since Eurozone countries borrow to cover their deficit spending). And when the government spends this money, it's putting 10,000 € of narrow money into the account of some lucky commercial bank. So the economy is right back where it started. Despite the government spending more than it expects to get back in taxes, fees, fines, etc., the narrow money supply is no bigger than it was before. Therefore the broad money supply is no bigger, and there's no economic growth effect.

Again, however, there's a catch, which a savvy government can exploit. Commercial banks, too, can buy government bonds, and they do so regularly. And when a commercial bank buys 10,000 € worth of government bonds, this doesn't necessarily mean the bank has 10,000 € less collateral for issuing loans. This isn't easy to explain, but here goes.

Two points need to be considered: banks buying government bonds; and the interest rate paid on bonds. First, although it's true that a commercial bank reduces its stock of narrow money when it buys a government bond, *the bond itself can serve as substitute collateral for the loans it issues.* Although the 10,000 € isn't in liquid form–it can't be divided up and spent as individual euros and cents and it's no use for reconciling the bank's accounts with other banks at the end of each working day–it's still an asset of the bank, and it contributes to the bank's financial soundness.

But let's consider the case of Spain, which overspent just over 5 billion euros in 2023 and financed this by borrowing, i.e., by issuing just over 5 billion euros worth of bonds. Spanish commercial banks hold only about 10% of these bonds[121], around 500 million euros worth. Therefore Spain's stock of narrow money gets a boost of only 500 million euros from its government's 5 billion euros of excess spending.

This brings us to the second point. One of the reasons Spain's commercial banks invest so little in Spanish government bonds is that the interest rate on bonds–or more accurately their "yield"–is relatively low. The interest rate on Spanish government bonds was 3.068% in early 2025, but the overnight interest rate was higher, at 3.4%. If a Spanish commercial bank invests some of its reserves in bonds, it might end up being short of the money it needs to reconcile its accounts with other banks at the end of each working day. It then has to borrow overnight from the central bank at 3.4% interest, while it's earning only 3.068% on the reserves it invested in bonds. This is not a good deal. Why invest in a bond that yields only 3.068%, if you then have to borrow money at 3.4% to clear your overnight debts?

Throughout 2024 the yield on Spanish government bonds was constantly below the European Central Bank's overnight rate. The highest yield was 3.1122%, on 10th June, and at that time the overnight interest rate was above 4.5%, so commercial banks lost, rather than gained, if they invested too much of their narrow money reserves in bonds. As of February 2025 the only Eurozone country with bond yields higher than 3.4% was Italy, at

[121] European Central Bank (2024a)

3.52%[122]. So apart from in Italy there was no incentive for commercial banks to invest the bulk of their narrow money reserves in government bonds. They do invest a small amount, because bonds are the most reliable form of investment. But not too much, or it could cost them when they reconcile their accounts with each other at the end of each working day[123].

What about the remaining 90% of Spanish government bonds, which aren't bought by commercial banks? Foreign investors hold about 40% of Spain's bonds. Since this is money coming into the economy from outside, this could theoretically give a boost of about 2 billion euros to the economy. However, there's a corresponding drag on the economy due to Spanish investors buying overseas countries' bonds.

A further 10% of Spain's bonds are held by banks within the wider Eurozone. This also has a cancelling out effect, since the criss-crossing of bond purchases between Eurozone countries tends to cancel out any specific boost to any particular country.

The remaining 40% are held by households, investment funds, insurance companies and pension funds. These don't boost the economy because, as explained above, they just swap one tranche of narrow money for another. Their benefit is that they provide a safe haven for the funds of these enterprises and households.

Overall, then, deficit budgeting only benefits Spain's economy by about 10% of the size of the deficit. Most of the benefits of deficit budgeting are cancelled by the drag on the economy caused by borrowing, or by the criss-crossing of bond purchases across borders.

Is government debt necessary?

But can a government run a budget deficit without financing it through debt? I've argued in Chapter 4 that the government of a state that issues its own sovereign currency can indeed do so, since such a state creates its own money by spending it into existence. I've argued that there's therefore no physical necessity for a government to borrow money from the private sector in order to finance a deficit. The rule of thumb is: (1) Spend as much as you need to, to ensure there's enough money in the economy to match its full capacity, and *don't dare spend any more than that* (!). (2) Use your

---

[122] Trading economics (2024)

[123] There's a detailed discussion of this in Wray (2015), pages 106-123.

other tools to keep inflation at the desired level: central bank bond purchases and sales, the central bank overnight rate, and tax rate changes for the longer term.

There are several other subtleties and nuances in this, which we'll look at in Chapter 11.

Summing up

Six main points stand out from the discussion above. First, in some ways the euro is a huge success story. Europe is a patchwork of dozens of countries with high levels of trade and commerce between them. Exchanging currencies is expensive, time consuming and wasteful. European nations also have a long history of making war on each other. The euro solves the problem of multiple currencies, while it also represents a new spirit of cooperation and friendship that breaks the pattern of centuries of war and destruction.

Second, with a joint currency there's a danger of cheating: creating more money than your fair share. The Eurozone solution has been to limit governments' debt and deficits, but this has put lower-performing countries in a stranglehold. The compromise solution of April 2024 softened this, but still prevented governments from spending the optimum amount to deliver "a balanced economy rather than a balanced budget", as Kelton so neatly expresses it.

Third, the long-running, deeply entrenched discourse that "there isn't enough money" for the things governments would dearly love to do fell into disrepute in mid-March 2025 within a few days of US President Trump's apparent withdrawal of US support for Ukraine's security. This is an important object lesson. It shows that when a falsely grounded but firmly held belief sanctioned by economists, central bankers and successive governments suddenly proves inconvenient, it can be abandoned overnight. It wasn't scientifically grounded, it was a myth. One wonders whether Europe's long years of austerity could have been avoided if this myth had been exposed earlier.

Fourth, we should be careful to avoid seeing figures such as "3% of GDP" as rules set in stone. These are useful averages, but different countries are at different stages of economic progress and need individually appropriate deficit rules, not hard-and-fast doctrines.

Fifth, the Eurozone therefore needs a more agile, politically astute and professionally competent body to oversee deficit and debt levels–rather than a set of hard and fast rules. The European Parliament should at least consider Piketty's suggestion and instigate a wide-ranging discussion on it.

Finally, the idea that Eurozone governments have to borrow in order to spend needs to be rigorously questioned. Euros are created out of nothing, and government borrowing has quite different functions than filling up the government's coffers–a topic we'll look at more closely in Chapter 11.

8. Foreign Exchange: How Money Shuffles Between Countries

Ever since countries have traded with one another, they've had to pay for goods across borders: they've been involved in foreign exchange. As far as we know, international trade between Mediterranean and ancient near eastern countries was flourishing at least as far back as the 3rd millennium BCE, some 5,500 years ago. Buyers and sellers therefore had to work out how to do commerce between currencies. The historian Haya Katz gives a detailed account of the cargo of a shipwreck from the 14th century BCE near the village of Uluburun, on what's now the Turkish Black Sea coast[124]. The wreck was discovered in 1982 by a local sponge diver, and the Turkish Institute of Natural Archaeology organised over 22,000 dives to catalogue its cargo.

The archaeologists concluded that the ship had most likely journeyed from Cyprus or Phoenicia, on the Palestinian coast, but its cargo came from even more distant lands. It included bars of copper and tin from mines in Cyprus and the southern Turkish coast; jars from Canaan in Palestine; glass from Egypt; blackwood, ivory, and ostrich eggshells from Africa; fruit and spices from the ancient near east; weapons from Mycenae and Italy; various weights and measures; and a trumpet of unknown origin. Clearly there were money exchange systems for selling and buying these goods between countries.

Katz also points to a remarkable list of cross-border trades recorded in the Old Testament book of Ezekiel, Chapter 27, dating from the 6th century BCE[125]. The chapter gives a list of imported goods and the countries they came from, in the city of Tyre on the Palestinian coast. The chapter was written as a tirade against Tyre for its practice of profiting from other nations' misfortunes, but Ezekiel inadvertently gives us a valuable insight into the extent of trade in the region at the time. He tells us that the ships in Tyre's merchant navy are constructed with timbers imported from Senir, Lebanon, Bashan and Cyprus, ivory from Africa, sailcloth from Egypt, and

---

[124] Katz (2008)

[125] Katz writes that this is in Ezekiel 26, but in English versions of the Old Testament it's Ezekiel 27.

awnings from Elishah. The goods in Tyre's local economy include bronze from Greece; horses and mules from Togarmah; ebony from Rhodes; coral, rubies, purple cloth and fine linen from 'Aram; wheat, honey, olive oil and confectionery from Israel and Judah; wine from Helbon, Izal and Zahar; sheep and goats from Arabia; and spices, gemstones and gold from Sheba and Ramah.

Although Ezekiel doesn't discuss how all this was paid for, his text assumes a successful and probably smooth method of international payments linking the ancient near east, parts of Africa, India and the Mediterranean, and extending deep into Asia.

Fast-forward to the 2020s and we have fully globalised trade involving 195 countries which use 180 different currencies, counting only those recognised by the United Nations[126]. But in today's world it's not just trade in goods that leads us to exchange money between currencies. There's also a huge international trade in money itself. We swap US dollars for euros, Chinese renminbi for British pounds, Chilean pesos for Japanese yen–and so on! Central banks buy foreign countries' government bonds, migrant workers send money home to their families, entrepreneurs in China invest in industries in Europe and Africa, while governments keep stocks of other countries' currencies as a hedge against their own currency going downhill.

The total value of these cross-border payments amounted to about $US 329 trillion in 2024 and is increasing by about $US 10 trillion per year[127]. The entire world's production of goods and services–its gross domestic product (GDP)–amounted to just over $US 115 trillion in 2024, so every year almost 3 times as much money is exchanged between countries as the monetary value of all the world's goods and services.

How does all this cross-border money exchange take place? Which countries lose out on it, who are the winners, and why?

Some readers might not find this subject interesting. But right now it's probably making you richer or poorer, depending on which country you live in. It's one of the reasons Donald Trump caused such a stir when he took office as US President for the second time. He complained about the US's negative trade balance: the fact that the US is spending almost $US 1 trillion more per year on exports than it's earning from imports. If you live in the US, this most likely affects you because, in a roundabout way, it could be

---

[126] UN (2025)
[127] Bank of England (2025)

making you poorer. Similarly, if you live in Uganda, Türkiye or Bulgaria. But if you live in China, Germany, Australia, Norway or Saudi Arabia, international trade is most likely making you richer.

The subject also affects you if you're an immigrant sending money home to family and friends in your home country. Let's go back to Ezekiel for a moment. In his report on the excessive wealth of Tyre he also mentions many different immigrant groups who lived and worked there. The oarsmen in Tyre's ships were immigrants from Sidon and Arvad. The sails were being repaired by craftsmen from Byblos. The soldiers in Tyre's army came from Persia, Lydia and Put, while the city guard included immigrants from Gammad, Arvad and Helek.

It's likely these people immigrated to Tyre for good paying jobs, much like millions do today. This has important implications for foreign exchange, because an ever-increasing trend today is that people who've immigrated to high-income countries are sending money home to family and friends in lower-income countries. These transactions are called "remittances", and according to the 2024 UN Sustainable Development Report[128] they amounted to the equivalent of $US 669 billion in 2023. That's about three times the total of all the development aid transferred from rich to poorer countries in that year (and a higher proportion today, since the US Trump Administration stopped its USAID overseas aid payments). So these millions of small remittances add up to a very big impact on people's well-being and opportunities.

In this chapter I'll talk mostly about these two issues: how foreign exchange makes some countries richer and others poorer; and how remittances work. But let's look first at the more technical issue of how money travels across borders.

How money crosses borders

We need to keep two things in mind. First, *only a small portion of the money that shifts between countries is in the form of cash.* Sure, British, European and Australian banks do keep stocks of US dollar notes and coins, Japanese yen and other prominent cash currencies, and do exchange them for other currencies, but this is only a very small part of the picture.

---

[128] UN (2024)

Second, this exchange of physical notes and coins is *the only part of international money exchange in which money itself moves between countries.* If you get your bank in England to exchange 10,000 British pounds for its equivalent in US dollars and send it to your sister's bank account in California, money does *not* float across the globe from one country to another. As the Bank of England explains:

> Currencies are closed-loop systems. Domestic payment systems are not traditionally directly connected with the systems of other countries so when making a transfer between two jurisdictions, the currency is not physically transferred overseas.[129]

If you live in the US, for example, you can't get a bank to shift US dollars to your daughter's bank account in Brazil. Apart from hard cash, all US dollars stay in the US, and all Brazilian reals stay in Brazil.

This is even the case in countries where it's possible to open a foreign currency account. For example, Lloyds International bank in the UK offers accounts in euros and US dollars, as well as in British pounds. But if you have US dollars in your Lloyds International bank in London, your dollars are not actually held in the UK in the same way that British pounds are–they're not electronic dollars in Lloyds' reserve account at the UK central bank, the Bank of England. If you're lucky, they're in a bank in the US, in an account that Lloyds International London owns there, operated under the strict rules of the US banking system. If you're not so lucky they're close to fictitious, a mere IOU issued by the bank, in the form of so-called "Eurodollars"–a topic we'll look at in some detail below.

So how does the vast bulk of money travel across borders? In a nutshell, it travels via forms of "near-money". In Chapter 1 I explained that, in addition to the fungible, liquid money in bank accounts and cash, there's a vast quantity of what's often called near-money: bonds, mutual funds, IOUs, credit default swaps, futures, and many other non-fungible paper assets. Most of this can flick around the globe as easily as an email. I'll now explain how this makes foreign exchange work, and how it makes it possible for vast inequalities to develop between countries.

---

[129] Bank of England (2025)

The puzzle of how money flows between closed loop currency systems

Let's begin with one of the simplest kinds of currency exchange methods. David, who lives in London, owns a rental flat in Melbourne, Australia. It's got draughty old single-glazed windows, and he's decided to get them replaced with triple-glazed, energy efficient ones. It's going to cost $A 36,000, equivalent to about £18,500. So he sends this money from his British account at Barclays Bank to his Australian account at National Australia Bank (NAB). He does this by using the services of an international currency exchange firm named Wise[130]. Wise's website requires him to pay £18,500 to Wise from his Barclays account in London, and within three hours his NAB account balance in Australia has increased by $A 36,000.

In this case, *no money actually moved from one country to another.* What actually happened was that the balance in Wise's UK bank account, held in the UK, increased by £18,500, and an hour or so later Wise's Australian bank account, held in Sydney, reduced by $A 36,000 as it transferred this amount into David's NAB account. Wise was thereby no richer or poorer than before (apart from its transaction fee), but the balance of its wealth had shifted from one of its branches to another. The vast majority of international payments happen like this. No money goes across borders, but people happily "send" money from one country to another.

How large sums of "money" flow between countries

On the scale of global foreign exchange transactions, this is a relatively small, so-called "retail" international payment. Retail international transactions are made by individuals and small-to-medium sized exporters, importers and cross-border firms. They usually involve an intermediate-sized agency such as Wise[131], Western Union[132], TransferGo[133], Instarem[134], or XE Money Transfer[135]. These agencies can handle transfers valued at up to about $US 5 million each, though this varies between agencies and currencies. Many commercial banks also deal in retail transactions, but their fees are generally higher than these agencies'. They all operate like the

---

[130] www.wise.com/
[131] www.wise.com
[132] www.westernunion.com
[133] www.transfergo.com
[134] www.instarem.com
[135] www.xe.com

description of David's transaction above. They have accounts in many countries and simply receive money into their account in the sender's country and currency, and pay out the equivalent amount of money from their account in the recipient's country and currency, less their transaction fee.

Very big international transfers valued at hundreds of millions of US dollars are serviced by a different layer of financial agencies known as "wholesale" agencies. Some of the largest of these are Citi[136] (called Citycorp or Citygroup in some countries), Goldman Sachs[137], JPMorgan Chase[138], HSBC[139] and Barclays[140]. These agencies are used by governments, for example, when they buy other governments' bonds worth many millions of dollars or even hundreds of millions.

These agencies can operate in much the same way as retail agencies but on a far larger scale. They have accounts in dozens of countries. They receive money from the sender in one country and that country's currency, and pay its equivalent to the recipient in the other country in that country's currency, less transaction fees. Some of them, however, operate in a far more esoteric way than this, using Eurodollars. In fact, most of the money that shifts between countries is in Eurodollars, and we'll get to this topic in a moment.

How money flows across borders

Getting back to our example of David sending money from the UK to Australia, you might ask, "But is this sustainable? What if thousands of people in the UK send tens of millions of pounds to Australia over a period of a week or so? Won't Wise's Australia account run out of money?"

The answer is both "no" and "possibly yes". No, because Wise's customers in Australia, Canada, New Zealand, Belgium, Britain, Europe, the US and other countries are using it to send money between countries all the time, and these criss-crossing transactions tend to balance each other out. Wise reports that every day it sends a total of around half a billion US dollars' worth of euros, Australian dollars, Ugandan shillings, Brazilian real, etc. between countries. Wise doesn't make public how much money it keeps in

---

[136] www.citigroup.com/global/insights/cross-border-payments-24x7
[137] www.goldmansachs.com/what-we-do/transaction-banking
[138] https://privatebank.jpmorgan.com/nam/en/services/banking/online-tools/how-to-pages/wire-money
[139] www.hsbc.co.uk/international/money-transfer/
[140] https://international.barclays.com/banking/international-payments/

reserve, but it doesn't need a reserve of hundreds of millions in each country because the values of most of these transfers are cancelling each other out, throughout the day.

This is similar to the situation we looked at in Chapter 2, with commercial banks' reserve accounts at the central bank, in any particular country. The commercial banks need to keep only a fraction of the total amount of their daily transactions in their reserve accounts, because most of the transactions that criss-cross the country in any one day tend to balance each other out.

So the first answer is no. All these millions of dollars, euros, yen, renminbi, etc. can criss-cross the planet without any money actually moving between countries, and this can balance out to keep all their branches more or less flush with money.

But the second answer is "possibly yes", because all this criss-crossing of international payments doesn't *perfectly* balance out, and over the medium to long term the imbalances become acute. This is where we begin to see how foreign exchange makes some countries richer and others poorer. Wise's account in Australia might reach rock bottom on a particular day because so many people have been sending money to firms and friends in Australia that Wise simply runs out of Australian dollars to pay the recipients. At the same time, Wise's account in the UK might be over-full, because so many people there have been sending money to Australia and other countries. How does Wise then shift *actual* money from one country to another to balance its accounts up? If cash is the only kind of actual money that crosses borders, and cash makes up only a few percent of international exchanges, where does the bulk of the money come from to balance up the shortfalls, and what kind of "money" is it?

The name's Bond

The easiest way for Wise to solve this problem is to use government bonds– which are a form of near-money. You'll remember from earlier chapters that a government bond is an IOU that a government issues, in order to borrow money. So here's an example of how these exchange agencies can use government bonds to keep a good level of money in their accounts in all the countries they're servicing. Wise in the UK pays the UK government, say, £10 million from its over-full account, and the UK government gives it 10 bonds valued at £1 million each (actually, Wise purchases these bonds by a roundabout route using what's called the "secondary market", but that's irrelevant to how the process works out).

These bonds are electronic credits (in past decades they were pieces of paper, but we now live in the digital age) and they can be sold or given to anyone anywhere in the world, like all forms of near-money. So, Wise's branch in the UK gives the bonds to Wise's branch in Australia, since both these branches are part of the same firm. Wise in Australia then sells them to the Australian government (or another dealer) and receives approximately $A 20 million in return. This tops up its account and it can now continue paying Australian dollars to people who are getting money sent from the UK.

Now let's step back and see what's happened.

1. The UK government now owes the Australian government £10 million (give or take what it previously owed or was owed). Expressed differently, the Australian government now owns £10 million more of the UK government's assets.
2. The UK banking system now has £10 million less in it than it did before Wise in the UK bought the bonds. That's £10 million less narrow money. That's because the only way to pay a government is to give it narrow money that it originally spent into existence, and which is dissolved back into nothing when it gets back to the government.
3. The banking system in the UK therefore has £10 million less narrow money to use as collateral for creating its own broad money by way of issuing loans. Remember that banks can generally issue loans totalling about 10 times the amount of narrow money they have in their reserve accounts. Therefore the UK economy could be weaker by about 10 times £10 million, around £100 million.
4. Meanwhile in Australia the banking system now has an extra $A 20 million. This is government-backed narrow money, and it can serve as collateral for the banks to issue loans of around $A 200 million. So the wider Australian economy could be about $A 200 million richer.

Point 1 above is where foreign exchange transactions make a *very* big difference to the wealth of nations. Of course, this example is only a small part of a much larger picture. There are dozens of foreign exchange firms constantly facilitating payments back and forth between many countries. But overall, if more money "goes out of" a country in a particular year than "comes in", that country gets poorer in that year. The official jargon is that its "current account balance" is negative in that year. On the other hand, if more money "comes in" to a country in a particular year than "goes out", it gets richer in that year. Its current account balance in that year is positive.

Countries with negative current account balances year after year are getting poorer and poorer compared to the rest of the world. The World Bank and several other reliable international institutions keep records of the current accounts of 202 countries and regions[141]. Here we see that the US's current account balance has been negative every year since 1992, and in 2023, the most recent year for which the World bank gives accurate figures, it was just over $US 0.9 trillion. If we think of this as accumulating from year to year, over the past 33 years the US has become about $US 17 trillion poorer in relation to the rest of the world. Keep in mind the fact that the US's entire GDP in 2023 was just under $US 27.4 trillion. So about 3% of its annual production of wealth and wellbeing is getting syphoned off to the rest of the world each year.

Other countries with negative current account balances in 2023 include France, suffering the equivalent of a $US 22.8 billion negative current account balance in 2023, the UK ($US 110 billion), Romania ($US 24.5 billion), Uganda ($US 4.2 billion), Türkiye ($US 45 billion) and Nigeria ($US 0.8 billion).

Countries with positive current account balances in 2023 include Australia ($US 21.4 billion), Switzerland ($US 67.8 billion), Portugal ($US 3.9 billion), Sweden ($US 40 billion), Thailand ($US 7 billion), Vietnam ($US 25 billion), China ($US 252 billion) and Japan ($US 151 billion). China's current account balance has been positive since 1994, and prior to that it was close to zero, so China has been getting cumulatively richer in relation to the rest of the world for at least the past 30 years.

I say "in relation to the rest of the world", because both China and the US have been getting richer in other ways *internally*, such as by becoming more productive. So this doesn't necessarily mean the US is getting poorer overall. But a portion of its newly created wealth is syphoned off each year. The internally produced wealth of a country is eroded if its current account balance is always negative. Wealth really does flow out of some countries and into others.

I emphasise this point because the leading proponents of modern monetary theory I mentioned in earlier chapters say it doesn't matter. The argument of L. Randal Wray and Stephanie Kelton goes like this: If China sells more

[141] See, for example, World Bank (2025).

of its goods to the US than the US sells to China, that simply means the US is getting the benefit of all these goods (cars, clothes, etc.) without effectively having to pay anything. Why? Because, say Wray and Kelton, the dollars the US citizens pay to buy them never actually leave the US. US wholesale and retail chains don't pay out US dollars to people outside the US when they buy Chinese goods. They pay them to the US branches of foreign exchange firms like Wise or Citicorp, so the dollars stay in the US[142].

In one sense that's true, since each country's money system is a closed loop. But modern monetary theorists don't seem to reckon with the fact that at another, higher level, "money" *is* going out of the US, in the form of government bonds (and other forms of near-money), *which are not part of this closed loop*. This "money" goes out because that's the only way the foreign exchange firms can keep their services going, as I explained above. The foreign exchange firms can't continue indefinitely having their branch in the loser country bloated with its currency and their branch in the winner country emptied of its currency, so they exchange their real money for near money in one country, and re-exchange the near-money for real money in the other country.

The US is a big, well-resourced country and there may be reasons not to be worried about its massively increasing foreign exchange deficit. If the US produces at least twice as much value of goods and services every year as people need, on average, does it really matter that 3% of this is syphoned off to other countries? But this is a serious, life-and-death problem for developing countries. Take Uganda, for example. I mentioned above that Uganda had a current account deficit of $US 4.2 billion in 2023. That was 8.6% of its GDP. Uganda can't afford to lose that much of the value of its production each year, since its GDP hardly covers the needs of its people.

It could be argued that there's a self-correcting mechanism for high-income countries that are suffering years of current account deficits, provided they have their own sovereign currencies and are regarded as stable and dependable. Examples are New Zealand and the UK. Running a current account deficit puts downward pressure on their currency's value, so the value of the British pound and New Zealand dollar tends to fall in relation to other currencies. This makes the UK's and New Zealand's imports more expensive, so the amount they import will reduce. Meanwhile, it makes their exports cheaper for other countries to buy, so the demand for them will

---

[142] E.g., Wray (2015), pages 121-134; Kelton (2020) pages 127-156

increase. These two effects together will reduce the UK's and New Zealand's balance of payments deficits. The downside of this is that the UK pound and New Zealand dollar become weaker than they otherwise would be, so the wages of people in the UK and New Zealand don't have the buying power, internationally, that they would otherwise have.

However, in low- or middle-income countries like Uganda, Türkiye, Uzbekistan, Equatorial Guinea or Fiji a negative current account balance is a very serious problem. In the last six months of 2023, Uganda's balance of foreign reserves fell by 12%, from $US 4.07 billion to $US 3.58 billion "because of external debt payments and the central bank's inability to buy foreign currency due to a slide in the Ugandan shilling."[143] Running a negative current account deficit can be disastrous for low-income countries.

There are, however, some creative moves to mitigate the problem. As I mentioned above, foreign exchange firms tend to get bloated with the local currency in countries that are suffering long-term balance of payments deficits. In Uganda, Citi (called Citibank Uganda Limited) puts some of its Ugandan shillings to good use in Uganda by lending them to Ugandan banks and even to the government for infrastructure projects. For example, in 2024 it lent the government 497 billion shillings–equivalent to about $US 130 million–to build the 97-kilometer long Lusalira-Sembabule road[144].

However, this means the Ugandan government owes Citibank Uganda Limited a very large sum of money, plus interest.

An alternative is for the Ugandan government just to let Citibank Uganda Limited and other international agencies own an ever-greater share of Uganda's shillings and encourage them to invest heavily in local projects. But this also has a downside as it shifts power and agency away from the government and local businesses, towards these overseas-owned finance companies.

At the highest level of the international currency exchange hierarchy, countries get richer by owning more and more of other countries' assets, or they get poorer and poorer by seeing more and more of their assets owned by other countries–and by multinational financiers. For countries with strong internal economies, such as the UK, the US and New Zealand, this may not be a serious problem. But for developing countries it's disastrous.

---

[143] Monitor, Ugandan Edition (2024)
[144] Nilepost (2024)

Eurodollars and the dominance of the US dollar in international trade

I mentioned above that any kind of near-money can cross borders and therefore be used for international trade. You buy the near-money in your own country using your own currency, and send it to the recipient in their country, where they sell it for their currency. Most of the near-money that flicks around the world in international trade is in the form of Eurodollars. This will be surprising to many, because most of us have never heard of Eurodollars, and they're hardly ever mentioned in economics textbooks.

What are Eurodollars? To begin with, they have nothing to do with the euro. They're called Eurodollars because they're a shadow form of US dollars that are believed to have been first created in Europe in the 1950s–though there are differing stories about their origins[145]. A Eurodollar is, essentially, an IOU denominated in US dollars but created by a bank outside the US and lacking any control or supervision by the US Federal Reserve. A balance of 100,000 Eurodollars in a customer's account in, say, Deutsche Bank in Germany essentially means "IOU $US 100,000, signed, Deutsche Bank". Deutsche Bank is thereby promising to pay to the account holder $US 100,000 in actual, physical cash if he or she demands it.

As I explained in Chapter 1, anyone can create money, just by writing an IOU, but the trick is to get people to believe you can honour it if you're ever required to. It follows that anyone, anywhere in the world, can write and issue an IOU denominated in US dollars (or any other currency). Banks in Europe cottoned on to this in the latter half of the 20th century, and more and more of them in more and more countries started offering Eurodollar accounts. These accounts gave commercial traders the advantage of being able to buy and sell goods priced in US dollars, across borders, without having to have a US dollar account in the US or ever having to touch a real US dollar. Here's how it works.

Suppose you live in Singapore and you want to buy a shipment of watches from Switzerland, and the shipment is priced in US dollars, at $US 50,000. You deposit 65,000 Singapore dollars in your Eurodollar account in Singapore, which shows up as $US 50,700. You get the bank to transfer 50,000 of this to the exporter's bank in Switzerland. After it's arrived in her account as $US 50,000, she withdraws it, not as US dollars but as Swiss currency, namely 38,682 Swiss francs, less bank charges. She's now got her

---

[145] Shenk (1998)

$US 50,000 worth of Swiss francs, and you've paid your $US 50,000 worth of Singapore dollars. If she wants, she can leave the $US 50,000 in her account and use it to buy, say, a shipment of bananas from Panama, which also has Eurodollar banks.

As with other international money flows, the bank in Switzerland doesn't have to worry about running out of Swiss francs, because millions of transactions like this are criss-crossing the globe every day, and they tend to balance each other out.

If you, the importer in Singapore, don't have any money but still want to buy the watches, you can borrow 50,000 Eurodollars from the bank, though at quite a high interest rate. The bank credits your account with $US 50,000, thereby creating this money out of thin air. It then debits it from your account and transfers it to the Swiss exporter's bank. You can pay back the money to your bank in Singapore using the equivalent amount of Singapore dollars when the watches arrive and you've sold them, hopefully at a profit.

As noted above, most of the "money" that shoots around the world in trade payments is in this form: Eurodollars. The daily volume of Eurodollars borrowed for international transactions is believed to be around 150 billion, amounting to about 55 trillion per year[146], which is about half the total value of the entire world's production of goods and services. These Eurodollars are not what you and I would usually class as money. They're really just a promise to pay US dollars if asked.

This huge sum total of fictitious US dollars is the core of what's often spoken of as US dollar dominance in world trade. The US dollar is the world's so-called "reserve currency"–not due to the number of actual US dollars circulating throughout the world, but mostly due to this huge virtual reality of bank-created IOUs.

Where Eurodollars differ crucially from actual US dollars is that Eurodollars are not backed by the US Federal Reserve, and the Fed has no authority to discipline or regulate the actions of the banks that issue these "dollars". In some countries, these banks' Eurodollar activities are regulated by their host countries' banking law, but in other countries it's a free-for-all. It's up to the customer to decide whether their Eurodollar bank is trustworthy.

---

[146] Afonso et al. (2024)

I should mention that economists took a long time to come to terms with the advent, nature and growth of Eurodollars. The leading Chicago neo-orthodox economist Milton Friedman attempted to explain the "first principles" of the Eurodollar market in 1969[147]. The first few pages of his article give a clear account of how the system works, and I'd recommend it as a useful introduction to the world of Eurodollars. But even Friedman seems to have misunderstood how these Eurodollar banks create new "dollars" out of thin air when they issue loans. The Austrian economist Fritz Machlup, who was President of the International Economic Association from 1971 to 1974, was somewhat more circumspect, publishing a paper in 1970 entitled "Euro-dollar creation: A mystery story"[148]. If you wish to follow up-to-date discussion and debate on Eurodollars, you could start with the website of the so-called "Eurodollar University"[149], which uses the analogy of a cosmic black hole as the basis of Eurodollar value. It's a black hole because there's really nothing to back up the value of these Eurodollars except the banks' promise to pay.

The quest to make remittances fairer

I explained above that many developing countries are suffering from long-term ongoing current account deficits. One small light at the end of the tunnel is remittances, the millions of small sums of money sent home by expatriate or immigrant workers every day. For example, the Bank of Uganda estimates that its expatriate workers send about $ US 0.6 billion home every six months. This slows down its fall in reserves by about 25%, and it makes Uganda's current account deficit 22% smaller than it would otherwise be. Even though this doesn't fill the gap left by trade imbalances and the extraction of Uganda's resources by overseas enterprises, it's a substantial contribution. I'll finish this chapter by briefly outlining some encouraging moves to make remittances to low- and middle-income countries easier and cheaper to send.

Remittances are usually sent by and to individuals who don't have access to agencies that charge low fees, especially for the small amounts they typically send. Even worse, some of these money transfers have to go through three or four different currencies and as many as five banks to get

---

147 Friedman (1969)

148 Machlup (1970)

149 https://www.eurodollar.university/

to their destinations, and it can take up to 10 days to complete the transfer[150]. Hence the high fees. Further, many of the recipients in low-income countries don't and can't have their own bank accounts, so the money has to be sent to an intermediary bank and paid to them in cash, with further fees deducted.

The UN reports that in 2023 the global average fee for sending the equivalent of a typical sized remittance of $US 200 was 6.18 %. That adds up to a loss of over $US 41 billion per year, in money that developing countries desperately need. The average fee for sending $US 200 to South Pacific Island nations was 8.33 % and for sub-Saharan Africa 7.63 %. In contrast, if a British resident with a bank account in London sends £ 20,000 to a recipient with a bank account in a high-income country like Australia or New Zealand, via an agency such as Wise, the fee will be about 0.33%.

As part of its sustainable development goals, the UN is working to get the average fee for small remittances to low-income countries reduced, initially to an average of 3.0 %. Current fees are lower than in previous decades, but still far too high. The reasons are summed up in the 2024 UN sustainable development report:

> Regulators need to address challenges such as limited competition, high compliance costs, account access barriers, transparency issues, and low digital and financial literacy. [151]

Currently the US is the largest source of remittances sent to low- and middle-income countries, at around $US 90 billion per year. The second largest is Saudi Arabia, at about $US 35 billion, followed by Switzerland, other Arab Gulf states, Germany and other European countries. Remittances, according to the UN, "have become the premier source of external finance for developing countries in the post-COVID-19 period."[152]

What's being done, then, to make it easier and cheaper for people to send small amounts home?

The good news is that a cluster of influential international bodies are cooperating with the UN to get these fees reduced. This includes the G20 group of industrial nations, the Bank for International Settlements (BIS), the Financial Stability Board (FSB), and the World Bank. The BIS, based in

---

[150] From a speech by Sir Jon Cunliffe of the Bank for International Settlements on 13 July 2020, reported in BIS (2020)

[151] UN (2024), page 29.

[152] UN (2024), page 42.

Basel, Switzerland, is a quasi-official body made up of representatives from the world's leading central banks. Its main aim is "promoting global monetary and financial stability through international cooperation"[153]. The FSB, also based in Basel, aims at "promoting global financial stability through strong financial sector policies"[154]. The World Bank is dedicated to reducing global poverty, and channels funds from high-income to low-income countries for this purpose[155].

Listening to speakers from these organisations and reading their reports reveals they're encouraged by the prospects of getting immigrants' remittance fees sharply reduced. They point out that the total value of remittances is about three times that of the world's entire overseas development aid, as I mentioned above, and they're only too well aware that wealth continues to drift upward from poor to rich countries. As we noted above, remittances are easily the largest force working against this drift, though it's still a losing battle.

These organisations are working on two main avenues to get remittance fees reduced: digitalisation; and local bank accounts.

The benefits of digitalisation came to light during the covid-19 pandemic. In the first six months of 2020 the total value of remittances to sub-Saharan African countries plunged by 40%, to middle eastern and north African countries by 20%, and to eastern European countries by about 10%. Dilip Ratha, who monitors global money flows for the World Bank, points out that this was because prior to the pandemic, much of the banking system didn't support remittances to low-income countries. Immigrants had to take cash to international transfer shops, where the agents used their own banking and international connections to get the money sent–for substantial fees. But during the pandemic people couldn't go to local transfer shops as much, so agencies developed online customer services, which turned out to be cheaper to run and more competitive.

Ratha's charts show that by mid-2020 the trough had bottomed out and the volume of remittances was steeply increasing in all global regions[156]. His charts also show that for almost all regions the percentage commission on a $US 200 remittance reduced during this period, by 0.5%–0.8%, with the largest reduction in transfers to sub-Saharan Africa. The BIS, FSB and

---

[153] https://www.bis.org/
[154] https://www.fsb.org/
[155] https://www.worldbank.org/ext/en/home
[156] Ratha (2022)

World Bank are consequently working to increase and improve digitalisation of remittances at all levels, and to reduce the size of commission fees.

An interesting development here is the advent of a new class of semi-digital remittance agencies that specialize in sending small sums of money. I call these "mini" agencies to distinguish them from the retail and wholesale agencies described above. An example is Sendwave[157]. Before the covid-19 pandemic, our Ugandan friend in England had to take cash to a transfer shop, which would use a complicated process involving banks and middle-agencies, and the total fees would be up to 20%. Now with Sendwave she does her part of the transfer online. She could use a retail agency like Wise for her remittances, but if she sends a modest amount such as £100 she gets a better rate with Sendwave: her £100 turns into 443,440 shillings with Sendwave compared to 441,498 shillings with Wise. If she were to send anything over £175 she'd get a better rate with Wise, but it would be difficult for her family in Uganda to receive the money.

These transfers with Sendwave are only "semi" digital because the money doesn't come directly into her cousin's bank account in Uganda. Instead, her cousin gets a text message from Sendwave and takes that and her passport or national ID card to any one of hundreds of shops or roadside stalls that deal in remittances. The shop or stall records the details of her text message and passport or ID card, and pays her the money in cash. The total fees amount to about 4%. There are so many local shops and stalls doing remittances as an extra service that it's often easier than buying an ice cream.

The other issue is the lack of bank accounts for people in the receiving countries. Having a bank account that's recognised by a transfer agency would cut out one more layer of middle-operators. It's not easy to get data on this, but some of the most difficult countries for low-income people to open bank accounts are believed to be West African Economic and Monetary Union countries such as Niger, Côte d'Ivoire and Guinea-Bissau, plus Southern African Development Community countries such as the Democratic Republic of Congo and Madagascar. In some regions you can open a bank account but the international transfer agencies might not recognise it as a safe place to send money to.

---

[157] https://www.sendwave.com/en

An emerging solution for people without bank accounts would be to use a so-called "digital currency". I'll say more about digital currencies in Chapter 9, but just briefly, a digital currency is narrow, high-powered money (central bank money, not broad, lower-powered money) that lives in a so-called "wallet" in your mobile phone. It's like cash, but digital. It's not to be confused with cryptocurrencies, which I'll discuss in Chapter 10. Nor is it to be confused with a digital transfer such as you can do with Wise or in part with Sendwave. A digital currency would work like this:

Suppose you live in Niger and don't have a bank account. Your uncle in Germany wants to send you, say, 200 € worth of West African francs (about 130,000 francs). At his end he uses an online agency such as Wise, to transfer the funds to a bank, earmarked for you, in your nearest town in Niger. You take your mobile phone to the bank, and the bank transfers the money electronically into the digital wallet in your phone. You can spend it in stages by presenting your phone to any person, shop or roadside stall that also uses digital currency. This would bypass a layer of middle-operators and reduce your fees dramatically.

The EU plans to introduce digital euros in 2027, and the hope is that in African countries, where mobile phones are now widely used, digital currencies will soon follow and that this will enable direct receipt of foreign remittances.

I'll finish this chapter with encouraging words from the European Central Bank. It recently published a working paper entitled "Towards the holy grail of cross-border payments."[158] The working paper opens with the words: "The holy grail of cross-border payments is a solution which allows cross-border payments to be (1) immediate, (2) cheap, (3) of universal reach, and (4) settled in a secure settlement medium, such as central bank money."

The search for the holy grail, it says, "has been ongoing for many centuries." But due to recent developments in secure digital currency transfer and extended banking in low-income countries, the European Central Bank suggests that "after more than a thousand years of search, the holy grail of cross-border payments can be found within the next ten years."

[158] European Central Bank (2022)

9. VIRTUAL CASH: THE ARRIVAL OF CENTRAL BANK DIGITAL CURRENCIES

We've all used cash, ever since we were children. We know the feel and power of the notes and coins in our wallets, purses and pockets. But today only about 5% of our spending is done with cash. Most of us in high- and middle-income countries now get paid with digital money. It goes straight into our bank accounts and we spend it using plastic cards and mobile phone apps. Unlike cash, this money doesn't literally change hands. It shoots across the internet from bank to bank, and from account to account, and to and from the central bank. But central banks around the world are now busily designing a new form of currency that, they say, will combine the best of these two types of money. At the same time, they say, it'll head off a challenge from cryptocurrencies, such as Bitcoin, which, they fear, is threatening to destabilise the global monetary system.

This new form of money is called "central bank digital currency", abbreviated to CBDC. It can also be called "digital cash". In this chapter I'll explain what this type of money is, what its pros and cons are, and the issues that need to be faced as it comes into being. But first, I'll set this in context by recalling some basic facts about money and the banking system.

Introducing digital cash, or "Central Bank Digital Currency" (CBDC)

So far in this book I've emphasised that anyone can create money or its equivalent by writing what amounts to an IOU. The trick is to get people to accept it as fulfilling the functions of money. I've also emphasised that governments have the edge in creating money today because a well-functioning state can never go broke. You can trust that the $100 in your purse or wallet, which your government created by spending it into existence via its central bank, will always be honoured by the state as payment for $100 worth of taxes (or fees, fines, student loan repayments, etc.).

I've also pointed out that there are two main *types* or *power levels* of money in modern states. There's narrow money, which the state creates by spending it into existence, and there's broad money, which commercial banks create by issuing loans and by crediting their customers' bank accounts. Narrow money is often called "high-powered" money, because it's created by the state and backed by the state. Broad money is often called "lower-powered" money, because it's created by commercial banks and has only their backing.

In addition to this, we can identify two main *domains*, or *realms*, in which money circulates. One is the central bank. The central bank is the government's own bank, and the government holds its bank account there. Every commercial bank also has an account at the central bank, and so do certain types of other commercial financial institutions. These banks and institutions *are required to* have an account at the central bank. No exceptions.

All the money in the accounts at the central bank is narrow money. No broad money ever gets there. What's more, about 95% of narrow, high-powered money never gets out of this domain into the wider economy. The only money that gets out is cold hard cash. The rest just goes back and forth between the accounts of the commercial banks, and between these and the government's bank account, and sometimes to-and-fro between these accounts and the central bank directly. That's why some economists call it "outside money": it spends its days outside the everyday economy that you and I participate in. It's stuck in the central bank for its entire lifecycle, and it exists only as electronic bytes on computer systems.

One of the main functions of the narrow money that lives in the central bank is to act as collateral for the broader money that commercial banks create, but more on that in a moment.

The other realm or domain in which money lives is the wider economy of everyday shopping, earning, manufacturing, paying rent, borrowing, paying debts, saving, getting a mortgage loan, gambling, betting on horses, buying shares, selling vegetables, giving pocket money to the kids, and all the other things we do in our everyday usage of money. I say "everyday" because there are other domains of money, so-called "near money" that go way beyond this into the realm of exotic financial instruments that we met in Chapter 2, which tend to cause booms and crashes, but we'll leave these out of the discussion for now.

The money in the everyday realm is almost all broad money, the electronic money created by commercial banks. It's often called "inside money" because it circulates inside the everyday economy, unlike "outside money" that circulates only within the central bank.

But note that a small percentage of this "inside money" is high-powered money, in the form of cold hard cash: notes and coins. Cash straddles both the domains. It's very special because although it's high-powered money, it operates in the realm where most of the load is carried by lower-powered, broad money. But unlike lower-powered, broad money, it's as good as the money in the central bank. The government *has* to honour it, regardless of whether the commercial banking system is booming or crashing.

When you buy $4 worth of bread using cash, it's very simple. You give the baker four one-dollar coins, and she gives you the bread. Only high-powered money changes hands. Further, because it's physical, material stuff, you can be anonymous. The internet can't spy on you, you bypass the banking system, and you don't make any demands on computers or the internet.

But when you use your debit card to buy bread for $4 it's much more complex. For a start, you're paying with broad money, though narrow money will also be involved in the background. Your debit card tells the baker's card-reader to start a rather contorted 4-stage process, which we looked at in Chapter 2. First, your bank reduces the balance in your current account (broad money) by $4. Second, the baker's bank increases the balance in her current account (broad money) by $4, less any commission her bank charges. Third, the baker's bank requests your bank to transfer $4 of *high-powered*, narrow money from your bank's account at the central bank, to the baker's bank account at the central bank. Fourth, this transfer happens at the end of the day's business. Or more correctly, it gets added to all the other narrow money transfers that have to be made at the end of the day, when all the banks have to clear their day's debts to each other.

This is a roundabout, complex process. It uses a lot of computing power, and it tracks precisely who bought what, where and when. Despite this complexity, the vast majority of everyday purchases are made like this. Fewer and fewer are being made with cash.

When I was a trainee engineer working for Telecom in the late 1960s, payday was an almost festive ritual. At about 10am a trolly came round the office, stacked with little brown envelopes, each with an employee's name on it, and each bulging with cash (high-powered money). The pay clerk handed me my envelope, and I divided the cash into two portions: one for the next fortnight's expenses, and one for saving. During the lunch break I banked the savings, along with queues of colleagues doing the same. If I'd estimated well, I didn't have to visit the bank again until the next payday in two weeks' time.

I'm not claiming this was better than today's electronic systems that use broad money. The fact is, though, that *there's a huge move today among central banks to make it possible for people to do all their shopping with high-powered money, as they did in the 1960s*–but to do it without having to keep notes and coins in their purses, pockets and wallets. The money they'll use is called "digital cash" or "Central Bank Digital Currency": CBDC.

Although almost all central banks worldwide are planning for this, most people I talk to have never heard of it. To date, the central banks of about 134 countries are developing, or at least seriously investigating, the possibility of introducing a CBDC[159]. The EU is already making plans to introduce a CBDC, a "Digital Euro" in 2027[160]. China has started a pilot scheme[161] as have about 40 other countries. At least three other countries have a CBDC up and running: The Bahamas, Jamaica and Nigeria[162]. There are now hundreds of published studies on the pros and cons of CBDCs and the range of technologies that could be used to run them, plus thousands of pages of progress reports from central banks, and no shortage of YouTube videos by supporters, enthusiasts, objectors and sceptics[163].

How a digital cash, or CBDC, will work

What exactly is a CBDC? To begin with, a CBDC is *not* the same thing as a cryptocurrency. The two are as different from each other as a state government apparatus is from a high-tech guru's basement office. A CBDC is state-created high-powered money that exists in digital form but operates outside the central bank, in the wider economy, performing the same functions as cold hard cash. Legally it's the same as the notes and coins in

---

159 PYMNTS (2024)

160 European Central Bank (2025)

161 Orcutt (2023)

162 PYMNTS (2024)

163 One of the most comprehensive and reliable overviews is provided by Dionysopoulos et al. (2024).

your wallet, purse and pocket. It's high-powered money, as reliable and enduring as the state. But materially it's similar to the digital bits and bytes that shoot around the internet when you use your debit card.

The basic idea with a CBDC is that some or all of your digital cash will live in an electronic wallet in your mobile phone. There are many possible ways it could be paid out and topped up, but the simplest is as follows.

When you buy your $4 worth of bread, the baker keys "$4" into her electronic CBDC reader, you open your CBDC app and hold your phone by the reader, your app asks if you approve the payment, and you click the "yes" button. The money then jumps (so to speak) from your phone CBDC wallet to the baker's CBDC wallet which is connected to her CBDC reader. It's very simple. There's no need for any wider internet tracking. You've given the baker $4 of your digital cash. The baker's software doesn't even need to know who you are.

When your digital wallet is running low, you first go to your banking app and tell your bank to transfer funds, say $500, from your current account into your CBDC account. And here's the crunch: *your CBDC account is held at the central bank, not at your own commercial bank.* From your bank's point of view it's as if you just transferred $500 to another bank. Your bank is now $500 poorer, as it's surrendered that money from its account at the central bank, and put it in your CBDC account at the central bank, which is completely separate from your bank. Your bank's total sum of reserves has been reduced by $500, and you've just swapped $500 of lower-powered, bank-created money for $500 of high-powered, super-safe high-powered money.

You then perform a second operation on your phone, requesting the central bank to top up your phone's CBDC wallet with at least some of the $500 in your CBDC account.

That's basically how the system will work–though different countries propose a range of variations of it, such as whether all your digital cash will live in your phone or some in the central bank.

There are three very big unresolved issues: what benefits might it bring; what are the possible risks and dangers; and what kind of digital technology will be used to run it?

The benefits of a CBDC

From the state's point of view the main benefit of a CBDC is that it will preserve and protect the power of central banks in managing and influencing the economy. We saw in Chapter 2 how central banks are mandated to keep the economy stable and healthy. The main way they do this is by influencing the interest rate that commercial banks must pay if they need to borrow money to reconcile their accounts at the end of each working day. If there's too much broad money in the wider economy, the central bank increases the overnight interest rate on the narrow money it lends to commercial banks when they need this to reconcile their accounts with each other at the end of each working day. Commercial banks recoup this by increasing the interest rate on the loans they give (broad money), which leads to lower demand for loans, which reduces the amount of money in the economy. If there's not enough money in the wider economy, central banks do the opposite.

This works reasonably well if all or most of the money in the wider economy is bank-created broad money plus some state-created high-powered money in the form of cash. But today there's an increasing amount of rogue money circulating in the economy, in the form of cryptocurrencies. Central banks have no control whatsoever over this stream of money, and it's guaranteed to increase the rate of inflation. Why? Because it's a simple case of more and more money chasing the same amount of goods and services.

I'll talk more about cryptocurrencies in Chapter 10. For now it's sufficient to say that central banks hope their CBDCs will head off competition from cryptocurrencies by giving people an easy, fees-free alternative to debit cards and physical cash.

An advantage for users is that a CBDC can be designed so that people who don't have bank accounts can use it. According to the American Bankers Association, 4.2% of US households were classed as "unbanked"–they didn't have a bank account–in 2023[164]. This represents 5.6 million households, about 10 million adults. With a CBDC these people could receive their wages, pensions, or social welfare payments directly into their phone wallets.

In low-income countries the percentage of unbanked households is much higher. For example, a survey in Uganda 2021 revealed that 87% of adults there didn't have a bank account[165]. The minority who did have one included

---

[164] Federal Deposit Insurance Corporation (2024)
[165] Agba (2022)

twice as many males as females, and three times as many urban dwellers as rural dwellers.

We saw in Chapter 8 that CBDCs could make remittances from immigrant workers to their family and friends in their home countries easier and cheaper. Recipients who don't have a bank account will only need a mobile phone, and mobile coverage is huge in sub-Saharan Africa. For example, Uganda now has close to 100% mobile phone network coverage and 81% of Ugandans have mobile phones[166].

There are different ways these people could receive remittances using a CBDC, but if the simplest system is used, all they'll need is a CBDC wallet in their mobile phone. They can take their phone to any bank, which can link up with the central bank to top up their phone wallet with the remittance money. When they go shopping, if some of the shops and roadside stalls they visit don't yet have CBDC readers, they can take their phone to a bank and exchange some of their CBDC for notes and coins.

A further benefit of CBDCs is that they'll eliminate the contorted system of payments we use with debit cards, saving administrative work and reducing the internet's energy consumption–though this advantage could be lost if central banks opt to use blockchain technology, which I'll describe in Chapter 10.

The Bank for International Settlements (BIS) has provided a very useful pyramid showing the consumer needs that a CBDC must satisfy. Here's a list of these needs, beginning with the most basic.

1. A CBDC needs to work like cash, with direct peer-to-peer payments.
2. It must be convenient, and enable immediate payments to be made at any time of day or night.
3. It must be resilient and robust: no crashes or breakdowns.
4. It must ensure privacy when being used lawfully.
5. Everybody must be able to have a CBDC–no bans, shut-outs or limitations.
6. Ideally it must work for cross-border payments.

[166] East African Communications Organisation (EACO) (2023)

The risks and disadvantages of CBDCs

The biggest risk with a CBDC is that it could weaken the banking system, thereby damaging the "memorable alliance" that our modern monetary system is built on (see Chapter 3) and possibly even tanking the economy. This is a hotly debated topic, with strong views each way. Some economists and bankers, including the highly influential Bank for International Settlements, warn that if too much money shifts from savings accounts to CBDC accounts, this will drain the reserves that commercial banks need as collateral for the loans they offer.[167] As we saw in Chapter 3, the entire capitalist money-creation system depends on commercial banks being able to create loan monies out of nothing, backed up by high-powered money in their accounts at the central bank. If their stocks of high-powered money are reduced, they'll have less collateral to back up the loans they offer. More subtly, they'll have less spare high-powered money in reserve to reconcile their accounts with each other at the end of each business day and will have to borrow heavily from the central bank to cover the gap[168]. This will put upward pressure on the overnight interest rate. The banks will have to pass this interest rate increase on to their customers when they offer loans, with the result that fewer people will borrow from them and those who do will borrow smaller amounts. This will reduce the amount of broad money in the economy, leading to economic stagnation. In the worst case it could lead to economic chaos and collapse. An interesting overview of this discussion is in the University of Reading's recent critical review of CBDCs, under the heading "CBDCs and financial stability"[169], but there are many other reviews and papers that also explain or discuss this risk.

Some economists argue that commercial banks could mitigate this risk by offering customers higher interest on their deposits. This would influence people to keep their money with their bank, rather than move it into a CBDC account. But there's also a move among central banks to offer interest on CBDC accounts[170]. This would increase the take-up of CBDCs and help fulfil central banks' aim of drawing people away from cryptocurrencies. But it could also start an interest rate war between commercial banks and the

---

[167] See, for example, McKinsey (2022); the Bank for International Settlements' CBCD Handbook (BIS, 2023); and a number of recent economics studies on "disintermediation" referred to in Dionysopoulos et al. (2024).

[168] For a fuller discussion of this issue see McKinsey & Company (2022).

[169] Dionysopoulos et al. (2024), Section 5.2

[170] See the discussion in, for example, Kumhof and Noone (2021), and the summary of a wider range of studies on the topic in Dionysopoulos et al. (2024).

central bank, as they compete for people's funds. This could put even more upward pressure on the interest rates that commercial banks charge on loans, thereby further reducing the amount and number of loans offered, thereby shrinking the supply of broad money further and leading to more stagnation.

On the plus side, from the central banks' point of view it would give them an additional tool to influence the amount of broad money in the wider economy and thereby influence the inflation rate. If the central bank increases the interest rate it pays on CBDCs, this will encourage people to shift money from their commercial bank accounts, to their CBDC accounts. Their commercial banks will therefore have to transfer some of their high-powered, narrow money from their accounts at the central bank, to their customers' CBDC accounts. This reduces their overnight reserves, thereby discouraging them from offering large loans in the broad money sphere.

Overall, it's difficult to avoid the conclusion that CBDCs will put a dampener on commercial banks' operations. As soon as the first tranches of narrow, high-powered money get shifted from banks' reserve accounts to CBDC accounts, the capacity of banks to offer broad money loans will go down, putting a dampener on the wider economy.

Note, in contrast, that cryptocurrencies are less of a problem for commercial banks overall, than for the central bank. If you buy a Bitcoin for $100,000 (today's price, approximately), then at the end of the business day this shifts $100,000 of narrow money from your bank's reserve account at the central bank, into the reserve account of the seller's bank at the central bank. Your purchase doesn't take $100,000 out of the total stock of narrow money in the accounts of the commercial banks, so it doesn't affect the total amount of loan monies they can offer or the interest rates they charge.

A problem for central banks is that the total value of cryptocurrencies keeps increasing, as more cryptocurrencies come into being and the largest ones increase in value and volume. It's as if new goldmines keep getting discovered *and* the price of gold keeps going up *and* gold is used to buy everyday goods. This puts extra purchasing power into the economy and drives up inflation. If central banks try to dampen this inflation by increasing interest rates, this punishes the banks and the users of regular money. Central banks therefore have a strong interest in drawing people away from cryptocurrencies, and they hope they can design and manage their CBDCs in such a way as to prevent or minimise disruption of the bank loan system.

How will CBDCs work in practice?

There's a busy and wide-ranging discussion on the nuts and bolts of how best to design a CBDC. I'll only look at two of the most pressing issues here: how your digital wallet will connect with the system; and who can have how much in their CBDC account.

On the first issue, there's a continuum of possible ways to design how your digital wallet connects to and communicates with the wider money system. The simplest is that your CBDC money lives entirely in the digital wallet in your mobile phone. You take it to a bank or other designated institution to top it up, either by transferring money to it from your savings account or, if you don't have a bank account, the bank gets your pension or wages electronically and tops up your digital wallet with them. Then, when you go shopping or pay your piano teacher, you put your mobile phone alongside their payment reader or mobile phone, press the right buttons, and your money skips from your device into theirs. If you lose your phone, tough luck. There's no record of your purchases in the cloud or in anyone's hard drive or database, so no-one can track your buying and selling. You don't need a bank account, and no-one apart from you knows or cares how much money you have in your wallet at any particular time. The central bank knows only the top-ups you made at the bank, but what you buy, or what your piano teacher earned from you, are known only to you and your shopkeepers and piano teacher.

The European Central Bank (ECB) has decided to offer this model as at least one option for their digital euro. They recognise, however, that they'll have to modify it if they want to track money-laundering or tax evasion[171]. It's not yet clear whether they can do this while still allowing pure offline peer-to-peer payments.

For these and other reasons, most central banks seem to prefer a more centralized form of connectivity. This would involve, as a minimum, a direct real-time connection between your phone and the central bank. In an extreme version of such a model, your digital wallet wouldn't be a wallet at all, just a record of your CBDC balance, which would be held in your own personal account at the central bank. Every time you pay or receive money the transaction would go through the central bank's electronic bookkeeping

---

171 European Central Bank (2024b)

system, much like commercial banks' transactions with each other at the end of each working day.

This has the advantage that if your phone's lost or stolen you can alert the central bank to freeze your account, then start again with a new digital wallet in a new phone. From the central bank's point of view, it gives them huge amounts of data on what's happening in the economy, at a very fine-grained level. This brings a big disadvantage to you, in that some future government could change the data protection laws and spy on all your past and present buying, selling and earning. Some bloggers fear the government could also programme your account to prevent you buying from certain sellers, and effectively control your financial life. Type the words "dangers of CBDC" into YouTube and you'll see how extreme some of the imagined scenarios are.

A disadvantage to society of a centralised CBDC system is that it will use a lot of computer power and energy compared to hard cash payments, which use none (apart from the amount to run the printing presses). On the other hand, it will use much less energy, per transaction, than today's debit cards, as it involves one loop rather than two. And it will use a minuscule amount compared to cryptocurrencies, as we'll see in the next chapter. A disadvantage, however, is that the central bank will suddenly have an extra x-million accounts to manage.

A third option being considered is to use blockchain technology[172]. Blockchain uses a large number of computers or servers across a wide geographical area to process and store transactions–rather than having them processed and stored on one centralised server. Blockchain is the system used by cryptocurrencies (described in Chapter 10). Blockchain can make it extremely hard for hackers to interfere with transactions or electronically steal money. Its big disadvantage is that it uses enormous amounts of computer power and makes huge energy demands, which frustrates moves to decarbonise the electricity system.

The issue of online security also comes into focus with CBDCs. Zhijun Zhang (also known as William Zhang) is the Lead Information security architect at the World Bank Group, and has worked on the online security of monetary systems in a range of organisations. He notes that "a CBDC can be quite complex and require the central bank to collaborate with a large number of market participants, thus introducing a large attack surface."

---

[172] A useful overview is provided by Auer and Böhme (2020), and a more up-to date survey in Dionysopoulos et al. (2024), Section 5.2.

CBDCs, he says, "could introduce security threats that are new to the central bank and other participants". These risks, he says, "must be recognized during the CBDC design, with countermeasures established along the lines of people, process, and technology."[173]

This covers only the main features of possible technologies and architectures for a CBDC. There tend to be almost as many possible variations on these architectures as there are central bankers and their programmers. The important issues to be decided are what we want a CBDC system to do, what we want to prevent it from doing, and what technologies best fit with these preferences.

How much can you have in your CBDC account?

As we saw above, because narrow money is mostly used as collateral for commercial banks to make loans, the more that gets syphoned off into CBDC accounts, the harder it is for banks to offer large loans at low interest, and the more this dampens economic activity. One possible remedy is to limit the amount of CBDC money that you and I can have in our digital wallets, a so-called "holding limit", or a limit on the size of our transactions, or both.

A holding limit is being considered by the European Central Bank, which established a workgroup to estimate how large each individual's holding limit of CBDC should be, so as to "ensure it can be widely used as a means of payment while still preserving financial stability and the transmission of monetary policy."[174] This will involve "a comprehensive monetary and economic assessment." So far there's no consensus on what the holding limit should be. Submissions are being put forward advocating anything from a few hundred euros to no limit at all.

The other type of limit is on the size of each transaction. Jamaica's CBDC, which is already up and running and is called "JAM-DEX", doesn't have a holding limit but has transaction limits: a daily cash-in limit of J$ 50,000 (about $US 327), and a daily cash out limit of J$ 100,000 (about $US 654). Jamaica's central bank has a website that describes its CBDC and gives answers to a range of frequently asked questions, from "What is a CBDC?" to "Can CBDC be used to facilitate overseas transactions?" (No, unfortunately,

---

173 Zhang (2024)

174 European Central Bank (2024b)

JAM-DEX can't)[175]. It's worth reading up on the structure of Jamaica's CBDC because its pilot phase was completed in 2022 and it's now up and running. An interesting feature of JAM-DEX is that the central bank uses intermediaries, called "CBDC wallet providers", to save it the administrative load of handling millions of CBDC accounts. You get your CBDC wallet installed on your phone from one of these providers, and the provider acts as a proxy for the central bank through the entire process of top-ups, tax compliance, and account management.

Summing up: So what happens now?

Central bank digital currencies–CBDCs–are not just a possibility, they're soon to be part of everyday life in many countries, if not most. The charge is being led by central banks, mainly due to the increasing effect of cryptocurrencies on central banks' ability to keep economies stable. Cryptocurrencies tend to behave like gold did in 16th century Spain. The more that's mined and the higher its market price, the more it causes inflation. Central banks want to draw the public away from cryptocurrencies so as to keep the "memorable alliance" intact, where the state has a monopoly on creating high-powered money and private banks use this money as collateral to create the lower-powered money that oils the wheels of the economy.

Other advantages of CBDCs are that they bypass heavy internet use, reduce transaction costs, and offer safe and easy payment methods for people who don't have bank accounts. This will be a huge advantage in many developing countries.

A risk of CBDCs is that they could severely weaken or even crash the banking system by drawing large amounts of high-powered money away from commercial banks' reserve accounts, into the CBDC accounts of millions of private individuals.

A further risk is online security. The more we substitute physical cash with digital money, the more opportunities we provide for hackers.

We've yet to see whether CBDCs will be popular enough to put a significant damper on the banking system. Nor do we know whether CBDCs will, as central banks hope, draw people away from cryptocurrencies. It's possible that the main allure of cryptocurrencies has to do with gambling: people's

---

[175] Bank of Jamaica (2023)

hope that their Bitcoins are destined to surge in value as time goes by. In the next chapter I'll address this question and others, as we look more closely at cryptocurrencies and the shiny yellow metal they attempt to imitate.

10. ALTERNATIVES TO MONEY: CRYPTOCURRENCIES, GOLD, AND ELVIS' BLUE SUEDE SHOES

On 12 January 2009 a computer programmer named Hal Finney produced the world's first 10 bitcoins[176]. A year and four months later, on 20 May 2010, the first significant purchase was made with the cryptocurrency: 2 pizzas for 10,000 bitcoins[177]. At the time that was about $US 40 worth. Today it would be hard to find anybody making a purchase worth 10,000 bitcoins because their total value would now be around $US 1 billion[178].

As of 22nd January 2023, there were 19,813,462 bitcoins in circulation, with a total market value of $US 2,082,160,462,945 (just over $US 2.08 trillion). That's about 30% higher than the UK government's annual budget. Bitcoin is now just one of hundreds of cryptocurrencies. The total market value of the leading 90 of these, as on 22nd January 2025, was $US 3,523,518,669,027 (just over $US 3.52 trillion), more than twice the UK government's annual budget. It's difficult to estimate the total market value of the full list of cryptocurrencies around the globe, but $US 7 trillion would be a conservative guess from the vast list available. This is more than the US federal government's annual budget, of $US 6.7 trillion.

Let's compare that with the total value of gold in the world, not counting underground or undersea deposits that haven't yet been found or mined. The firm Visual Capitalist estimates there are 201,296 tonnes of gold in use or storage today[179]. At today's value of $US 88 per gram[180], the total value of all that gold comes to just over $US 17 trillion. It took human society thousands of years to accumulate that much gold. It's taken cryptocurrencies just 16 years to accumulate about 40% of that value. In Chapter 3 we saw the economic disruption that sudden influxes of gold can lead to. It's no wonder, as we saw in Chapter 9, that central bankers are worried about the

---

[176] Peterson (2014)
[177] Becker (2019)
[178] CoinMarketCap (2025)
[179] https://www.visualcapitalist.com/sp/chart-how-much-gold-is-in-the-world/
[180] https://www.gold.de/kurse/goldpreis/gramm/

sudden surge in buying power that this ballooning cryptocurrency value could lead to.

When Finney produced the first bitcoins, he was using open-source software he'd downloaded from a web server named SourceFog[181]. The software's origin stemmed from work by an anonymous programmer, or group of programmers, using the pseudonym "Satoshi Nakamoto". An article had been published in 2008 under Nakamoto's name setting out the architecture for a distributed computer system, a large number of geographically distributed computers operating in sync and copying their data to each other. In each of these computers the data would be bunched in blocks, and each new block would join the others in chronological order, making a long chain. Computer programmers call this "blockchain" [182]. Nakamoto brought this system into existence on the internet in January 2009, together with a blueprint for a cryptocurrency that would be called Bitcoin, with the challenge for anyone to use it to produce the first tranche of 50 bitcoins (note that it's customary to write "Bitcoin" when referring to the system or general topic of Bitcoin, but "bitcoin" when referring to one or more of the coins–though the distinction is often blurred, as you may notice in the narrative below).

I'll explain how this chain of blocks works in just a moment. First, another pressing question: Are cryptocurrencies money?

Are cryptocurrencies money?

So far in this book I've argued that money, especially as it exists today, is a form of IOU, a promise to pay. The money we use every day is the state's promise to write off the tax we owe. When the state creates $10,000 by paying a security guard (for example), the guard is happy to be paid in this way and values the money. Why? Because she can use it to pay her tax bill. If she's already paid her taxes, the money's still valuable because she can use it to pay her landlord. The landlord will be glad to accept it because he also has to pay taxes. If he's already paid his taxes, he can use the money to pay the hotel bills on his holiday, and the hoteliers can use it to pay their taxes, and so on. Economists and social historians such as Keynes, Ingham, Wray, Kelton, Graeber and many others argue that money has always

[181] https://sourceforge.net/directory/windows/?q=bitcoin
[182] Nakamoto (2008)

functioned much like this–as an IOU issued by the state–even during the ancient eras of gold and silver coinage.

In this chapter I'm going to suggest this picture needs to be extended, because cryptocurrencies and gold do act like money to some extent, even though they're not, essentially, IOUs. This relates to my suggestion in Chapter 5, that there's an aspect of the prevailing understanding of modern money that needs further exploration: what I called the "power and oomph" of money. I suggested the practice of creating IOUs, or promissory notes, is rooted in the real, almost tangible everyday phenomenon of obligations people have to each other. Obligations aren't a new thing that humans suddenly developed when they first used money, around 5,000 years ago. As far as we know, people have always kept tallies, at least informally, of their obligations to each other.

Modern money therefore draws on a deep, primitive, instinctive human practice and uses it to facilitate market exchange, state power and many other aspects of life. I'm going to suggest that cryptocurrencies and gold also draw on this practice, but that they additionally draw on another primitive, instinctive human practice, namely the gambling instinct.

But first let's look at the assumptions and rationale behind cryptocurrencies, then at how they work, then at the most recent research on why people invest in them and accept them as payment. I'll focus almost entirely on Bitcoin because it's the largest and best-known cryptocurrency, but note that there are variations and nuances between Bitcoin and some of the other cryptocurrencies.

What are the principles of Bitcoin?

The rationale for Bitcoin and other cryptocurrencies is rooted in a cluster of concerns, beliefs and human instincts, some of which are repeatedly made clear, though others are seldom stated upfront.

First, when Nakamoto designed Bitcoin, it was planned to mirror gold. As time goes by, more gold is discovered and mined, but the new amounts tend to get smaller, because all the easy finds have already been unearthed. Eventually the new finds will dwindle to a small trickle and, at least in theory, come to an end at some time in the future. The World Gold Council[183] estimates there's still about 58,000 tonnes of gold left in the

[183] https://www.gold.org/who-we-are/what-we-do?gad_source=1

ground (if only they'd tell us where!). This would imply that 78% of all the gold on planet earth has already been found and mined. Its supply will therefore always be limited, so its price will remain high–as long as people continue to value it as precious, necessary and irreplaceable.

Nakamoto wanted a form of digital money that mimics this ever levelling-off trajectory, except that Gold tends to be unearthed in fits and starts, whereas Nakamoto designed Bitcoin to have a much smoother trajectory. The number of bitcoins will gradually increase to a maximum of 21 million. The increases come via a process called "mining", which I'll explain in a moment. The number of coins allowed to be mined halves every few years, so the trajectory of growth slows down. It's expected that 99% of bitcoins will have been mined by 2032, then the trajectory will trail off and the very last coin is likely to be mined by about the year 2145. As of January 2025, just under 94.35% of bitcoins had been mined, so the increase is now very, very slow.

Bitcoins are therefore rare and limited in supply, like gold. In 1971 President Nixon realized that gold and US dollars were going in opposite directions: gold was getting more and more scarce per head of population, while dollars were getting more plentiful. The US couldn't keep giving away an ounce of the US's stock of gold for just $US 35, so Nixon took the dollar off the gold standard. Today an ounce of gold is selling for over $US 3,000, so we can see how far the trajectories of gold and dollars have diverged.

Nakamoto reasoned that Bitcoin's value would follow a similar trend as gold but over a much shorter period of time, namely 150 years compared to around 8,000. So far, this has happened overall, though there've been big fluctuations in Bitcoin's value. Since people know there's always going to be a limited supply of bitcoins and that this supply will stop increasing in the near future, Nakamoto reasoned this would keep its value high.

A second rationale for Bitcoin and other cryptocurrencies is the desire to operate a secure currency outside the state apparatus–again mimicking gold. This presented a complex digital problem. The payments we make with our debit cards are processed via an electronic system that encompasses commercial banks, the state's central bank, and software providers who have these institutions' trust. This system is subject to government oversight and, since the state makes and enforces the laws of the land, this puts it in a powerful position of control over the money system. Nakamoto wanted a money system that was free from state control.

Further, because the state has the means to enforce its laws, there are strong disincentives against hacking the state money system. Nakamoto wanted a system that was just as secure but without centralized state control and protection. That's where blockchain, a globally distributed system, and mining come in.

The nuts and bolts of Bitcoin's blockchain

Blockchain was originally developed by Stuart Haber and W. Scott Stornetta in 1991. Nakamoto developed a distributed, decentralized form of it in 2008, in the now famous paper "Bitcoin: A Peer-to-Peer Electronic Cash System"[184]. Here's how it works.

As Bitcoin transactions take place around the world, they're stored digitally, in ten-minute time intervals, in a temporary list. For each transaction the list records the number of bitcoins that changed hands, the coded ID of the seller, and the coded ID of the buyer. This process only lasts 10 minutes, then a new list is started.

The 10-minute list is now an almost complete "block". It now gets processed by hundreds of thousands of computer-savvy people called "miners". But note well: *The term "miners" is misleading*, and this is where it's easy to get confused about cryptocurrencies. It's better to think of these people as digital accountants or bookkeepers or record keepers. Their job is to compete against each other to crack a complex digital code that will seal off the 10-minute block and attach it to the chain of all the other 10-minute blocks of Bitcoin transactions that have taken place in the past. So let's see what happens.

The new 10-minute list is visible to all the Bitcoin miners throughout the world–hundreds of thousands of them, competing against each other to be the one that cracks the code. Each miner has a computer, or server or cluster of computers. The great chain of all the previously completed blocks is stored on their hard drives, in order, from the earliest to the second-most recent. To date that's about 740,000 blocks, all lined up in a chain, identically, on all the miners' hard drives.

The miners now compete against each other to discover a very long random number, called a "hash", that will be automatically placed at the end of the new block, to close it off. The closed off block then attaches itself to the end

[184] Nakamoto (2008)

of the chain as it's copied to the hard drives of the computers of all the miners around the world. This provides a secure record of all the Bitcoin transactions that have ever taken place.

Whoever gets the random number first wins that round, and is rewarded by being given some newly created bitcoins. They've successfully "mined" these–which is why they're called miners, even though they didn't actually do the job of creating new bitcoins.

That's how the number of bitcoins steadily increases. But the number of newly mined bitcoins for each block diminishes over the years, as we noted above, so the value of the successful miner's reward depends on the price of a bitcoin steadily increasing.

Of course, computer power is increasing exponentially from year to year. Moore's Law says it tends to double about every 18 months, so miners are continually upgrading their computers to make it easier to crack the code to find the hash. But the Bitcoin system compensates for this by making the hashes longer and longer as time goes on. It's all nicely balanced so that it will always take about 10 minutes to crack the code.

This makes Bitcoin a distributed, global system that exists right outside any particular state. It also prevents what's called "double spending". Even though there's no central record of how many bitcoins you possess at any particular time, the chain of blocks contains precise information on every bitcoin the person with your code number ever spent or received, and the code number of whoever you spent it on or received it from. Therefore you can't spend the same coin twice, unless you've earned it back before you re-spend it, and that will show up in the record.

Further, it's very hard for a hacker to invade the blockchain and steal bitcoins (by doing false transactions), because the blockchain is copied in identical form on hundreds of thousands of miners' computers and servers. A hacker would need to invade the majority of these simultaneously. Alternatively, as hackers are now realising, they can attempt to hack one of the international cryptocurrency exchanges that own large numbers of bitcoins that are used for financial trading.

Nakamoto's intention, however, was that the structure of Bitcoin and the architecture of its blockchain accounting system would enable it to be safe and secure even though it's outside the state money system. Assuming that it usually is safe, why do people trust cryptocurrencies and invest so much money in something that doesn't seem to have any intrinsic value? And what will happen when all the coins are finally mined?

Why do people trust and invest in cryptocurrencies?

The economist Z. John Zang recently reviewed a slew of studies on what motivates people to invest in cryptocurrencies, focusing particularly on Bitcoin[185]. He concluded that trust in Bitcoin is more a matter of faith than cold hard logic. "Bitcoin," he said,

> … has no intrinsic value that lies beyond the collective faith amongst investors in its long-term survival. That faith is held together by a shared goal by many to create a currency free from any government control and by the ingenious technical design of its creator.

He also observed that "Bitcoin is always in a fragile price equilibrium and may move in a jiffy from one equilibrium to another supported by investors' beliefs." Moreover, he warned, "it is not hard to see that Bitcoin prices will continue to swing widely and wildly, and that doubters and believers will always abound." Zang is certainly correct about the swings in value. Just while working on this chapter, from early January till late February 2025, Bitcoin suddenly lost 13% of its value, then regained about half of this.

Although Bitcoin mimics gold in terms of its rarity and its tendency to suffer huge swings in value, a major difference is that Bitcoin has no intrinsic uses. Gold can at least be used to fill tooth cavities, protect vulnerable electrical connections, and decorate palaces and human bodies. This is still enigmatic, however, because the world's current stock of 201,296 tonnes of gold is far, far more than is needed for these uses. Most of the value of gold isn't based on its intrinsic worth but on a similar faith to that which supports Bitcoin and the thousands of other cryptocurrencies now on the market. It's interesting to recall that when the Spanish conquistadors were looting gold from South America in the 16th century, South Americans expressed surprise that anyone could find the shiny yellow metal so enthralling. There was far more of it than they needed for their jewellery and palace decorations. Apparently, it had never occurred to them to use it as money.

In short, Bitcoin has nothing to back it up apart from people's belief that *other* people will always regard it as valuable. Regular money is completely different. It's backed up by the state's promise to accept it as payment for

---

[185] Zang (2023)

taxes. No matter what you or others believe about it, this process always works. But Bitcoin's value is only as good as people think its value is.

But Zang hints at another motivation for buying bitcoins: *the gambling instinct.* This is a motivation that pervades the entire world of financial markets. Many people think Bitcoin will make them rich. If the price keeps going up, at least in the long term despite temporary troughs, every dollar invested in Bitcoin today will translate into many, many dollars in future years.

Even though this belief is also based on the faith that other people will share this belief, it seems to be a basic human instinct, at least among a large number of people. The gambling instinct is largely what fuelled the huge bubble in the derivatives market in the early 2000s, which collapsed when investors suddenly started to believe that other investors believed it was overheated–as we saw in Chapter 2.

I've argued throughout this book that the substance of regular money is rooted in the human practice and instinct of obligation and entitlement. When the government spends $1000 into existence, it's putting itself under an obligation. It's declaring, "The State owes you $1000 worth of tax credits." Bitcoin shares this practice to some extent, just like an IOU. If you own a bitcoin, the community of bitcoin owners has an obligation to pay you a certain amount of regular money if you offer that coin for sale. The bitcoin serves as an entitlement, the Bitcoin community's IOU to you.

But I'm also suggesting that Bitcoin and other cryptocurrencies are rooted in a further human characteristic, the gambling instinct. If central banks want to head off the challenge of cryptocurrencies, as we discussed in Chapter 9, they'll need to address this instinct. Their own CBDCs will be solid, dependable and efficient. They'll fulfil all the functions of regular state money. But they'll be irrelevant to investment addicts. They won't appeal to the gambling instinct.

Until recently, the gambling instinct has been satisfied through an array of financial instruments: shares, credit default swaps, speculative real estate, mutual funds, and many shades of exotic investment options. Although these can have the potential to destabilize the wider economy, *they don't threaten the heart of the monetary system* because you can't do your daily shopping with them. Cryptocurrencies bring the same gambler satisfaction as these instruments, but they operate within the ordinary money system because you can buy and sell things with Bitcoin. Each bitcoin can be divided up into 100,000,000 portions, each called a "Satoshi", just as a payment of $1,000,000 can be divided up into 100,000,000 payments of 1 cent each.

In this respect bitcoins are like new tranches of gold that suddenly arrive on the stage and put upward pressure on the prices of everyday goods, from bread and butter to luxury cars. This is the danger that central banks are worried about. But they'll need to engage with the gambling instinct if they want to head off the challenge.

What could make Bitcoin crash?

I asked above what will happen post-2145 when all the bitcoins are finally mined. What will be the motivation of the hundreds of thousands of Bitcoin miners around the world, when there can be no newly mined bitcoins to reward them for cracking the hash code that completes the new block of transaction records that gets attached to the great blockchain of Bitcoin? Won't they just give up and stop? If they do, no-one will be completing the new blocks. The new blocks won't be getting attached to the chain of previous blocks, and the system will break down. I've looked in vain for an answer in the learned literature on Bitcoin, but can't find one. The nearest I've found is "The miners will probably get a fee."

It costs a lot to be a Bitcoin miner, continually upgrading your computer's central processing unit to take advantage of Moore's Law, writing and rewriting your code to crack the hash quicker than your competitors, teaming up in great clusters to share the load with other tech wizards (with whom you'll have to share the reward), spending hours staring into a screen. If miners are to continue in this pursuit, they'll need to be rewarded.

But if they get a fee, it'll have to be paid for in bitcoins. Presumably it'll be a commission for each new block completed. But it can't be made up of newly mined bitcoins, as there'll be no more to be mined. It'll have to come as a surcharge on each new Bitcoin transaction. This means that the ratio between ordinary users' and miners' total stock of bitcoins will start to fall, and keep on falling ad infinitum. You won't be able to use Bitcoin without the miners syphoning off more and more of your bitcoins. Eventually Bitcoin will be an elitist quasi-currency that extracts money from ordinary people to the ever-richer miners.

Perhaps I've painted too bleak a picture. But if Bitcoin users start to see this and believe it, or something like it, I strongly suspect that Bitcoin's days will be numbered. And if Bitcoin users start to think that other Bitcoin users are going to see this and believe it, Keynes's prophecy will once more come true: the market will tend to do what people think that other people think the market's going to do.

Bitcoin and energy consumption

But there's a more immediate problem with the sustainability of Bitcoin: its exponentially increasing energy consumption. The Judge Business School at Cambridge University has been tracking the estimated electricity consumption of the world's Bitcoin miners since 2019. The miners' consumption basically follows an exponential curve, increasing each year by an ever-greater amount[186]. Consumption in 2019 was estimated at 54.63 Terawatt-hours (TWh), rising to 121.13 TWh in 2023. This was higher than the Netherlands' entire electricity consumption in that year.

A little bit of mathematics shows that if this trend continues, in the year 2030 consumption will be 469 TWh, higher than that of France. In 2040 it will be 3,556 TWh, almost as high as that of the US. In 2050 it will be 25,977 TWh, which is about equal to the entire world's annual electricity consumption. By 2060 it will be more than seven times the entire world's electricity consumption, and in 2145, the year the last Bitcoin is expected to be mined, it will be 4.12 trillion TWh. This is equivalent to 164 million years of current global electricity consumption. Obviously, this is impossible in the real world. Such a system simply isn't sustainable.

And note that this unsustainability isn't just to do with avoiding climate change. Even if all the electricity consumed by Bitcoin miners were carbon-neutral, and even if it didn't divert carbon-free electricity from other sectors like transport, industry and home heating, planet earth simply couldn't supply that much energy per year, or anything near it.

This isn't just a pure modelling exercise based on theory. There's a good reason why the miners' electricity consumption is increasing. I mentioned above that computer processing power tends to double every 18 months, and that miners need the most up-to-date processors to compete against each other. This increasing processing power speeds up their code-cracking, but it

[186] Judge Business School (2025)

also demands more electricity[187]. The miners *have* to get on this bandwagon to be able to compete with each other. Bitcoin is designed that way.

Of course, this simple mathematical model doesn't take account of restraints that would naturally arise if Bitcoin electricity consumption were to threaten general electricity supply. But at a certain point, we can expect a kind of showdown between Bitcoin and global energy needs.

So, at some point in the next few decades, I suspect the process of Bitcoin mining, which includes the recording and blockchain archiving of all Bitcoin transactions, will almost certainly begin to break down. Who knows what form such a breakdown might take? For example, miners could start to withdraw because it's too hard to get the energy their processors need. As soon as this starts, some bitcoin owners will suspect a looming crisis and start to sell. Then, assuming Keynes was right, this will start a fall in confidence, leading to more selling, and possibly a collapse in Bitcoin values. Whatever way the collapse comes, Bitcoin is simply not sustainable.

Can cryptocurrencies be hacked?

Another looming crisis for Bitcoin, along with most other cryptocurrencies, is the increasing power of hackers. On 3 March 2025, North Korean government hackers stole $US 1.5 billion worth of cryptocurrency, equivalent to about 15,000 bitcoins, from a Dubai-based cryptocurrency exchange named Bybit. The hackers were then able to sell most of the bitcoins and other crypto-coins on to other cryptocurrency users before the hack was foiled. All bitcoin users are anonymous, so the coins can't be traced. Prior to this, the largest hack was in March 2022, when North Korean state-backed hackers stole $US 625 million from the Axie Infinity gaming platform. A total of about $US 3.4 billion worth of cryptocurrencies was stolen by these and other hackers in 2022, and it's now believed that North Korea is rapidly advancing in its cryptocurrency hacking skills. Cryptocurrency agencies are a major target for hackers, as this bypasses the need to invade globally distributed blockchains, and the hackers effectively get online access to super-large cryptocurrency wallets.

With hacking becoming more prevalent and successful, a likely cryptocurrency mining energy crisis looming, and a tendency to crash or surge in value depending on what people think that other people are thinking, future

[187] A couple of my own scientific publications on this general phenomenon in computing are Galvin (2015) and Galvin and Gubernat (2016).

confidence in Bitcoin and other cryptocurrencies could prove flaky. And if confidence falls, value falls, with no solid backup for the coins' value.

I'll now shift gear and say a few final things about the shiny yellow metal that Bitcoin was designed to mimic.

Gold and its glittering but muddled history

Throughout most of the history of Western, near Eastern, north African and Asian civilization, there's almost always been a popular view that gold is the basis of money, often with silver playing a supporting, companion role. Even today, many economics faculties teach their students that money was originally gold or some other valuable commodity, and that it came to be used as money as a way of making barter easier. If you had a spare cow but needed three more chickens, but people in your community generally regarded a cow as worth 27 chickens, then, rather try to find someone who was short of a cow but had 27 spare chickens and then re-trade 24 of the excess chickens, you could use a neutral commodity like gold. Sell the cow for nine pieces of gold, buy three chickens for one piece of gold, and keep the other eight pieces of gold for a rainy day. Gold would be acting as money.

Actually, there's no evidence that this is how money began. As John Maynard Keynes noted in the 1930s and other economists have confirmed since, money was already well established before there were written records, so we simply don't know how it started[188]. The earliest gold or silver coins we know of were minted in Lydia (now western Türkiye), around 700 BCE. They were made of an alloy of silver and gold called electrum, which occurs naturally. The coins quickly spread to Classical Greece, and philosophers including Plato (428-348 BCE) and Aristotle (384-322 BCE) discussed and debated how it was that these not-very-useful pieces of metal could hold such sway in the marketplace. In 2013 the Canadian social scientist Mark Peacock brought together the main strands of evidence of early coinage, in his book *Introducing Money*, and this still seems to be the best account of early coinage on offer[189].

If we follow the history of metal coinage in European, Middle Eastern, Asian and North African countries, two quite different phenomena seem to

---

[188] Keynes (1930); and see reviews of studies in Schmandt-Besserat (2019); Ingham (2020), pages 16ff.
[189] Peacock (2013)

have coexisted. On the one hand, a king, queen or other sovereign ruler would mint tranches of identical coins, usually stamped with their own image and a written declaration of their value, in denarii, shekels, drachmas, guanzi, pounds, talars, etc., depending on the sovereign and realm. The first tranches of these coins would usually have a fixed amount of gold or silver (or both), and the proportion of this would be lower for coins of lesser value. It would therefore look at first as if the sovereign ruler was simply making it easy for people to use precious metals in the marketplace, since they'd all assume there was just the right amount of precious metal in each coin to match the value stamped on it.

But as time went on, the coins got debased: newer coins had less and less precious metal in them, but the image of the sovereign ruler and their alleged value were still stamped on them. As we saw in Chapter 5, the Roman denarius was originally minted in 211 BCE to make it easier for landowners to pay their wealth taxes, and over the next 400 years the proportion of precious metal in it got lower and lower, but it was still worth one denarius.

The economist L. Randal Wray discusses this phenomenon in depth[190]. Based on the history of coinage, he finds that the decisive factor that made a coin valuable was the ruler's stamp on it, not the metal in it. One of his observations is that in Greece and other regions of ancient Europe, coins actually made up only a small portion of what passed as money. Most of it was in the form of "money tokens": written records including tally sticks and the equivalent of IOUs. This was also the case in Lydia, mentioned above as the oldest known kingdom where coins were used. Wray points out that this was also the case in most societies at least up until the late 19th century.

Wray also suggests that rulers put precious metals in their coins as "a conscious thumbing-of-the-nose against the elite who placed great ceremonial value on precious metal." The rulers did this, says Wray, to demystify gold and silver and make these metals serve a commonplace purpose, passing through everybody's hands and not just prettifying the elite. He concludes that "since coins are really nothing more than tokens of the city's authority, they could have been produced from any material."

Why, then, was gold so coveted in ancient Europe, the Near East, China, the Muslim countries, India, and of course, the world today? I can only conclude it has much the same appeal as Bitcoin. First, people see it as a

---

[190] Wray (2015), pages 158-172

store of value that will survive through all the trials and tribulations of nation states. If a country collapses, so do its written promises of payment on tally sticks, IOUs and the like. But gold will still shine. Its value is not set by the state but by people acting independently.

Second, it's in limited supply, as we noted above. Therefore, people assume, the demand for it will always exceed the supply, and those who hold it now will get richer as time goes on. Both gold and Bitcoin are enticing for the gambling instinct.

Also like Bitcoin, the value of gold is only as high as people think that other people think it is–which is why it repeatedly surges and plunges in value.

Unlike Bitcoin, however, gold isn't heading for a likely eventual breakdown. Gold miners can always be rewarded with state-backed money, as long as there's more gold to mine. With gold there isn't an energy consumption time-bomb: the act of recording sales and purchases of gold won't demand any more energy in 2145 than it did in 2024. It might cost significantly more to dig up the earth's remaining unmined gold, and it's likely to cause more and more pollution and greenhouse gas emissions, but it won't cost any more to write down or key in who sold what gold to whom.

Gold, then, is likely to outlast Bitcoin and other cryptocurrencies.

And what about Elvis' blue suede shoes?

Finally, I should mention another class of contenders for the gambling instinct and investors' hopes that certain elite items will increase in value at a far greater rate than everyday commodities. This includes art objects like Rembrandt's "Adoration of the Kings", which sold at Sutherby's on 6 December 2023 for £11,000,000, and pop memorabilia like Elvis Presley's original pair of blue suede shoes, which sold at auction at Henry Aldridge's on 28 June 2024 for £ 120,000.

Since Bob Dylan is currently in vogue, I should also mention that an original hand-written draft of his lyrics for "Mr Tambourine Man" recently sold at Julien's Auctions in Nashville for $US 508,000. But not to be outdone, Rory Gallagher's 1961 Fender Stratocaster guitar sold for £ 889,400, and Kurt Cobain's Martin D-18E acoustic guitar sold for over $ US 6 million in 2020.

These items have a similar appeal to gold: a store of value that doesn't depend on state support, and the possibility of getting rich (or even richer, since you have to be rich to start with, to bid at one of these auctions). But these items also suffer the same Keynesian paradox: they're only as valuable as people think other people think they are, and their value could collapse like exotic financial instruments did in 2008.

They do, however, have an extra appeal. You can enjoy admiring them and showing them to your guests, and perhaps even impress your friends with some cool blues licks on Rory Gallagher's guitar. Or you can simply enjoy owning them if they really appeal to you–though it's difficult to see how Elvis' blue suede shoes have any intrinsic value in and of themselves.

Summing up

And so to sum up. Bitcoin, gold and pop or art memorabilia have several things in common. None of them is money in the traditional sense, but people see them as a store of value that's independent of the vicissitudes and rise and fall of nation states. Their value depends on other people thinking that other people will continue to think they're valuable, but when a chink arises in this lattice, prices tend to tumble.

Art and pop memorabilia can have an intrinsic value, the joy and pleasure of staring at them and showing them off. To some extent that might make their monetary value a bit more stable than gold and a lot more stable than Bitcoin.

All three of these types of assets benefit from their limited supply. There can only be 21 million bitcoins, there's probably only about 260,000 tonnes of gold on planet earth, and there's only one "Adoration of the Kings" and probably only one pair of Elvis' blue suede shoes.

But of all these, Bitcoin is the most precarious. Bitcoin depends on a method of recording transactions that will no longer be supported after about 2145. It's becoming increasingly vulnerable to state-backed hackers. More worryingly, planet earth simply won't be able to supply its ever-higher electricity demands for more than the next one or two decades.

11. GOVERNMENT DEFICITS, DEBT AND MONEY CREATION: MISSING AN OPPORTUNITY?

During the first half of 2025 a crisis began to evolve regarding US government debt. The US Federal Reserve (the US's central bank, known as the "Fed") reported that at the end of April 2025 this debt totalled $US 36,214,310,000,000, or just over $US 36.2 trillion[191]. It had risen from $US 23.2 trillion in April 2020, an average increase of $US 2.6 trillion per year, or over 10% per year.

To put this in perspective, US government debt in April 2025 was equivalent to around 121% of US GDP. The US government owed more to its creditors than the country's entire annual production of goods and services.

The interest rate the government has to pay on its debt varies according to when each tranche of debt was issued. In April 2020 the US government could issue 10-year bonds (called "treasuries") for an interest rate of just over 1% per year. But for 10-year bonds issued in April 2025 it had to pay around 4.4% interest per year, with a further rise to just under 4.44% for bonds issued in June 2025.

Because of the way the bond market works, these increases in interest affect the value of debt that has been issued in earlier years. For example, if you can get 4.44% interest per year by lending the government money right now, you're unlikely to want to buy bonds from someone who bought them in 2020, as those bonds are only paying about 1% per year. The market value of these older bonds therefore falls. Someone who bought $10,000 worth of 10-year government debt in 2020 may find it's now worth much less than that on the open market.

It would be fairer to compare the interest rate on 5-year bonds issued in April 2025, with the interest rate on 10-year bonds issued in April 2020, since both have 5 more years to run. But this is almost as bad for the holder

191 StLouisFed (2025)

of older bonds, since the interest rate on 5-year bonds issued in April 2025 was just over 4%.

The interest rate on government debt is called the "yield". Generally, the less confidence investors have in a government's bonds, the higher the yield. These steadily increasing yields have led a number of prominent economists, investment fund managers and columnists to begin sounding the alarm about the ability of the US to service its debt.

A further issue is that in the year from mid-2025 to mid-2026, about 32% of existing US government bonds will mature and need to be replaced with new bonds. The US government will therefore need to borrow a further $US 38 trillion in addition to the regular borrowing it undertakes, to finance its ongoing budget deficit.

US government *debt* is increasing because of the US government's high annual budget *deficit*. The deficit, as explained in Chapter 4, is the excess of government spending over government income (mostly from taxes) in any particular year. This was around $US 1.75 trillion in 2024, or 6.28% of GDP[192]. The government's annual deficit averaged around 0% of GDP from 1950 to 1970, then about 2.5% of GDP from 1970 to 2000. Since then, it's more-or-less steadily increased, except for two sudden, steep increases, from which it quickly bounced back. One was in 2010 during the great financial crisis: the other was in 2020 during the covid pandemic.

These sudden, steep increases and recoveries are regarded as normal by Keynesian economists, who argue that government spending should be counter-cyclical: it should increase to make up for a downward plunge in the economy, and reduce when the economy is strong.

However, some economists and commentators are worried that there's no credible rationale for the current steady increase in government deficits. It seems, quite simply, that the government's regular, routine spending is out of sync with its (too small) tax revenue.

The US Government Accountability Office[193] is a nonpartisan federal agency that "provides fact-based, nonpartisan information to Congress". It commented, in February 2024:

---

192 St Louis Fed (2025a)

193 https://www.gao.gov/

"The federal government is on an unsustainable long-term fiscal path that poses serious economic, national security, and social challenges if not addressed. And the longer we wait to act, the more dire the consequences will be on the economy and the public."[194] This sentiment was continually repeated in the press during the first half of 2025.

Government deficits and debt in general

For almost all governments, deficit budgeting is the norm. In 2023 all Eurozone countries reported a budget deficit. The lowest was Portugal's, at 1.2% of its GDP. Italy's was the highest, at 7.2%. Germany's so-called constitutional "debt-brake" limited its federal government deficit to 0.35% of GDP, but exceptions bought it to 1.85% of GDP. The debt brake was removed in April 2025, and a back-of-the-envelope estimate suggests the deficit could now reach over 7% of GDP. Meanwhile the UK's budget deficit was 4.8% of GDP in 2023, New Zealand's 2.4%, China's 3.8% and Japan's 2.3%. Australia ran a budget surplus of 0.9% of GDP in 2023, but this was an exception, as its deficit averages around 2% of GDP each year.[195]

As I've suggested in earlier chapters, there needs to be a certain level of government deficit each year, on average, because that's the essence of how the money supply grows from year to year. The money supply has to steadily and persistently increase, to cater for an acceptable level of inflation and a realistic level of GDP growth. Therefore, the state has to continually inject more money into the economy than it takes out through taxes, fees, fines, etc. But this brings two main issues into focus.

Perhaps the most obvious of these issues is that under current practices, government deficits lead to government debt. As we saw above, US federal government debt had accumulated to 121% of US GDP by the end of 2024. China, the UK, Italy and Portugal had government debt in a similar range (between 90% and 140% of their respective GDPs), while Japan's reached as high as 234.9%. Government debt levels for Germany, Australia, New Zealand and Switzerland were lower but still considerable[196].

Modern monetary theorists such as Stephanie Kelton and L. Randal Wray argue that government debt isn't a problem because money is created by

---

[194] Cited in Winograd and Bingham (2024).
[195] Trading Economics (2025).
[196] IMF (2025)

governments, so they can always create more, to service and pay off their debts[197]. But this doesn't take account of the inflationary effect of injecting more and more money into the economy. It's fine to create new money to facilitate an acceptable level of inflation and a realistic amount of GDP growth. There might also be occasions when extra money creation is needed to finance an entrepreneurial project that will benefit society and effectively pay for itself over time, such as constructing a new railway line or establishing a technical university. But to create new money just to cover the excesses of a profligate government simply bloats the money supply: more and more money chasing the same volume of goods and services.

The second issue is more subtle than this: how to work out just how large a government deficit needs to be, to meet the needs for an acceptable level of inflation plus realistic GDP growth. I'm going to suggest it's helpful to identify three areas of legitimate government spending, then set the discussion of deficits and debts in that context.

Legitimate areas of government spending

First, there needs to be regular, routine government spending just to keep the state apparatus running and in good order: education, the police, the arts, the military, roads, railway lines, and so on. This, I suggest, needs to be covered by taxation and other regular government income. I'd argue that if a government can't run its country's normal, everyday state apparatus without a deficit, it's either spending too much or taxing too little.

Second, as I've already mentioned, a small amount of deficit spending is necessary, to keep the money supply growing sufficiently, to cater for an acceptable level of inflation and a realistic level of GDP growth. But I'm going to suggest that this portion of the budget shouldn't be financed by going deeper into debt. Instead, it should be covered by new money creation, in conjunction with the central bank. Actually, as we'll see, in most countries it's already financed this way, but by a back-door route that hides what's really happening. More on this below.

Third, again as I've mentioned above, a percentage of deficit spending may be needed for socially beneficial entrepreneurial projects. This would mostly apply to ventures such as a new education initiative, a new hospital, or research and development for renewable energy or defence technology. It would also apply to counter-cyclical spending, such as occurred during

[197] Kelton (2020)

covid or the great financial crisis. It seems sensible for projects like this to be funded by borrowing–issuing new government bonds–because these ventures are likely to bring a financial return, at least over time. Further, if some of these projects are likely to add to GDP growth, this would also increase the amount of new money needing to be created, as in the above paragraph.

This three-way split might sound rather tidy and idealistic. In practice it's likely to be very difficult and challenging. This is partly because the calculation of how much new money is needed to cater for inflation and growth is dizzyingly complex. But the biggest difficulty is a set of traditional assumptions about the relationship between governments and their central banks, and the practices that go with these. The rest of this chapter explores these issues and makes suggestions for improving the coordination and cooperation between governments and central banks. The aim is to see whether and how government deficits, debt levels and bond purchases could become much more socially useful and economically sustainable than at present.

Central banks, inflation and GDP growth

As I've pointed out, the money supply needs to increase, on average, year after year, to cater for inflation and GDP growth. How does this happen if governments always finance their deficits by borrowing money, thereby clawing it back from the same economy they're spending the excess into?

The answer is that *central banks increase the money supply by a back-door method.* It's part of what they call their "open market operations". They create money out of nothing, and use it to buy government bonds on the open market, often called the "secondary" market.

Let's go back a step. When a government runs a budget deficit, it finances this by issuing bonds. Most governments offer these bonds for sale by auction to a select group of major banks and financial institutions, who bid against each other to establish the interest rate, or yield, on this new tranche of government bonds. This is called a Dutch auction because the seller aims to have to pay the lowest interest rate, rather than get the highest price.

These banks and institutions that have bought the newly issued bonds then offer them for sale on the open market (the "secondary" market), to *all* willing buyers, who effectively bid against each other in what amounts to a regular marketplace–the winners are the buyers who offer the highest prices for the bonds.

The central bank participates as a buyer in this secondary market. It creates new money (out of thin air) and uses it to buy government bonds that have already been issued and sold. It thereby injects newly created money into the economy.

So, by a back-door method, the state (in the form of the central bank) injects the new money into the economy that the state (in the form of the government) failed to inject because it slavishly borrowed to finance the part of its deficit that was needed, to facilitate acceptable inflation and realistic GDP growth.

Two major issues arise from this: How does the central bank work out how much money to inject into the economy? And how could this practice be vastly improved by better coordination and cooperation between governments and their central banks?

Working out how much new money is needed

It would be a simple matter if a central bank could say, "Our inflation target is 2%, and the economy is capable of 1% GDP growth this year, so we'll increase the narrow money supply by 3%." But the life of central bankers is much more challenging. To begin with, inflation and GDP growth are related more closely to how much money is *spent*, than how much money there *is*. They're also related to the amount of *new broad* money that commercial banks create by issuing new loans, and this is affected by *interest rates*, as well as the amount of *narrow* money these banks have as collateral in reserve in their accounts at the central bank.

Let's look first at the spending rate. Spending doesn't necessarily correlate with the amount of broad money there is in the wider economy. This is mostly because people save some of their money and spend only a portion of it, and also because there are other forms of money available for spending alongside broad money (such as cryptocurrencies). The Bank of England and many other central banks therefore use a parameter called the "divisia" to estimate the likely relationship between spending and the broad money supply[198], together with other measures of money supply that are available

[198] Hancock (2005), McLeay et al. (2014)

to potential spenders[199]. In a nutshell, money that's held as physical cash or in current accounts can be spent immediately, whereas money in savings accounts must first be transferred to cash or current accounts, and this becomes more difficult depending on the saving account's degree of lock-in. Meanwhile, monetary assets such as shares or mutual funds must first be sold and converted to regular money, before they can be spent. The divisia gives an overall figure for the likelihood of spending at any moment in time, based on these parameters.

It's worth mentioning here that some economists and central banks use the term "M1" to mean all the money that's available for spending at any particular moment in time. This includes all physical cash, plus all the money in all the current accounts in commercial banks. You can spend this right now, without having to shift money from one account to another. The term "M2" is often used to mean all the M1 plus all the broad money in savings accounts–namely the sum total of fungible money in the economy. The terms "M3" and "M4" extend this to include various types of near money. But I've been warned by a prominent former central banker to be cautious with these "M" labels as they're used so differently by different countries' central banks and by different economists.

In brief, then, one of the tasks of the central bank is to estimate the divisia, the ratio between the amount of money immediately available for spending, and the total broad money supply.

The central bank then has to estimate how the size of the broad money supply will be affected by the size of the narrow money supply plus other reserves owned by commercial banks. Recall that the amount of broad money commercial banks create, by issuing loans, depends, in part, on the size of their reserves. If they follow the guidelines of the Bank for International Settlements (BIS), they'll tend to have about 10 times as much money out on loan as they have in reserve. A 1% increase in the narrow money supply might lead to a 1% increase in the broad money supply, but that amounts to about 10 times as much increase in broad money in dollar terms.

But this is further influenced by interest rates. This is where the skills and experience of central banks is paramount: they have decades of experience in influencing commercial banks' loan practices by setting overnight interest rates, as we saw in Chapter 2. The overnight interest rate is the

---

199 Center for Financial Stability (2025)

amount the central bank charges commercial banks to reconcile their reserve, narrow-money accounts with each other at the end of each working day. And the higher the overnight interest rate, the higher the interest commercial banks tend to charge for loans to their customers, therefore the less loan money is likely to be created, therefore there's less money for households and businesses to spend.

Note that this will also influence the divisia, because people are more likely to shift money to savings accounts if interest rates are higher.

In summary, this is a complex task, but it's probably the best approach available for matching the increase in state spending to the needs of the economy for its inflation target and GDP growth. Central banks have probably the best pool of skills and expertise to work out how much new money needs to be injected into the economy.

Where this practice falls short

However, there's a gaping flaw in this practice, which I've already mentioned in previous chapters: there's no political input on who gets the new money the central bank creates in its open market operations. The central bank simply buys government bonds from whoever's willing to sell them, thereby putting newly created money into their hands. This can be seen as a missed opportunity. The point of government budgeting is not just to put money into the economy in general, but also to *target* money to where it's likely to be most effective in achieving the country's social and economic goals. The need to increase the money supply is an opportunity to target worthy projects, such as a new research center, a national cycling route, an upgraded missile defence shield, new social housing, or an extension to a hospital–or increased funding to local government if some such projects have to be initiated on that level.

Likewise, the government might be thwarting its own aims when it *borrows* the money to cover this part of its deficit. Although only a select few financial institutions are allowed to bid for the new bonds, the bonds are then sold off to whoever wants to buy them. This could draw money away from socially useful projects, such as from a business that would otherwise be using the money to upgrade a production line or fund technology education for its workers.

What this amounts to is that opportunities are missed because governments fail to create new money directly. Instead, they issue new bonds to borrow money from whoever's willing to lend it, then leave their central banks to create the required amount of new money and to inject it into the economy by buying government bonds back from whoever's willing to sell them. In the next section I suggest a novel approach that could solve this problem.

Coordination and cooperation between governments and their central banks

If governments were to find a way of cooperating and coordinating more effectively with their central banks, the current practice outlined above could be altered. The central bank could estimate the amount of new money that needs to be created in a particular year to cover an acceptable level of inflation and a realistic level of GDP growth. This would take into account the divisia and the likely effects of interest rates and near money, as explained above. But instead of injecting the money into the economy by buying government bonds, *the central bank would simply report this figure to the government.* The government would then budget for a deficit of this amount and instruct the central bank to simply spend it into existence alongside the rest of government expenditure.

This would facilitate precise targeting of the recipients of the newly created money, in line with the normal precise targeting of government expenditure in general. It would also have a further positive effect, which we'll look at toward the end of this chapter, namely a reduction in government debt.

How realistic is it to expect such cooperation and coordination? There's a dominant, prevalent discourse among central bankers, economists and politicians, that central banks should be "independent" of government, much like the judiciary[200], and the degree of independence has tended to deepen over time. The economist Davide Romelli documents legal steps in 155 countries from 1923 to 2023 that indicate steadily increasing central bank independence[201]. In this framework, governments deal exclusively with fiscal policy (decisions about the budget, spending and tax revenue), while central banks deal exclusively with monetary policy (managing the money supply, interest rates and inflation).

Central bank independence is often framed as a necessary fact of life, and its main justification is that it avoids government pressure to increase the money supply unduly. Recent historical research by economist Carola

---

[200] Romelli (2022)
[201] Romelli (2024)

Binder reveals that, where central banks have been subject to pressure or interference from governments, this has usually resulted in higher than desirable inflation[202]. In 2025 we saw the stern resistance of US Federal Reserve Bank chairman, Jerome Powell, to President Trump's attempts to persuade him to reduce interest rates. If he'd given in, this would have put upward pressure on inflation[203]. We saw a similar contest during Trump's first term of office, though mostly only via his many public tweets[204].

Nevertheless, some scholars suggest the relationship between governments and their central banks should be more nuanced than hard-and-fast independence. Social scientist Carlo Tognato, for example, investigates the discourse and practices of central bank independence in terms of culture and "symbolic performance". He argues that the notion of absolute central bank independence is driven as much by a culture of privilege and exclusivism among the banking and investment community, as by the avoidance of economic danger that would arise if central banks and their governments acted more cooperatively[205].

The New Economics Foundation (NEF) recently published a major study that gives details of differing features of the relationship between governments and their central banks during the years 1945 to early 2025[206]. Despite Romelli's finding of ever-increasing, legally based central bank independence, the authors of the NEF study offer abundant evidence that elements of cooperation and coordination between governments and their central banks have never gone away. This cooperation was especially active and effective in the years 1945-1980, including during the oil price shocks of the 1970s, and it's frequently reemerged in more recent years. The NEF notes that a strong emphasis on central bank independence developed in the 1980s, and that this gave cooperation a bad press. Along with economists such as Gerald Epstein, the NEF suggests the post-1990s heavy emphasis on central bank independence is "highly idiosyncratic", "dramatically different from the historically dominant theory and practice of central banking" and broadly counterproductive[207].

What examples are there of cooperation and discoordination, and what effects have these had? In the 1930s-1970s it was common for central banks

[202] Binder, (2021)
[203] Zahn (2025)
[204] Bianchi et al. (2023)
[205] Tognato (2012)
[206] Prieg et al. (2025)
[207] Epstein (2006)

and their governments to achieve coordination between fiscal and monetary policy by buying and selling government debt[208]. In the UK, for example, during Clement Attlee's government (1945-1951) the Bank of England used this strategy to support a 2.5% interest rate target. This, together with the moderately high inflation it led to, helped the UK government pay off the large debt it had incurred during the Second World War.

The NEF report argues that this type of approach contributed to historically high economic growth among high-income countries in 1945-1980. Its downside was that inflation, averaging around 4.5%, tended to erode private sector savings, but this did not stop households accumulating wealth and rapidly increasing their share of home ownership.

But with the shift to central bank independence in the 1990s, most central banks were mandated to target inflation directly, mostly using interest rate management, so this form of cooperation ceased. Independence led to a mixture of serious dis-coordination and forms of ad-hoc coordination during and after the great financial crisis of the late 2000s and early 2010s. In the UK, for example, the government of Prime Minister Gordon Brown initially took the lead in mitigating the effects of the crisis. Effectively using taxpayers' money, Brown's government bailed out Northern Rock in September 2007, then nationalised it in February 2008. Then in October 2008 the government guaranteed depositors' funds in the collapsing Iceland bank Landsbanki, again using taxpayers' money. It wasn't until March 2009 that the Bank of England began its quantitative easing programme, creating new money and injecting it into the economy via bond purchases. These two quite different approaches, one from government, the other from the central bank, don't give the impression of a coordinated effort. The government would have had to go less deeply into debt if there had been coordinated cooperation from the beginning, with the central bank creating reserves for Northern Rock by buying assets, much like it does in quantitative easing.

Not only dis-coordination, but even oppositional strategies were seen in responses to the ongoing financial crisis in the early 2010s. At that time it became common for governments to implement austerity, *reducing* government funding for everyday economic life, while their central banks implemented quantitative easing, massively *increasing* commercial banks' reserves with newly created money. Austerity had severe social consequences, perhaps most severely in the case of Greece, while quantitative easing often

[208] Ryan-Collins and Van Lerven (2018)

saved financial institutions from their own follies[209]. More generally, the two approaches tended to work against each other on the macro-level. Central banks were busily increasing the money supply while governments were busily reducing it.

Nevertheless, there are still post-1990s examples of increased cooperation. Nick de Boer, a professor of constitutional law in the Netherlands, has identified recent moves by the European Central Bank (ECB) to act in greater cooperation with Eurozone governments and their fiscal policies[210]. This is mostly driven by the ECB rather than governments, and runs in two directions: monetary-to-economic coordination, where the central bank seeks to influence governments' economic policy making; and economic-to-monetary coordination, where the ECB bases its monetary policy measures on governments' economic policy decisions.

Other studies of the Eurozone have identified ongoing "soft" bilateral coordination between governments and central banks, within the framework set by the EU's Economic and Financial Committee and its Economic Policy Committee[211].

The NEB study notes episodes of more overt cooperation between central banks and their governments during the covid years, both within and beyond the Eurozone. For example, the Bank of England funded and incentivised small-to-medium enterprises, enabling the government to avoid extra debt to do this. It also created new money to buy corporate debt (rather than just government debt) and lightened some of the rules for commercial bank loan collateral, thereby increasing the broad money supply without the need for extra government spending[212]. A publication of the UK House of Commons Library indicates that this gave the UK government room to spend over £400 billion on public services, business, and individual support[213].

The NEF study sums up its assessment of the history of government and central bank interactions over the past decades with the words:

---

[209] See, for example, discussion on the European Central Bank's QE programme in Fontan (2018).

[210] de Boer et al. (2024)

[211] E.g., Gortos (2020)

[212] Bank of England (2020; 2020a).

[213] Brien and Keep (2023).

> … it is possible to design a governance framework that permits improved monetary-fiscal coordination, while protecting democratic mandates and central bank independence.

My own assessment is that, while we can understand economists' legitimate fear that direct government interference in central bank's monetary policy could severely damage an economy, there are areas where their close cooperation and coordination can be both sensible and economically advantageous. I'll now outline a possible framework for cooperation in managing the portion of government deficit that's needed to keep the money supply in step with sensible levels of inflation and GDP growth.

Outline of a possible framework

(a) Technical staff from the government and the central bank would estimate a desired level of inflation (currently around 2% in most countries, but this is not a law of nature) and a realistic level of GDP growth, given the potential capacity in the economy (natural resources, technology, research and development, human resources, plant and equipment, etc.). The government and the central bank would strive to reach agreement on this.

(b) Technical staff at the central bank would then estimate the additional amount of narrow money needed to increase the broad money supply to a level that can facilitate these levels of inflation and growth. This is not a simple matter. As noted above, it involves estimating the influence of interest rates on the amounts commercial banks issue as loans, given their levels of reserves, as well as estimating the divisia and its effects on spending. However, central banks are skilled at doing this, as it guides their approach in open market operations.

We should note that in some situations the "additional amount of narrow money needed" will be negative. This may be the case, for example, in the wake of long periods of quantitative easing, when banking sector reserves are awash with narrow money created by the central bank in its attempts to induce banks to lend more generously. After such a period, the task may be to reduce the narrow money supply, so as to put negative pressure on inflation but still allow for economic growth.

(c) Assuming an additional amount of narrow money is needed, this portion of the government's deficit would be funded by new money creation. Suppose, for example, the government deficit is expected to amount to 5%

of GDP, but the additional amount of narrow money needed is equal to only 2% of GDP. In that case, only the 2% is funded by new money creation.

(d) The remaining portion of the deficit, in this case equivalent to 3% of GDP, would be funded by government borrowing. However, there would need to be strong and credible justification for this portion of the deficit. As suggested above, it would not be merely to generate a feel-good factor or make up for gaps in regular spending (which can be funded by a realistic tax take) but would need to be highly likely to stimulate genuine societal benefits and pay for itself over time.

A process such as this would be more complex in Eurozone countries, since the players include not only member governments and their central banks, but also the ECB, which sets deficit and debt rules, plus the European Parliament together with its relevant committees. But as we saw in Chapter 7, the debt rules were relaxed in April 2024 and again in early 2025 when the EU approved a set of "New Fiscal Rules"[214] designed "to foster investment" and "strengthen the social dimension" of the Eurozone[215].

Further changes in Eurozone debt and deficit rules that came into effect in March 2025 (in response to President Trump's trade tariffs and prevarication on European defence) have begun to open a door that could help to enable an approach such as that outlined here. The new rules allow member countries to further relax both deficit and debt limits in the event of major shocks. This includes a Eurozone-wide "general escape clause" for responding to recession or a systemic crisis, as well as a "national escape clause" for individual countries to respond to temporary exogenous shocks[216].

The main aim of this cooperative approach would be to enable governments to do their democratically appointed job of targeting new money to where they see specific needs, rather than leaving the central bank to inject the required amount of new money blindly into the general economy. But there's a further advantage: it will substantially reduce government debt.

---

[214] European Parliament (2024)
[215] European Parliament (2024a)
[216] ECB (2025).

Government debt and central bank bond buying

Let's begin with US government debt. Because the US central Bank, the Fed, buys government bonds as outlined above, around 15% of US government debt is currently owned by the Fed. This means, effectively, that the state owes itself this money–about $US 5.7 trillion–so it's not really part of US debt. If you owe yourself $US 5.7 trillion it shouldn't be a problem for you or anyone else.

A further 6% of US government debt is owned by federal government departments[217]. The social security department, for example, uses government bonds as a safe haven for the large contributions it receives and holds in the years prior to workers' retirement. This is simply a case of one arm of the government being in debt to another arm.

A more realistic figure for US government debt would therefore be around 97% of GDP rather than 121%. This is still high and may be problematic in the long term, but it's significantly lower than the figure we see repeatedly in the press.

Japan is a more extreme case, where the central bank often buys up to 70% of government debt in any particular year. On 30 April 2025 Japan's central bank owned 570 trillion yen out of the total government debt of 1,318 trillion yen, or 43.2%[218]. The Japanese state's total debt was therefore not 234.9% of GDP as frequently cited in the press, but 133.4%, a substantially lower figure.

For the UK, the Bank of England currently owns about £621 billion worth of the total £2,600 billion of government debt, or 23.9%[219]. This brings the UK's total state debt to 79% of GDP, considerably lower than the popularly heard figure of 103.9%.

For Eurozone countries the picture is more complex, because these countries' central banks tend to buy government bonds issued by each other's governments as well as their own, and the European Central Bank (ECB) began buying member countries' government debt in March 2015 in the wake of the global financial crisis[220]. A useful rule of thumb is that about 27% of Eurozone governments' debt is held by Eurozone central banks and

---

[217] US Treasury (2025).
[218] Bank of Japan (2025).
[219] House of Commons Library (2024)
[220] ECB (2016)

the ECB, so the actual indebtedness of Eurozone member countries is probably around 73% of the popularly stated figures.

The approach outlined above therefore wouldn't reduce the amount of debt the *state* owes non-state investors, but it would substantially reduce the *government* debt figures in the popular press and in financial circles. This is likely to have a significant impact on market confidence because, as Keynes observed, the market tends to respond to what investors think other investors are thinking regarding confidence and dependability.

Still a place for government bonds

But this doesn't mean there's no place for government bonds. I mentioned three broad categories of government spending above: regular, routine spending to keep the state up and running; extra spending to facilitate inflation and GDP growth; and socially entrepreneurial spending. When the latter is likely to bring a financial return over time, it could be financed by government debt.

In this sphere, government debt provides a valuable service. Government bonds are about the most reliable investment a business or household can ever make. Although they're lacklustre because they don't surge and dip like gold and cryptocurrencies, they're as reliable as the state itself. Investors aren't going to make a fortune with government bonds as they might with real estate or shares, but government bonds are very unlikely to crash and leave investors bankrupt. That's why insurance companies, pension funds and commercial banks invest a large portion of their funds in government bonds. For example, many people started paying into an employer pension fund at about age 20, and they can trust that when they retire they'll have a pension, because a considerable portion of their contributions has been invested in government bonds

Concluding remarks

In recent years, a number of high-income countries have incurred very high levels of government debt, which is increasingly seen as unsustainable. Government debt is the result of government deficits, but a portion of government deficit must inevitably be financed by newly created money. This is because the state must steadily increase the money supply to cater for an acceptable level of inflation and realistic GDP growth. But governments habitually fail to take responsibility for this new money creation. Instead, they finance their deficit by issuing new bonds, and leave it to the central bank to inject the requisite amount of new money into the economy by buying back government bonds in their "open market operations". This has two problematic effects.

First, it fails to target the new money to the sections of the economy where it can be most socially and economically beneficial, while also drawing money away from sectors and institutions that could have put it to better use.

Second, it over-bloats government debt. In fact, this portion of government debt is fictitious, because it's owned by the countries' own central banks– or in the case of Eurozone countries, a large portion is shared amongst their central banks and the European Central Bank. But it's popularly seen as part of government debt and thereby contributes to economic uncertainty.

This chapter has suggested a form of increased cooperation between governments and their central banks which could eliminate these problems. The central bank would use its professional skills to estimate the amount of new money needed, and the state would simply spend this into existence as part of the deficit in the government's budget, targeting it to where it's most needed. Any extra government deficit would require debt financing, by issuing bonds, but this should only be for projects that can be expected to pay for themselves over time.

Some commentators may object to the approach suggested in this chapter on the grounds that it would compromise central bank independence. But history shows that the desire for pure central bank independence is based on a narrow ideological viewpoint, and there are plenty of examples of constructive cooperation between governments and their central banks over the past 100 years, including in recent years. The approach suggested in this chapter would require sensible cooperation, while still respecting the boundaries between each party's responsibilities.

12. CONCLUDING COMMENTS AND ONGOING CHALLENGES

I began the research for this book after working in an economics faculty in Germany for almost a decade and realising that my colleagues and I weren't equipped to have a clear, logical, fact-based discussion on the topic "What is money?" I'd trained originally in engineering and later in social psychology and policy studies, and the faculty had hired me to help bring those disciplines into economics-based research on energy and climate change mitigation. This worked well for questions of so-called "micro-economics", such as how much it will cost to insulate an apartment building, how much return the owners will get on the resulting energy savings, and what might motivate them to insulate the building even at a financial loss. But it bothered me that the teaching in faculties such as this appeared to assume there was a limited supply of money "out there" and that governments always had to cut back in one area to be able to spend in another. To me this didn't square with the obvious fact that the world's economies are getting bigger every year: there's more and more money in the world, and new industries and technologies are arising without stealing funding from everyday life and luxury. There was something about money that didn't fit the idea of a limited and scarce resource "out there".

Then in 2020, during the US election campaign that led to Joe Biden's presidency, a social science colleague in the US, Prof Noel Healy, asked me to join with him in writing a paper on the proposed "Green New Deal". The Green New Deal was a modern, climate-friendly version of US President Franklin Delanor Roosevelt's 1930s "New Deal". The New Deal had been a Keynesian-inspired money-creation scheme to pump money into the US economy to lift it out of its deep depression doldrums and get people back to work. It led to substantial developments in infrastructure, national parks and public amenities, as well as providing millions of jobs. It carried over into the US Second World War effort, providing enormous amounts of new money that powered a huge expansion of the US defence industry and the massive payrolling of military personnel. How did they do it? Part of the answer is they created lots and lots of new money, out of nothing.

That's not the whole story, because they also had to dampen the inflationary effects of this extra money, and in the unique situation of wartime it was politically acceptable to put price controls on everyday goods. They also pulled a lot of the money back by issuing bonds and increasing taxation. But the money didn't come from goldmines or appear by magic. It was created out of nothing.

Most of the existing research on a Green New Deal was grounded on "modern monetary theory" (MMT), which I've mentioned in various parts of this book. Modern monetary theorists' basic tenet is that money is created by the state by spending it into existence and is dissolved back into nothing by the state when it collects taxes, fees and fines. These theorists are quick to point out that this is not a new approach which they're advocating or arguing for, but merely a *description* of what actually happens in practice. They're not saying the state *should* create money out of nothing, but that the state simply *does* create money out of nothing–and dissolves it back into nothing when it collects taxes, fees, fines, etc.

We drew on this insight when we wrote our paper, *The Green New Deal in the United States: What it is and how to pay for it*.[221] It was published toward the end of the presidential candidate selection process and quickly became one of the journal's most downloaded papers of that year.

I continued to explore MMT and found many profound insights in it, but I had serious misgivings about some of its more prescriptive ideas, as you'll have noticed throughout this book.

At the same time, I pursued recent writings from other theorists on the theme "What is money?". The work of Geoffrey Ingham has been especially enlightening. Similar to me, Ingham is trained in the social sciences but worked in a university economics department. This gave him a novel perspective on what's credible and questionable about the understanding of money that's regularly taught in universities. In particular, I've been inspired by how Ingham developed his insight that money is, essentially, an IOU, that anyone can create money, and that the trick is to get others to accept it as money.

This led me to a wider, critical study of how governments and central banks work in tandem in modern economies, and what hinders them from making full use of the power of money in a world where there are easily enough material resources for everybody to have a decent life (and for us to save

---

[221] Galvin and Healy (2020)

the planet[222]). One thing led to another and I found myself exploring issues such as the day-to-day working of central banks, the monetary basis of capitalism, how outmoded and inappropriate our tax system is, how foreign exchange works, what's good and bad about the euro, the mechanisms and weaknesses of cryptocurrencies, and the soon-to-arrive world of central bank digital currencies.

I also gave extra thought to the social basis of money as debt, obligation or an IOU, leading to the chapter on the power and oomph of money. I hope this will provoke discussion and add to our understanding of what money essentially is–and I'm looking forward to feedback on it.

Another point I hope to provoke discussion on and get engaging, thoughtful, critical feedback on is my claim that a government doesn't have to go into debt to finance the portion of its budget that will increase the money supply just enough to cater for economic growth and an acceptable level of inflation–as explained in Chapter 11. It seems to me this is a clue that could enable a major shift in the way money is made to work for all of us. It calls for more active cooperation and coordination between governments and their central banks, but without governments bullying central banks into loosening the money supply for short-term political gain. It would aim to utilize the best of central bankers' skills alongside the need for governments to ensure that every dollar, yen, euro or renminbi of the budget hits its most useful target.

On both these points I very much hope economists will look at this objectively and critique what I'm actually saying, not some contorted version of what bloggers claim I'm saying. We'll see.

More generally, I want this book to help people from all walks of life get a clearer understanding of money, and I want it to start a discussion on countering the misunderstandings of money that dominate among many politicians, bloggers, and even economists. I'll sum up the main issues now.

The end of the gold standard

As I've noted several times in this book, on 15th August 1971 President Richard Nixon took the US dollar off the gold standard. Since then, the validity of the US dollar as a means of payment for everyday goods and services has depended entirely on the US government's promise to honour

[222] One of my early attempts at exploring this is Galvin (2020).

it as a tax token. Since most of the world's major currencies were tied to the US dollar in the decades from the late 1940s to 1971, these also lost their relationship to the value of gold.

One of the basic tenets of this book is that we need to get to grips with the idea of currencies whose values float free of any fixed standard. This is the first step in understanding modern money. There's no specific precious metal, substance, object or measuring stick anywhere in the world that sets the value of our currency firm and steady. Accepting this basic idea is the start of a journey of understanding what money is and how it works.

In fact, we can take this even further. For most of its long history, money hasn't usually been tied to the value of precious metals. Emperors, kings and queens often launched a new coin that originally contained its equivalent value of gold or silver, but this was soon debased. It was the emperor's stamp that gave the coin its value, not the metals in it. Precise gold standards tend to be the exception rather than the rule.

The stop-start gold standards in the US, Britain and other countries in various periods of the 19th and 20th centuries helped satisfy some of the need for widespread belief in the stability of a country's currency. But gold standards never worked successfully for long, for two reasons. One is that the value of gold fluctuates out of step with the needs of an economy, as Britain found during the First World War and President Nixon found in the early 1970s. The other is that the value of gold is itself based on myth and the suspension of belief. As Wray points out, gold is "bright and shiny, … doesn't rust, is easy to clean up, can be smashed into impossibly thin sheets, and looks good in ears and teeth and on fingers." But there's far, far more of it in the world than is needed for these practical tasks, so its price is kept artificially high by a "propensity of governments to lock most of it up behind bars (in places like Fort Knox)."[223]

However, this doesn't mean our currency's value is completely arbitrary. I've argued in this book that the credibility, reliability and value of a currency rest on the credibility and reliability of the person or institution who issues it as an IOU. Anyone can issue an IOU. An IOU is as good as the trustworthiness of the issuer, together with whatever enforcement agencies you can call on to make the issuer honour their promises. Chapter 5 is important in this regard, on the power and oomph of money. People have always created obligations and entitlements, one to another. Money is

223 Wray (2015) page 48

a formalisation of this. If you issue someone with an IOU, you're putting yourself under an obligation to them, and at the same time they get an entitlement in relation to you.

For a country, money is the state's IOU. A five-dollar note means "IOU five dollars' worth of tax write-offs, signed, The State."

So, we need to move forward from the comforting but false notion that somewhere there's an objective standard that gives our currency a reliable value. Money is essentially a social obligation and it's only as good as the reliability of the body that issues it as their IOU.

Governments don't have to get money from somewhere outside themselves

The second basic tenet I've argued for in this book is that the state doesn't have to get money from somewhere outside itself. The state creates money by spending it into existence, and the state dissolves it back into nothing by clawing it back in taxes, fees, fines, student loan repayments, bond sales, etc.

Some bloggers will howl with derision at this statement. They'll argue that a government can only spend money it already has in its account at the central bank. They'll say it gets this money from your taxes, fees, fines, borrowings, bond sales, etc., and that all this is recorded in the government's account book.

In the sense of traditional bookkeeping this may look credible. Governments keep account of what they spend and what they receive, they do their spending and receiving via their account at the central bank, and they record their spending and revenue in their account books. But the entries in the account book are not the money itself. If you're paid a 100 euro note for playing the violin at a concert, you (should) write it up in your account book, but that's just a record of what happened. The money itself doesn't live in the account book, it lives in your purse or wallet. Similarly, the government's money doesn't live in its account book. That's just a record of its comings and goings.

And this points to a further difference. In your case, as a private citizen, you can only have money in your purse that you got from somewhere else. But the state's central bank can and does conjure money out of nothing, to enable the government to spend what it wants to spend, or to tweak the economy, as with open market operations, or to save the banks from crashing the economy, as with quantitative easing. And the state dissolves money back into nothing when there's too much of it for the health of the economy. The state doesn't have to get money from outside itself to be able to spend. Never.

And of course, there's one final difference between a private citizen and the state, that trumps all. The state creates the most powerful, reliable money there is, and this money is the basis on which all other money rests.

Government debt, deficits and bonds

This leads to the third great misunderstanding I've tried to counter in this book: the illogic associated with government deficit, debt and bonds. You'll remember in Chapter 11 I explained this contorted logic. Every government has to spend more than it gets back in taxes, fees, etc. in any particular year, to allow for an acceptable level of inflation and a realistic amount of GDP growth. Therefore it has to incur a budget deficit of a few percent, on average, each year. The habitual practice is that it finances this part of its deficit by borrowing from the private sector, i.e. by issuing bonds and going deeper into debt. This by itself would stifle economic growth because the money the government borrows comes out of the very economy it's hoping to grow. So the central bank quietly steps in to save the day. It creates new money, to buy government bonds back from the public (on the so-called "secondary market"), thereby injecting money into the economy to compensate for the money the government took out of the economy as payment for its bonds. There's now more money circulating in the economy than there was the year before, so the economy can grow from year to year and accommodate the desired level of inflation. But the elected government loses its agency to decide where that extra money goes, and where the money comes from that finances its bonds. An additional problem is that this amplifies government debt by putting the government in debt to its own central bank, and leads to popular misconceptions of how indebted a government actually is.

I've argued in this book that we could well do without this charade, and I suggested an alternative approach based on active cooperation and coordination between a government and its central bank.

I've also argued that this does not give governments a mandate for excessive deficit budgeting. Most of the government's budget is for routine spending and should be covered by taxes (and fees, fines, etc.) but not borrowing.

Another portion is needed, as outlined above, to cater for inflation and GDP growth. A third portion can be for socially entrepreneurial investments that can pay back over time, and this can be funded by borrowing.

I'm aware that the second of these represents a departure from current practice, and I'm looking forward to feedback on it. Governments' practice of going deeper into debt to cover each year's budget deficit is deeply entrenched. It's supported by a standard narrative that's repeated over and over again by economists, columnists, bloggers and politicians: "The government will have to increase its debt to finance that deficit." This is treated as if it's an obvious, self-evident fact, even though it's based on the false notion that governments have to get their money from somewhere outside themselves in order to spend. I don't expect the argument in this book to collapse this narrative overnight, but I'd like to see economists and others seriously discuss the point I'm making.

Getting the taxes right

Along with MMT theorists and an increasing number of other economists, I've argued in this book that modern money is, effectively, a tax token. Money gets its reliability and credibility from the fact that the state promises to accept it as payment for our tax liabilities (and fees, fines, etc.). Along with these writers I've also argued that the main reason taxes are necessary is to withdraw money from the economy to give space for the state to spend new money into the economy, targeted to where the elected government sees the needs.

But I've taken this a step further, arguing that this lays upon a government the awesome responsibility of deciding who should pay how much tax, based on what forms of enrichment. In doing this, in Chapter 6 I set our current tax system in its historical context. Today in most countries, over 60% of tax is income tax (including social security tax), but this is an historical anomaly. To begin with, throughout most of history the bulk of tax, in most societies, has been based on wealth. The richer you were, the more tax you paid. This seemed just and fair in most societies even if they didn't have welfare systems anything like as comprehensive as some of today's.

Second, I pointed out that in the 1950s-1970s, most of the increase in wealth came from ordinary work income. To get richer in those decades all you had to do was keep a steady job, save, buy a house, and keep saving. Today, however, most of the increase in income comes from what can broadly be termed “financialization”. If you already have money, you can make more money by clever investments. Money breeds money. The annual increase in wealth among the richest 1% is phenomenal, while the meagre wealth of the poorest 50% is stagnating or going backwards. And yet the taxes on the richest amount to only a few percent of their annual increase in wealth, while the poorest pay at least 20% on their income, due to sales taxes.

I would strongly argue that this is not consistent with society’s intentions for the nature of money. Taxation–the mechanism designed to give money its credibility–has morphed into a system of gross exploitation and injustice.

Fortunately, due to the intensive, detailed investigative work of Prof Gabriel Zucman and others at the Paris School of Economics, there’s now a blueprint for how we can radically reform the tax system without being foiled by the super-rich–without the multi-billionaires winning the cat-and-mouse game of finding ways to avoid and evade the proposed new taxes. This is designed as an international dragnet to prevent the super-wealthy avoiding tax by shifting their residence or parking their money in tax havens. It’s already gained the support, in principle, of the G20 group of the world’s leading economies, and specifically the governments of Brazil and Spain, and the former German social democrat government.

It’s too early to see how willingly our elected governments will support this scheme. They’ll have to resist being bought off by the super-rich. Already the US seems a lost cause, and Germany’s new government is led by a party that’s more likely to reduce taxes on the rich than move to taxing wealth itself.

But there are two reasons I think this topic is important for this book. First, as I imply above, it’s intrinsic to the meaning and functioning of money. Money gets its credibility from taxes. Second, if taxes are unfair, it’s not just the distribution of wealth that’s unfair, it’s *money itself that’s unfair.* It means that the ten-dollar notes in your purse or wallet are objects of injustice. Their value is supported by a cruelly unfair system that would make even the ancient Romans balk–and certainly the early Muslims and Christians, as well as Judaism’s ancient prophets like Ezekiel, Micah and Amos.

I want this book to provoke discussion about the mechanisms of money creation, central bank functions, foreign exchange practices, debt-deficit-bond relationships, cryptocurrencies and central bank digital currencies, among other topics. But we also need to foster discussion on the justness or unjustness of the tax system, or we're missing half the picture.

A final challenge to critics

I'm hoping this book will attract plenty of solid, critical discussion. I'd like to hear what different readers find enlightening or bizarre in it, what they agree with or disagree with. But I very much hope that those who disagree with things in this book will represent the book accurately. I hope they'll aim their shots at what I've actually said, not at a half-baked version of what I've said. For example, in this book I've repeatedly argued that in countries that run their own currency, the state spends money into existence, so there's no physical or material limit on how much money it can create in its own currency. When I mention this to some of my economist friends, they immediately howl it down as hyper-inflationary, citing Zimbabwe's multi-trillion percent inflation of the 2000s or the runaway inflation of Germany's Weimar Republic in the 1930s. But what I've been saying throughout is *not* "Governments should create as much money as they like". I've merely explained the mechanism by which money comes into existence. If critics read the book carefully, they'll see I repeatedly argue that the state should create *just the right amount of money* to match the capacity of the real economy to utilize it. Too much, and inflation goes too high. Too little, and people miss out on the abundant resources the planet has to offer them, the economy stagnates, and we risk causing deflation.

That's just an example. I hope the book will stimulate discussion based on what it says, not what it carefully avoids saying. It seems to me there's enough material in the book that'll seem strange or surprising in its own right, without needing to misunderstand or distort it. After all, we all use money every day, but how many of us have had the opportunity to get to grips with what it actually is?

BIBLIOGRAPHY

Afonso, Gara, Cisternas, Gonzalas, and Riordon, Will. 2024. "Who Is Borrowing and Lending in the Eurodollar and Selected Deposit Markets?" Liberty Street Economics, Federal Reserve Bank of New York. May 13, 2024. Accessed 13 July, 2024. https://libertystreeteconomics.newyorkfed.org/2024/05/who-is-borrowing-and-lending-in-the-eurodollar-and-selected-deposit-markets/

Agba, R. 2022. "Survey–87% of Ugandans don't have a bank account." New Vision, December 11 2022. Accessed 15 June, 2025. https://www.newvision.co.ug/category/news/87-of-ugandans-lack-bank-accounts-survey-NV_149445

Alkhateeb, Firas. 2017. Lost Islamic History: Reclaiming Muslim civilisation from the past. London: Hurst and Co. ISBN 978-1-84904-689-3

Winograd, Eric and Bingham, Chris. 2024. The US National Debt: Debt or Alive? Alliance Bernstein. https://www.alliancebernstein.com/corporate/en/insights/investment-insights/the-us-national-debt-debt-or-alive.html

Auer, Raphael and Böhme, Rainer. 2020. The Technology of Retail Central Bank Digital Currency. BIS Quarterly Review, March 2020. Accessed 16 July, 2025. Available as SSRN: https://ssrn.com/abstract=3561198

Austin J. L. 1955. How to do things with words: The William James Lectures delivered at Harvard University in 1955. Oxford UK: Oxford University Press.

Bank for International Settlements. 2024. "Pillar 2 framework–Executive Summary." Bank for International Settlements, 2024. Accessed 09 February, 2025. https://www.bis.org/fsi/fsisummaries/pillar2.pdf

Bank of England. 2020. "Term Funding Scheme with additional incentives for SMEs (TFSME)–Market Notice". Bank of England. Accessed 09 February, 2025. https://www.bankofengland.co.uk/markets/market-notices/2020/term-funding-scheme-market-notice-mar-2020

Bank of England. 2020a. "Bank of England announces supervisory and prudential policy measures to address the challenges of Covid-19." Bank of England. Accessed 20 March, 2025.

https://www.bankofengland.co.uk/news/2020/march/boe-announces-supervisory-and-prudential-policymeasures-to-address-the-challenges-of-covid-19

Bank of England. 2025. "Cross-border payments." Accessed 10 May, 2025. https://www.bankofengland.co.uk/payment-and-settlement/cross-border-payments

Bank of Jamaica. 2023. "CBDC Frequently Asked Questions. Downloadable booklet." Accessed 10 May, 2025. https://boj.org.jm/wp-content/uploads/2022/08/CBDC-FAQs-Booklet.pdf

Bank of Japan. 2025. "Japanese Government Bonds held by the Bank of Japan (as of April 30, 2025)." Accessed 03 March, 2025. Link to datasheet in https://www.boj.or.jp/en/statistics/boj/other/mei/index.htm

BBC. 2022. "How much market chaos did the mini-budget cause? BBC News, 17 October 2022". https://www.bbc.com/news/63229204

Becker, Ben. 2019. "Bitcoin history tied to Jacksonville; why the government may fear cryptocurrencies' potential." Accessed 06 June, 2025. Action News AJX, 01 November 2019. https://www.actionnewsjax.com/news/local/bitcoin-history-tiedto-jacksonville-why-the-government-may-fear-cryptocurrencies-potential/1004080886/

Berkeley, Andrew, Ryan-Collins, Josh, Tye, Richard, Voldsgaard, Asker and Wilson, Neil. 2022. The self-financing state: An institutional analysis of government expenditure, revenue collection and debt issuance operations in the United Kingdom. UCL Institute for Innovation and Public Purpose, Working Paper Series (IIPP WP 2022-08). https://www.ucl.ac.uk/bartlett/public-purpose/publications/working-papers/wp2022-08

Bianchi, Francesco, Kind, Thilo, and Kung, Howard. 2023. Threats to central bank independence: High-frequency identification with twitter. Journal of Monetary Economics 135: 37-54. https://doi.org/10.1016/j.jmoneco.2023.01.00

Binder, Carola. 2021. Political Pressure on Central Banks. Journal of Money, Credit and Banking 53(4): 715-744. https://doi.org/10.1111/jmcb.12772

BIS (Bank for International Settlements). 2020. "Cross-border payment systems have been neglected for too long." Accessed 14 June, 2025. https://www.bis.org/cpmi/speeches/sp200730.htm

BIS (Bank for International Settlements). 2023, "Project Polaris, Part I: A handbook for offline payments with CBDC." 10 June, 2025. https://www.bis.org/publ/othp64.htm

Brien, Philip, Keep, Matthew. 2023. Public spending during the Covid-19 pandemic. House of Commons Library. https://researchbriefings.files.parliament.uk/documents/CBP-9309/CBP-9309.pdf

Bruce, Andy 2024. "UK debt hits 100% of GDP, adding to1930 Rachel Reeves' headache." Reuters, Macro Matters. 20 September, 2024. Accessed 07 November, 2024. https://www.reuters.com/world/uk/uk-debt-hits-100-gdp-adding-rachel-reeves-headache-2024-09-20/

Carter, Zachary 2020. The Price of Peace: Money, democracy and the life of John Maynard Keynes. New York: Random House.

Center for Financial Stability. 2025 "CFS Divisia Monetary Data for the United States, June 2024." Center for Financial Stability. Accessed 10 July, 2025. .https://centerforfinancialstability.org/wp/

CBS News. 2009. "Ben Bernanke's Greatest Challenge." CBS News 12 March, 2009. Accessed 02 February, 2025. https://www.cbsnews.com/news/ben-bernankes-greatest-challenge/

Charotti, Carlos, Palma, Nuno and Pereira dos Santos, João. 2022. American Treasure and the Decline of Spain. CEPR Discussion Paper No. DP17020, Available at SSRN: https://ssrn.com/abstract=4069806

CoinMarketCap. 2025. "All Cryptocurrencies" (data table updated daily). Accessed 20 July, 2025. https://coinmarketcap.com/all/views/all/

Dionysopoulos, Lambus, Marra, Miriam and Urquhart Andrew. 2024. Central bank digital currencies: A critical review. International Review of Financial Analysis 91: 103031. https://doi.org/10.1016/j.irfa.2023.103031

de Boer, Nick, Grünewald, Seraina and van`t Klooster, Jens. 2024. The law and politics of independent policy coordination: fiscal and sustainability considerations in the European Central Bank's monetary policy. EBI Working Paper Series 2024 No. 174. https://papers.ssrn.com/sol3/papers.cfm?abstract_id=4827387

Doll, Ignacia Olivera. 2024. "New Argentine Currency Launched to Offset Milei's Shock Therapy." Bloomberg, 3 September 2024. Accessed 10 July, 2025. https://www.bloomberg.com/news/features/2024-09-03/usd-ars-argentine-peso-alternative-emerges-in-la-rioja-the-chacho

East African Communications Organisation (EACO). 2023. "Communications Sector Regional Report." (undated). Accessed 09 July, 2025. https://eaco.int/29thAssemblies/files/StatisticsFullReport.pdf

Elliot, Larry. 2024 "At last G20 is showing how to finance an assault on poverty." The Guardian, 14 April 2024. Accessed 14 April, 2024.

https://www.theguardian.com/business/2024/apr/14/at-last-g20-showing-how-finance-assault-poverty-lula

Elliot, Larry 2024a. "Rachel Reeves goes back to the future with a tax and spend budget." The Guardian, 30 October, 2024. Accessed 30 October, 2024. https://www.theguardian.com/uk-news/2024/oct/30/rachel-reeves-goes-back-to-the-future-with-a-tax-and-spend-budget?CMP=share_btn_url

Epstein, Gerald. 2006. "Central Banks as Agents of Economic Development." United Nations University Research Paper No. 2006/54. Accessed 30 October, 2024. https://www.wider.unu.edu/sites/default/files/rp2006-54.pdf

European Central Bank. 2016. "The ECB's asset purchase programme: an early assessment." European Central Bank Working Paper Series, No. 1956, September 2016. Accessed 09 July, 2025. https://www.ecb.europa.eu/pub/pdf/scpwps/ecbwp1956.en.pdf

European Central Bank. 2020. "Asset Purchase Programmes." (undated). Accesssed 08 March, 2025. https://www.ecb.europa.eu/mopo/implement/omt/html/index.en.html

European Central Bank. 2022. "Towards the holy grail of cross-border payments." Working Paper Series No 2693 / August 2022. Accessed 08 July, 2025. https://www.ecb.europa.eu/pub/pdf/scpwps/ecb.wp2693~8d4e580438.en.pdf

European Central Bank. 2024. "Key ECB interest rates." (undated) Accessed 08 July, 2025. https://www.ecb.europa.eu/stats/policy_and_exchange_rates/key_ecb_interest_rates/html/index.en.html

European Central Bank. 2024a. "Who buys bonds now? How markets deal with a smaller Eurosystem balance sheet." (undated) Accessed 10 April, 2025. https://www.ecb.europa.eu/press/blog/date/2024/html/ecb.blog20240322~54dcd060b1.en.html

European Central Bank. 2024b. "ECB publishes first progress report on digital euro preparation phase." Accessed 10 April, 2025. https://www.ecb.europa.eu/press/pr/date/2024/html/ecb.pr240624~7b3d7581e6.en.html

European Central Bank. 2025. "Digital Euro." Accessed 10 April, 2025. https://www.ecb.europa.eu/euro/digital_euro/html/index.en.html

European Parliament. 2024. "New EU fiscal rules approved by MEPs." Press release, 23rd April 2024: Accessed 19 November, 2024.

https://www.europarl.europa.eu/news/en/press-room/20240419IPR20583/new-eu-fiscal-rules-approved-by-meps

European Parliament. 2024a. "Deal on EU economic governance reform." Press release, 10th April 2024. Accessed 19 November, 2025. https://www.europarl.europa.eu/news/en/press-room/20240205IPR17419/deal-on-eu-economic-governance-reform

Eurostat. 2024. "Natural gas price statistics." Accessed 10 February, 2025. https://ec.europa.eu/eurostat/statistics-explained/index.php?title=Natural_gas_price_statistics

Federal Deposit Insurance Corporation. 2024. "FDIC Survey Finds 96 Percent of U.S. Households Were Banked in 2023." Accessed 10 July, 2025.
https://www.fdic.gov/news/press-releases/2024/fdic-survey-finds-96-percent-us-households-were-banked-2023

Federal Reserve. 2020. M1 "Money Stock." US Federal Reserve Bank, Economic Research. Accessed 20 July, 2025.
https://fred.stlouisfed.org/series/M1NS

Federal Reserve. 2024. "All Employees, Total Nonfarm." Accessed 10 February, 2025. https://fred.stlouisfed.org/series/PAYEMS

Federal Reserve. 2024a. "Do the Rich Pay Their Fair Share?" Accessed 10 February, 2025. https://www.federalbudgetinpictures.com/do-the-rich-pay-their-fair-share/

Fernandes, Rodrigez and Aalbers, Manuel. 2024 Financialization and housing: Between globalization and Varieties of Capitalism. Competition and Change 20 (2):
https://doi.org/10.1177/1024529415623

Fontan, Clement. 2018. Frankfurt's double standard: the politics of the European Central Bank during the Eurozone crisis. Cambridge Review of International Affairs, 31(2): 162–182.
https://doi.org/10.1080/09557571.2018.1495692

Francis G. N. Li, A.Z.P. Smith, Phillip Biddulph, Hamilton, Ian G. Robert Lowe, Mavrogianni, Anna, Oikonomou, Eleni, Raslan, Rokia, Stamp, Samuel, Stone, Andrew, Summerfield, A.J., Veitch, David, Gori, Virginia and Oreszczyn, Tadj. 2015. Solid-wall U-values: heat flux measurements compared with standard assumptions, Building Research & Information, 43(2): 238-252:
https://doi.org/10.1080/09613218.2014.967977

Friedman, Milton. 1969. The Euro-Dollar Market: Some First Principles. Reprinted in: Federal Reserve Bank of St. Louis Review, 1971, pp. 16-24.

https://web.archive.org/web/20150920044229id_/https://research.stlouisfed.org/publications/review/71/07/Principles_Jul1971.pdf

Galvin, Ray. 2015. The ICT/electronics question: Structural change and the rebound effect. Ecological Economics 120: 23–31. http://dx.doi.org/10.1016/j.ecolecon.2015.08.020

Galvin, Ray, Gubernat, Andreas. 2016 The rebound effect and Schatzki's social theory: Reassessing the socio-materiality of energy consumption via a German case study. Energy Research & Social Science 22: 183–193. http://dx.doi.org/10.1016/j.erss.2016.08.024

Galvin, Ray. 2023. How prebound effects compromise the market premium for energy efficiency in German house sales, Building Research & Information. https://doi.org/10.1080/09613218.2023.2176284

Galvin, Ray. 2020. Yes, there is enough money to decarbonize the economies of high-income countries justly and sustainably. Energy Research & Social Science 70: 101739. https://doi.org/10.1016/j.erss.2020.101739

Galvin, Ray and Healy, Noel. 2020. The Green New Deal in the United States: What it is and how to pay for it. Energy Research & Social Science (67): 101529. https://doi.org/10.1016/j.erss.2020.101529

Graeber, David (2011) Debt: The first 5000 Years. London: Penguin Books.

Guardian. 2024. "Rachel Reeves tells cabinet UK still faces £100bn black hole over next five years." Guardian 15 October 2024. Accessed 15 October 2024. https://www.theguardian.com/uk-news/2024/oct/15/rachel-reeves-tells-cabinet-uk-still-faces-100bn-black-hole-over-next-five-years

Guardian. 2024a. "Sweden and Norway rethink cashless society plans over Russia security fears." 30 October 2024. Accessed 30 October 2024. https://www.theguardian.com/world/2024/oct/30/sweden-and-norway-rethink-cashless-society-plans-over-russia-security-fears

Hancock, Matthew. 2005. "Divisia money. Bank of England". Quarterly Bulletin, Spring 2005. Accessed 09 July, 2025. https://papers.ssrn.com/sol3/papers.cfm?abstract_id=698782

He Tai Ōhanga, The Treasury. 2024 "Financial Statements of the Government of New Zealand for the Year Ended 30 June 2024." Accessed 02 March 2025. https://www.treasury.govt.nz/publications/year-end/financial-statements-2024

House of Commons Library. 2024. "What are gilts? A simple guide." Accessed 05 March 2025. https://commonslibrary.parliament.uk/what-are-gilts-a-simple-guide/

IMF (International Monetary Fund). 2024. "Central Government Debt: Percent of GDP." Accessed 05 March 2025. https://www.imf.org/external/datamapper/CG_DEBT_GDP@GDD/CHN/FRA/DEU/ITA/JPN/GBR/USA

IMF (International Monetary Fund). 2025. "General government gross debt: Percent of GDP." Accessed 07 July, 2025. https://www.imf.org/external/datamapper/GGXWDG_NGDP@WEO/OEMDC/ADVEC/WEOWORLD

Ingham, Geoffrey. 2004. The Nature of Money: New Directions in Political Economy. Cambridge UK: Polity Press.

Ingham, Geoffrey. 2005. Concepts of Money: Interdisciplinary Perspectives from Economics, Sociology and Political Science. Cheltenham, UK: Northampton, MA: Edward Elgar

Ingham, Geoffrey. 2008. Capitalism. Cambridge UK: Polity Press.

Ingham, Geoffrey. 2020. What is Political Economy? Money. Cambridge UK: Polity Press.

Investing.com. 2025. "European Government Bonds." Assessed 29 July 2025. https://www.investing.com/rates-bonds/european-government-bonds

IPPR 2024. "Entrepreneurs say raising capital gains tax wouldn't stop them investing." 17 October 2024. Accessed 20 November 2025. https://www.ippr.org/media-office/entrepreneurs-say-raising-capital-gains-tax-wouldnt-stop-them-investing

Judge Business School. 2025. "Cambridge Bitcoin Electricity Consumption Index; Total Bitcoin electricity consumption." Accessed 20 March 2025. https://ccaf.io/cbnsi/cbeci

Kelton, Stephanie. 2019 "There are no inherent tradeoffs between fiscal and monetary policy." Bloomberg 21 February 2019. Accessed 20 March 2025. https://www.bloomberg.com/opinion/articles/2019-02-21/modern-monetary-theory-is-not-a-recipe-for-doom

Kelton, Stephanie. 2020. The Deficit Myth: Modern Monetary Theory and the Birth of the People's Economy. New York: Public Affairs. ISBN-13: 978-1541736184

Kelton, Stephanie. 2022. "How Are You Going to Pay for It? The Macroeconomic Benefits of Student Debt Cancellation." In: Care, Climate, and Debt. Edited by B.CZ. Wilson, 165–181. Palgrave Macmillan: Cham. https://doi.org/10.1007/978-3-030-96355-2_9

Keynes, John Maynard. 1930. A Treatise on Money. London: Macmillan.

King Darwin L, Case Carl. 2020. A brief history of taxation of the American colonies prior to the revolutionary war. Journal of Business and Accounting 13(1): 154-175. ISSN: 1944-2874.

Kinkartz Sabine 2024. "What is Germany's debt brake?" Deutsche Welle In Focus, 03 May 2025. Accessed 07 July 2025. https://www.dw.com/en/what-is-germanys-debt-brake/a-67587332

Kishtainy, Neill. 2017 A Little History of Economics. New Haven: Yale University Press.

Krugman, Paul. 2024 How the 'unforced error' of austerity wrecked Britain. Guardian 26 June, 2024. Accessed 07 July, 2025. https://www.theguardian.com/politics/ng-interactive/2024/jun/28/how-the-unforced-error-of-tory-austerity-wrecked-britain

Kumhof, Michael and Noone, Clare. 2021. Central bank digital currencies—Design principles for financial stability. Economic Analysis and Policy 71: 553–572. https://doi.org/10.1016/j.eap.2021.06.012

Lagos, Ricardo. 2006. "Inside and Outside Money. Federal Reserve Bank of Minneapolis, Research Department Staff Report 374." Accessed 20 July 2024. https://researchdatabase.minneapolisfed.org/concern/publications/kd17ct00b?locale=zh

Leigh, Andrew. 2024. The Shortest History of Economics. Exeter, UK: Old Street Publishing. ISBN978-1-913083-49-6.

Lyttkens, Carl Hampus. 1992. Effects of the taxation of wealth in Athens in the fourth century B. C. Scandinavian Economic History Review, 40 (2): 3-20: https://doi.org/10.1080/03585522.1992.10408249

McKinsey & Company. 2022. Central bank digital currencies: An active role for commercial banks. Accessed 20 July, 2024. https://www.mckinsey.com/industries/financial-services/our-insights/central-bank-digital-currencies-an-active-role-for-commercial-banks#/

McLeay, Michael, Radia, Amar and Thomas Ryland. 2014. "Money creation in the modern economy." Bank of England Quarterly Bulletin, 2014 Q1, 14 March 2014. Accessed 20 July, 2024. https://www.bankofengland.co.uk/quarterly-bulletin/2014/q1/money-creation-in-the-modern-economy

Monitor, Ugandan Edition. 2024. "Uganda's forex reserves drop 12% due to debt payments." 09 April 2024. Accessed 20 March 2025. https://www.monitor.co.ug/uganda/business/finance/uganda-s-forex-reserves-drop-12-due-to-debt-payments-4585254

Morony, Michael. 2004, Economic Boundaries? Late Antiquity and Early Islam. Journal of the Economic and Social History of the Orient. 47(2): 166-194. https://doi.org/10.1163/1568520041262288

Machlup, F. 1970. Euro-dollar creation: A mystery story. PSL Quarterly Review. 23(94) https://doi.org/10.13133/2037-3643/11742

Nakamoto, Satoshy. 2008. Bitcoin: A Peer-to-Peer Electronic Cash System. Reprint in: Modern Economy 6 (7), 20 July 2015. https://web.archive.org/web/20100704213649/https://bitcoin.org/bitcoin.pdf

Neate, R. (2024) "World's five richest men double their money as poorest get poorer." The Guardian, 15 January 2024. https://www.theguardian.com/inequality/2024/jan/15/worlds-five-richest-men-double-their-money-as-poorest-get-poorer

Nilepost. 2024. "Citi Boosts Govt With Shs497bn Loan for Lusalira-Sembabule Road Project." Accessed 30 April, 2025. https://nilepost.co.ug/business/225847/citi-boosts-govt-with-shs497bn-loan-for-lusalira-sembabule-road-project

Office for Budget Responsibility. 2024. "Economic and fiscal outlook October 2024." Accessed 30 November, 2024. https://obr.uk/efo/economic-and-fiscal-outlook-october-2024/

Office of national Statistics. 2023. UK government debt and deficit: December 2023. Accessed 30 November 2024. https://www.ons.gov.uk/economy/governmentpublicsectorandtaxes/publicspending/bulletins/ukgovernmentdebtanddeficitforeurostatmaast/december2023

Office of National Statistics. 2024. "Unemployment rate (aged 16 and over, seasonally adjusted): %" 11 November 2025. Accessed 14 December 2025. https://www.ons.gov.uk/employmentandlabourmarket/peoplenotinwork/unemployment/timeseries/mgsx/lms

OECD. (Organisation for Economic Cooperation and Development). 2023. "Revenue Statistics 2023: Tax Revenue Buoyancy in OECD Countries." Accessed 02 February, 2025. https://www.oecd.org/content/dam/oecd/en/topics/policy-sub-issues/global-tax-revenues/revenue-statistics-highlights-brochure.pdf

Orcutt, Mike. 2023. What's next for China's digital currency? MIT Technology Review, August 3, 2023. https://www.technologyreview.com/2023/08/03/1077181/whats-next-for-chinas-digital-currency/

OXFAM. 2024. "World's top 1% own more wealth than 95% of humanity, as 'the shadow of global oligarchy hangs over UN General Assembly,' says Oxfam." 23 September 2024. Accessed 30 March 2025. https://www.oxfam.org/en/press-releases/worlds-top-1-own-more-wealth-95-humanity-shadow-global-oligarchy-hangs-over-un

Palley, Thomas. 2020. What's wrong with Modern Money Theory: macro and political economic restraints on deficit-financed fiscal policy. Review of Keynesian Economics 8(4): 472–493. https://doi.org/10.4337/roke.2020.04.02

Patel, Rupal and Meaning, Jack. 2022. Why Can't We Just Print More Money? Economics in ten simple questions. London: Cornerstone books. ISBN 1529159067

Peacock, Mark. 2013. Introducing Money. Cambridge, UK: University of Cambridge Press.

Peterson, A 2014. "Hal Finney received the first Bitcoin transaction. Here's how he describes it." Washington Post, 3 January 2014. Accessed 10 November 2025. .https://www.washingtonpost.com/blogs/the-switch/wp/2014/01/03/hal-finn

Pettifor, Ann. 2018. The Production of Money: How to bread the power of bankers. London: Verso. ISBN-13: 978-1-78663-135-0

Piketty, Thomas. 2014. Capital in the Twenty-First Century. Cambridge (MAS) and London: Harvard University Press.

Piketty, Thomas. 2020. Capital and Ideology. Cambridge (MAS) and London: Harvard University Press.

Piketty, Thomas, Saez, Emmanuel and Zucman, Gabriel. 2023. Rethinking capital and wealth taxation. Oxford Review of Economic Policy, 2023, 39, 575–591. https://doi.org/10.1093/oxrep/grad026

Prates, Daniele. 2020. Beyond Modern Money Theory: A Post-Keynesian approach to the currency hierarchy, monetary sovereignty, and policy space. Review of Keynesian Economics 8(4): 494–511. https://doi.org/10.4337/roke.2020.04.03

PYMNTS. 2024. "Report: Digital Currency Projects Underway in 134 Countries." 17 September, 2014. Accessed 02 February, 2025. https://www.pymnts.com/cbdc/2024/report-digital-currency-projects-underway-in-134-countries/

Ratha, Dilip. 2022. "Remittances during COVID 19 Crisis and Beyond." G24 Session "Remittances and Migration for Development", March 29, 2022 Accessed 30 March 2025. https://g24.org/wp-content/uploads/2023/09/Dilip_Ratha_Remittances_G24_March29_2021.pdf

Reich, Robert. 2016. Saving Capitalism: For the Many, not the Few. London: Icon Books. ISBN 1785781766

Romelli, Davide. 2022. The political economy of reforms in Central Bank design: evidence from a new dataset. Economic Policy, 37 (112): 641–688. https://doi.org/10.1093/epolic/eiac011

Romelli, Davide. 2024 Trends in Central Bank Independence: A De-jure Perspective. BAFFI CAREFIN Centre Research Paper No. 217. https://papers.ssrn.com/sol3/papers.cfm?abstract_id=4716704

Ryan-Collins, Josh and Van Lerven, Frank. 2018. Bringing the helicopter to ground: A historical review of fiscal-monetary coordination to support economic growth in the 20th century'. UCL Institute for Innovation and Public Purpose Working Paper Series (IIPP WP 2018-08). https://www.ucl.ac.uk/bartlett/public-purpose/wp2018-08

Saez, Emmanuel and Zucman, Gabriel. 2021. How to Get $1 Trillion from 1000 Billionaires: Tax their Gains Now. Working Paper, University of California, Berkeley. https://eml.berkeley.edu/~saez/SZ21-billionaire-tax.pdf

Schatzmiller, Maya. 2011. Economic Performance and Economic Growth in the Early Islamic World. Journal of the Economic and Social History of the Orient. 54(2) 132-184. https://doi.org/10.1163/156852011X586831

Schmandt-Besserat, Denise. 2019. "Tokens: their Significance for the Origin of Counting and Writing." Accessed 30 March 2025, https://sites.utexas.edu/dsb/tokens/tokens/

Schönhärl, Korinna, Hürlimann, Gisela and Rohde, Dorothea. 2023. Histories of Tax Evasion, Avoidance and Resistance. London and New York: Routledge.

Shaw, William Arthur. 1896. The History of Currency, 1252–1894: Being an Account of the Gold and Silver Moneys and Monetary Standards of Europe and America, Together with an Examination of the Effects of Currency and Exchange Phenomena on Commercial and National Progress and Well-being. Putnam. Archived from the original on 12 May 2021. Accessed 18 August 2024 via Google Books. https://web.archive.org/web/20210512150410/https://books.google.com/books?id=GrJCAAAAIAAJ&pg=PA44#v=onepage&q&f=false

Shenk, Catherine R. 1998. The Origins of the Eurodollar Market in London: 1955–1963. Explorations in Economic History 35: 221–238, Article No. EH980693

StLoiusFed (Federal Reserve Bank, St Louis). 2025. "Federal Debt: Total Public Debt (GFDEBTN)." Accessed 14 June 2025. https://fred.stlouisfed.org/series/GFDEBTN

StLoiusFed (Federal Reserve Bank, St Louis) 2025a. "Federal Surplus or Deficit [-] as Percent of Gross Domestic Product (FYFSGDA188S)." Accessed 14 June 2025. https://fred.stlouisfed.org/series/FYFSGDA188S

Statista. 2024a. "Value of assets on the balance sheet of the Federal Reserve from August 2007 to May 2024." Accessed 20 June 2025. https://www.statista.com/statistics/1121448/fed-balance-sheet-timeline/

Statista. 2024b. "Wealth distribution in the United States in the second quarter of 2024." Accessed 20 June 2025. https://www.statista.com/statistics/203961/wealth-distribution-for-the-us/

Steel, Catherine. 2013. Hungry City: How food shapes our lives. London: Vintage books.

Tcherneva, Pavline and Tymoigne, Eric. 2024. Seismic shifts in economic theory and policy: From the Bernanke Doctrine to Modern Money Theory. Journal of Post Keynesian Economics 47(4): 853–874. https://doi.org/10.1080/01603477.2023.2225518

Tognato, Carlo. 2012. Central Bank Independence: Cultural codes and symbolic performance. New York: Palgrave Macmillan.

Trading Economics. 2024. "Bonds." Accessed 10 December, 2024. https://tradingeconomics.com/bonds

Trading Economics. 2025. "Government Budget." Accessed 10 June, 2025. https://tradingeconomics.com/country-list/government-budget

UK Parliament. 2024. "War and the coming of income tax." Accessed 20 November 2024. https://www.parliament.uk/about/living-heritage/transformingsociety/private-lives/taxation/overview/incometax/

UN. 2024. "The Sustainable Development Goals Report (United Nations)." Accessed 10 December 2024. https://unstats.un.org/sdgs/report/2024/The-Sustainable-Development-Goals-Report-2024.pdf

UN. 2025. UN "Operational Rates of Exchange." Accessed 10 June 2025. https://treasury.un.org/operationalrates/OperationalRates.php

US Treasury. 2025. "Monthly Treasury Statement, Bureau of the Fiscal Service." Accessed 10 Maz 2025. https://www.fiscal.treasury.gov/reports-statements/mts/previous.html

Vogl, Joseph. 2017. The Ascendancy of Finance. English translation by Simon Garnett. Malden (MA): Polity Press. ISBN13:978-1-5095-0930-0-pb

Weinberg, John. 2013. "The Great Recession and Its Aftermath." Federal Reserve History. Accessed 30 March 2025. https://www.federalreservehistory.org/essays/great-recession-and-its-aftermath

Wittgenstein, Ludwig. 1953. Philosophical Investigations: The German Text, with a Revised English Translation. Oxford UK: Blackwell. ISBN 9780631231592.

Wray, L. Randal. 2015. Modern Money Theory: A primer on macroeconomics for sovereign monetary systems. Second Edition. Basingstoke UK: Palgrave Macmillan.

World Bank. 2025 "Current account balance (BoP, current US$)–United States." World Bank Open Data. Accessed 10 July, 2025. https://data.worldbank.org/indicator/BN.CAB.XOKA.CD?locations=US

Yueh, Linda. 2018. The Great Economists: How their ideas can help us today. London: Penguin Random House

Yulu, Chen. 2014. Chinese Currency and the Global Economy: The rise of the Renminbi. New York: McGraw Hill.

Zahn, Max. 2025 "Fed holds interest rates steady, defying pressure from Trump." ABC News 08 May, 2025. Accessed 09 May 2025. https://abcnews.go.com/US/fed-expected-hold-interest-rates-steady-defying-trump/story?id=121510718

Zang, Z. J. 2023. Cryptopricing: Whence comes the value for cryptocurrencies and NFTs? International Journal of Research in Marketing 40: 22-29. https://doi.org/10.1016/j.ijresmar.2022.08.002

Zhang, Zhijun William. 2024. "CBDC Security." In: Web3 Applications Security and New Security Landscape. Future of Business and Finance. Edited by Ken Huang, Carlo Parisi, Lisa JY Tan, Winston Ma and Zhijun William Zhang. Chapter 5. Springer, Cham. https://doi.org/10.1007/978-3-031-58002-4_5

Zucman, Gabriel. 2015. The Hidden Wealth of Nations: The scourge of tax havens. Translation from the French by T L Fagan. Chicago and London: University of Chicago Press.